ANTONIO GR
A New Introdu

Austria
Switzerland
Trafoi
TRENTINO
LOMBARDY
VENETIA
Turin
Milan
Venice
ISTRIA
France
PIEDMONT
Parma
EMILIA-
ROMAGNA
Genoa
Ferrara
Bologna
Nice
LIGURIA
Florence
Livorno
TUSCANY
MARCHE
Ancona
Elba
Adriatic
Corsica
UMBRIA
Rome
ABRUZZI
LAZIO
Sea
Gaeta
Sardinia
CAMPANIA
APULIA
Ghilarza
Sorongo
Naples
BASILICATA
Turi
Ales
Bugerru
Iglesias
Cagliari
CALABRIA
Usticia
Palermo
Sicily
Mediterranean
Sea

ANTONIO GRAMSCI
A New Introduction

Paul Ransome

HARVESTER
WHEATSHEAF

New York   London   Toronto   Sydney   Tokyo   Singapore

First published 1992 by
Harvester Wheatsheaf
Campus 400, Maylands Avenue
Hemel Hempstead
Hertfordshire, HP2 7EZ
A division of
Simon & Schuster International Group

© 1992 Paul Ransome

All rights reserved. No part of this publication may be reproduced, stored in a retrieval system, or transmitted, in any form, or by any means, electronic, mechanical, photocopying, recording or otherwise, without prior permission, in writing, from the publisher.

Typeset in 10/12 Ehrhardt
by Pentacor PLC, High Wycombe

Printed and bound in Great Britain by
Biddles Ltd, Guildford and King's Lynn

British Library Cataloguing in Publication Data

A catalogue record for this book is available from the British Library

ISBN 0–7450–1111–X (hbk)
ISNB 0–7450–1112–8 (pbk)

1 2 3 4 5   96 95 94 93 92

For John and Evelyn Ransome

Contents

Preface	ix
Acknowledgements	x
Abbreviations	xi
Chronology	xii
Introduction	1

1	***Central themes and debates***	**9**
	The development of the Gramsci industry	9
	Themes and debates	19
	Summary	26
2	***The development of modern Italy, 1861–1914***	**30**
	Summary	49
3	***Gramsci's Life and Work, 1891–1937***	**54**
	Gramsci's early life and education, 1891–1911	55
	Gramsci and the 'bienno rosso' in Turin, 1911–21	61
	Gramsci and the PCI, 1921–6	86
	Prison, 1926–37	104
4	***Ideology and the concept hegemony***	**113**
	Marx: the pejorative use of the concept ideology	114
	Lenin and Lukács: an extension of the concept ideology	121

	Discussion and summary	126
5	*The concept hegemony: a variable definition*	132
	Hegemony and 'historical bloc'	133
	Civil society, political society and the State	138
	'War of position' and 'war of manœuvre'	144
	Summary	150
6	*Structure and superstructure*	156
	Preliminary issues	157
	The formation of political consciousness	162
	Norberto Bobbio: Gramsci and the conception of civil society	166
	Jacques Texier: Gramsci, theoretician of the superstructure	170
	Summary	174
7	*Political consciousness: eduction and the intellectuals*	179
	The common school	179
	The intellectuals	186
	Discussion	191
8	*Political participation: the council movement and the political party*	201
	The factory councils	202
	The political party	209
	Summary	223
Conclusion		227
Further reading		230
Bibliography		238
Index		245

Preface

The purposes and intentions of this book are set out in the Introduction which follows. As an additional guide to readers who already have a knowledge of Gramsci's work, however, it might be useful to say briefly what the book *does not* seek to do. In the first place, no attempt is being made to provide a comprehensive summary of every aspect of Gramsci's thought. Because of the need to be selective, accounts of Gramsci's philosophy and his relationship with the work of Benedetto Croce, his work in the fields of cultural and artistic criticism, and some aspects of his analysis of Italian history are not specifically included. In the second place, no attempt is made either to develop a far-reaching revision of how Gramsci's work should be interpreted, or to recruit his thinking for particular theoretical or political purposes. Thirdly, because the book is intended to be of use to readers who may have a minimal understanding of Marxism and of political theory more generally, these issues are discussed in relatively simple terms. The following is therefore intended to provide a starting point for further study and discussion rather than a series of neatly formed conclusions.

Acknowledgements

Inevitably, any book builds upon the ideas and research of its predecessors, and I would therefore like to acknowledge the work of all those authors referred to in the text. In particular, I would like to thank Lawrence & Wishart for permission to quote from the following English translations of Gramsci's work: *Selections from the Prison Notebooks*, edited and translated by Quintin Hoare and Geoffrey Nowell Smith (London, 1971); *Selections from Political Writings: 1910–1920*, selected and edited by Quintin Hoare, translated by John Mathews (London, 1977); and *Selections from Political Writings: 1921–1926*, translated and edited by Quintin Hoare (London, 1978).

In addition, I would also like to express my gratitude to Gavin Mackenzie and Conrad Lodziak who offered much valuable advice and helpful criticism during the preparation of the manuscript, to Paul Ginsborg and John Thompson who encouraged me at the outset, and to Nick Stevenson whose conversation provided a much needed diversion. Needless to say, the shortcomings of the text are entirely my own.

Finally I would like to thank Jackie for being the best possible friend and companion throughout.

Abbreviations

CGL   *Confederazione Generale del Lavoro*
CGT *Confédération Générale du Travail*
CIL   *Confederazione Italiana del Lavoro*
FIOM *Federazione Impiegati Operai Metallurgici*
KPD *Kommunistische Partei Deutschlands*
PCI   *Partito Communista Italiano*
PNF *Partito Nazionale Fascista*
PSI   *Partito Socialista Italiano*
SPD *Sozialdemokratische Partei Deutschlands*
UIL   *Unione Italiana di Lavoro*
USI   *Unione Sindicale Italiana*

SPN   *Selections from the Prison Notebooks*
SPWI *Selections from Political Writings: 1910–1920*
SPWII *Selections from Political Writings: 1921–1926*

Chronology

1860 Gramsci's father, Francesco Gramsci, born at Gaeta

1861 Unification of Italy
Gramsci's mother, Giuseppina Marcias, born at Ghilarza

1864 Marx founds First International Working Men's Association

1869 German Social Democratic Workers' Party formed

1870 Rome becomes capital of Italy

1871 End of Franco-Prussian War
Unification of Germany
Paris Commune

1878 Congress of Berlin

1881 French invasion of Tunisia

1882 Triple Alliance between Germany, Austria–Hungary and Italy (renewed 1887, 1891, 1902, 1912)

1883 Francesco and Giuseppina married

1889 Second International formed in Paris

1890 German Social Democratic Party (SPD) formed (splits in 1917 into SPD and anti-war Independent Social Democratic Party [USPD])

1891 Antonio Gramsci born at Ales, 22 January

CHRONOLOGY

1892 Italian Socialist Party (PSI) formed

1893 Independent Labour Party formed in Britain

1895 *Confédération Générale du Travail* (CGT) formed in France

1896 Italian defeat at Adowa

1898 Family moves back to Ghilarza
Gramsci enters primary school
Social Democratic Workers' Party formed in Russia

1903 Gramsci suspends education
Russian Social Democratic Workers' Party splits into Mensheviks and Bolsheviks

1905 Enrols at Santu Lussurgia secondary school
Miners strike at Bugerru
St Petersburg Revolution

1906 *Confederazione Generale del Lavoro* (CGL) formed in Italy

1908 Awarded secondary school certificate in September
Moves with brother Gennaro to Cagliari
Enters Dettori state *liceo*

1910 First article published in *L'Unione sarda*, 26 July

1911 Italian invasion of Libya, war with Turkey
Wins Turin University scholarship, enrols on Modern Philosophy course, 16 November

1913 Becomes member of PSI

1914 'Red Week' in Italy in June
Outbreak of First World War

1915 University education ends in April
Italy enters war in May following signing of the Treaty of London
Zimmerwald Conference of Second International in September

1916 Kienthal Conference of Second International in April, Lenin calls for formation of new Third International

Gramsci begins career as journalist for *Il Grido del Popolo* and *Avanti!*

1917 'February Revolution' in Russia

United States enters war in April

Italy suffers heavy defeat at battle of Caporetto in November

'October Revolution' in Russia

Gramsci becomes Secretary of the Turin section of the PSI

1918 Trotsky signs Treaty of Brest-Litovsk with Germany in March

End of war with Armistice on 11 November

Revolutionary uprisings throughout Germany

1919 Berlin uprisings organised by Spartakus League and German Communist Party (KPD) of Rosa Luxemburg and Karl Liebknecht. Demonstrations suppressed and Luxemburg and Liebknecht murdered

Italian Popular Party formed

General Confederation of Industry (Confindustria) formed by Italian industrialists

Mussolini forms first *Fasci Italiani di Combattimento* in Milan

First Congress of Third International (Comintern) held in Moscow in March

First edition of *L'Ordine Nuovo* in May
Factory Council Movement begins in Turin

1920 First strike in Turin in April
PSI National Congress held in Milan during strike

Second Congress of the Comintern in July, Lenin puts forward the 'Twenty-one Conditions'

Second strike and factory occupations in Turin and Piedmont district in September

1921 Congress of the PSI held at Livorno in January
Italian Communist Party (PCI) formed

Third Congress of Comintern in Moscow in July, Lenin puts forward policy of 'united front'

PSI expelled from Comintern

National Fascist Party (PNF) formed

1922 Congress of PCI in Rome in March, 'Rome Theses' put forward by Bordiga and Terracini

PCI Central Committee elects Gramsci as next representative on the Comintern's Executive, travels to Moscow in May

Meets and marries Julia Schucht

Congress of PSI at Rome in October, Turati's reformists expelled and form Unitary Socialist Party, while 'Terzini' form on left of PSI under Serrati

Fascist 'March on Rome' in October, Mussolini becomes prime minister

Fourth Congress of the Comintern in November

1923 Comintern ratifies new leadership of the PCI in June

Second defeat of Communist uprisings in Germany

Gramsci moves to Vienna in December

1924 Lenin dies on 21 January

Gramsci elected to parliament in April

Matteotti murdered in May

Fifth Congress of the Comintern in Moscow in June

Gramsci becomes Secretary-General of the PCI

First son Delio born in August

1925 Comintern Executive meets in Moscow

Julia, Delio and Eugenie come to Rome in October

1926 Congress of the PCI at Lyons in January

Gramsci returns to Rome in May to speak in parliament

Julia, Eugenie and Tatiana go to Trafoi on the Swiss border in July

Gramsci joins them before returning to Rome in August

Second son Giuliano born

	Gramsci arrested on 8 November, sent to penal island of Usticia
1927	Moved to San Vittore prison in Milan in January
1928	Trial in Rome, sentenced to twenty years, four months and five days
	Arrives at Turi prison on 19 July
	Sixth Congress of the Comintern in Moscow, united front replaced by 'left-turn'
	Stalin assumes complete control of the CPSU
1931	Leading members of the PCI executive expelled
	Togliatti remains as leader of the Party
1933	Gramsci collapses and is moved to special clinic at Formia in December
1935	Moves to Quisisana clinic in Rome
1937	Suffers brain haemorrhage and dies at 4 a.m. on 27 April

Introduction

Anyone who studies the way society works, how relative stability is maintained and how, at the same time, society continues to change and develop, will immediately be struck by the increasing popularity of the work of Antonio Gramsci. The close association of Gramsci with a new paradigm in Marxism, and the possibility of applying his ideas to contemporary political developments in a relatively straightforward way, has meant that references to Gramsci's terminology and theory now abound in the contemporary literature. Anyone who wishes to understand Gramsci's original ideas is therefore faced with the perplexing task of having to disentangle Gramsci from both the work of his forebears and the claims of his successors. The aim of this book is to resolve some of these difficulties by providing a clear and uncomplicated introduction to Gramsci's life and work, to explain and define his terminology, and to show how his ideas have contributed to recent developments in Marxist theory. By adopting a largely descriptive and definitional approach to the subject matter, it is hoped that this discussion will also provide a valuable starting point not only for approaching other more specialised material on Gramsci himself, but also for developing an understanding of the Marxian perspective as a whole.

Initially, the continuing popularity of Marxism in general, and of the work of Gramsci in particular, may seem somewhat surprising since many of the predictions made by Marx and his advocates have not been fulfilled. Capitalism has continued to dominate the world economic system, while those countries which have adopted a socialist or communist philosophy, most notably the Soviet Union, are associated with totalitarianism and authority, rather than with equality and freedom. The recent collapse of many communist regimes in eastern Europe, and the imminent transformation of the former Soviet Union itself into a market economy, would seem to sound the death knell of Marxism. Despite this apparent failure, many writers have continued to adopt a Marxist view of society, arguing that although the soviet-style organisation of society has not lived up to expectations, the Marxist perspective continues to provide an important basis from which to analyse the processes of social development and change. Although capitalism has succeeded in sustaining vigorous economic growth and prosperity in the West, it is clear that this prosperity has not been distributed equally either within particular societies or between one society and another. The prosperity of the minority, in other words, still largely depends on the poverty and exploitation of the majority. In view of these obvious shortcomings, many crucial questions remain to be answered as to how capitalism has become so dominant, and why so many individuals continue to support it by participating in a system which seems to act against their own best interests in so many ways. The process of posing these questions correctly, and of providing answers to them which are relevant to contemporary society, has resulted in a continuous evolution within Marxist theory itself. Of all the revisions and reinterpretations which have been made during the last fifty years, the work of Gramsci now stands out as being of seminal importance. The conceptual tools and terminology developed by Gramsci now provide the central core of what can be called a new orthodoxy in Marxism.

Studying the work of Antonio Gramsci presents a number of difficulties, however. These are associated first with the somewhat enigmatic nature of the texts themselves and second with their very popularity. With regard to the first set of problems, the circumstances in which Gramsci developed and recorded his thoughts were far from ideal. It must be emphasised that Gramsci was himself a political activist who had direct personal experience of trying to instigate radical change within his own society. He was a central figure in Italian politics during the particularly volatile period of the *bienno rosso*, the red years of 1919–20, and was deeply involved in the formation of the Italian Communist Party in 1921. Following his arrest in 1926, he spent the rest of his life living, studying and writing under appalling prison conditions, before dying of a brain haemorrhage in 1937 at the age of forty–six. Of necessity, therefore, many elements of his thought, particularly those concerned with the actual conduct of revolutionary politics, were developed under the pressure of constantly changing circumstances and a highly charged political atmosphere. For a large part of his life, in other words, he simply did not have the time to indulge in the niceties of academic study and clarity of exposition.

Inevitably, this has given rise to considerable confusion and debate over how his work should be interpreted. Various authors have outlined the possible chronological stages in Gramsci's intellectual development, and have suggested that inconsistencies and deviations regularly occur within his work. Others have suggested that Gramsci's best known writings, the *Quaderni del Carcere* or *Prison Notebooks*, written between 1929 and 1935, represent the clearest and most mature summary of his ideas, while the earlier writings, largely comprised of articles in *Avanti!* and in *Il Grido del Popolo*, approximately during the period 1914–19, and later in *L'Ordine Nuovo*, founded by Gramsci in 1919, together with public and private correspondence, are necessarily less amenable to consistency of interpretation.

The *Prison Notebooks* themselves, however, present the reader with a number of difficulties since Gramsci was forced to express himself in terms which would not attract the attention of the prison censor. So, for example, Marxism is referred to as 'the philosophy of praxis', while Lenin and the Bolsheviks are referred to as Ilich and 'the majoritarians' respectively. In addition, a number of linguistic problems arise since it is not always possible to find an exact English equivalent which can capture Gramsci's original meaning. So, for example, the Italian word '*dirigere*' can be variously translated as 'to direct, lead, rule', but can also carry the same meaning as the word '*egemonia*' (hegemony), a term which Gramsci uses in a particularly innovative way. As if in anticipation of these difficulties Gramsci forewarns the reader:

> It is clear that the content of posthumous works has to be taken with great discretion and caution, because it cannot be considered definitive but only as material still being elaborated and still provisional. One should not exclude the possibility that these works, particularly if they have been a long time in the making and if the author never decided to finish them, might have been repudiated or deemed unsatisfactory in whole or in part by the author. (*SPN*, p.384)

Finally, as Morera has recently pointed out:

> The scope of Gramsci's thought is far too wide for any specialist to assess his contribution. He writes on philosophy, history, politics, and even grammar. . . . Given then both the scope of the notebooks, and their unfinished and inconsistent character, the interpreter is put in the difficult position of evaluating the relevance of many passages whose meaning is obscure and of dealing with topics of which he or she knows little. (Morera, 1990: 3–4)

Despite these ambiguities and indeed largely because of the variability of use which they encourage, Gramsci's work has become heavily integrated into the mainstream of contemporary Marxism. This leads us to the second problem faced by anyone wishing to study Gramsci's work: his popularity.

Perhaps the most important development in Marxist theory during the past twenty years or so has been a decisive shift away from an uncritical belief in the all-powerful influence of the 'structural' economic institutions of society, towards a more forthright acknowledgement of the influence of non-economic or superstructural institutions. The latter have now been promoted to a position of great significance, acquiring in the process their own forms of 'determinism'. The institutions of government, the legal system, education, and the mass media, and the processes of communication and meaning-formation which they construct and transmit, are seen as having a very powerful effect upon the way in which individuals interpret the world around them.

The historical rationale underlying this change in emphasis is that, since the Second World War, the capitalist system has been able to maintain its dominant position not solely as a result of its control over economic practices, but through the *ideological* recruitment of the mass of the population. It has achieved a threshold of consent above which the majority of the population has come to express approval of the primary constituents of the capitalist world-view. Most significantly, this form of ideological consent is not limited to individuals who to a greater or lesser extent benefit from capitalist society, but also extends into the consciousness of individuals who do not. In part as a consequence and in part as a stimulus to this change of focus within Marxism, the concepts of ideology and hegemony have been invoked in order to articulate this revitalised theoretical and polemical discourse. This has inevitably resulted in considerable interest in the writings of Gramsci, a large part of which concentrate specifically upon the relationship between structure and superstructure, and upon the role of ideology.

At the same time, the emergence of a number of 'alternative' social movements which are not based solely upon economic issues tends to support the Gramscian view that social change is not exclusively dependent, as Marx had suggested, upon conflicts between strictly defined and mutually exclusive *economic* classes. Issues such as the rights of women, racial equality, the welfare of the young, the elderly and the disabled, and, perhaps most evidently, a growing feeling of impotence in the face of widespread ecological change, may signify the emergence of a new and 'universal' world-view of the kind outlined by Gramsci. In the light of these historical and theoretical developments, it is evident that an understanding of Gramsci's life and work has become indispensable to anyone who wishes to participate in the analysis and critique of contemporary society.

This book is set out in such a way as to give a clear introduction not only to the theoretical issues and debates which surround Gramsci's work, but to the social and historical context of Gramsci's own life. To achieve this balance between background and theory, the first part of the book is taken up with a largely descriptive account of the political and social circumstances of Gramsci's life and intellectual development. This provides a basis from which to understand the more analytical discussion which follows. In order to make the discussion as straightforward as possible, each of the later chapters concentrates upon a particular aspect of Gramsci's thought. In each case, the terms used by Gramsci are clearly defined together with a brief consideration of their wider implications. Each chapter concludes with a summary of the main ideas which have been put forward. Although the subject matter of each chapter tends to follow on from the previous one, the topics are discussed in a relatively self-contained way so that, if necessary, each chapter can be read in isolation from the rest.

More specifically, then, Chapter 1 places the book in context by tracing the development of interest in Gramsci's work since it first became available during the late 1940s. It will be shown that the reception of Gramsci's work in Italy stimulated much discussion and debate, particularly over the extent to which Gramsci does or does not adopt a straightforward Leninist perspective. The chapter goes on to discuss the impact of Gramsci's work upon the development of

Marxist thought in Britain. It is suggested that interest in Gramsci was closely associated with a number of trends which either directly or indirectly reflected his own concerns. The development of a 'culturalist' perspective in the work of E.P.Thompson and Raymond Williams, a new and rigorous theoretical critique of 'labourism' in the work of Perry Anderson and Tom Nairn, and the emergence of a Eurocommunist perspective within the British Left were particularly important in this respect. Finally, it will be shown that by posing the problem of the relationship between the economic and non-economic institutions of society in a different way, and by emphasising the role of ideology and consent in the maintenance of social control, the Gramscian perspective has become central to the new paradigm in Marxist thinking.

Chapter 2 provides a brief account of social and political developments in Italy from its unification in 1860 to the outbreak of the First World War in 1914. This was a particularly volatile period in European history characterised by a complex blend of economic and social development and continuing international struggles for colonial supremacy. This period also saw the emergence of increasingly militant working-class organisations, advocating the transition of society from capitalism to socialism. These developments inevitably made a strong impression in Italy and set the political agenda within which Gramsci's own development as an activist took place. Chapter 3 gives a descriptive account of the historical circumstances of Gramsci's life and work. This includes a biography of Gramsci himself, and a summary of the major political events which were taking place in Italy and elsewhere in Europe during this period. Particular attention is given to Gramsci's participation as a political activist during the 1920s, and to the way in which he tried to adapt Lenin's political strategy to events in his own country. These issues are illustrated by reference to the body of political writings which Gramsci produced during this period.

Of all the concepts used by Gramsci, the notion of hegemony is perhaps the best known. Indeed 'Gramsci' and 'hegemony' are often taken to be synonymous. Unfortunately, however, this concept is notoriously difficult to define. Aside from the problems of translation, Gramsci uses the term in a particularly innovative way to encompass a wide range of meanings and circumstances. Its popularity, and the rather taken-for-granted manner in which it is sometimes used, makes it especially important to consider the notion of hegemony in some detail. Chapter 4 introduces the concept hegemony by suggesting that this concept can usefully be seen as an extension of the concept of ideology found in Marx, Lenin and Georg Lukács. Chapter 5 then goes on to provide a definition of the concept hegemony as used by Gramsci himself. It is suggested that in common with all 'concepts', hegemony can best be understood as a composite expression, a linguistic shorthand describing a variety of elements in combination. A definition of the principal constructs which appear throughout Gramsci's writing – namely: 'historical bloc', civil society/political society and 'war of manoeuvre/war of position' – are given here. To illustrate the problematic nature of Gramsci's terminology, this chapter includes a brief discussion of Perry Anderson's seminal article 'The Antinomies of Antonio Gramsci'. It will be argued that despite the considerable flexibility or 'slippage' which tends to arise in the Prison Notebooks, Gramsci is able to sustain an extremely useful means of analysing the processes of social reproduction and social change.

Chapter 6 approaches the notoriously controversial issues associated with the relationship between the economic and non-economic institutions of society. Gramsci develops a particularly novel approach to this problem by suggesting that the economic institutions of 'civil society' are at least as much superstructural as they are structural. This apparent deviation from Marx has inevitably caused much debate. By way of describing the main issues involved here, this chapter includes a brief discussion of the alternative interpretations of Gramsci put forward by Norberto Bobbio and Jacques Texier. It is suggested that Gramsci's analysis can be regarded as less dissimilar to Marx's understanding than it might at first appear.

It is well known that Gramsci attaches great significance to the need for widespread educational and cultural development among the mass of the population. The institutions through which this can be achieved, and the agents who help nurture the development of a new hegemony, namely the intellectuals, all receive close attention in his writings. For the sake of analysis it is useful to discuss these issues, first, in terms of the development of political consciousness and, second, in terms of political participation. To this end, Chapter 7 provides an account of Gramsci's theory of educational development and his suggestions for the formation of a 'common school'. A key feature of this process of enlightenment is that individuals can develop a clear and truthful understanding of reality only on the basis of personal experience. This chapter then goes on to describe Gramsci's analysis of those individuals who play a specifically intellectual role in society. The distinctions he draws between 'organic' and 'traditional' intellectuals are discussed, together with a brief analysis of the importance of working-class intellectuals in the business of conducting a revolution.

Having looked at the principles of education and political consciousness, Chapter 8 gives an account of the institutions through which individuals can further develop and express their political consciousness in practical terms. Although Gramsci consistently refers to the leading role of working-class organisations in revolutionary change, he is less consistent as to what form they should take. Broadly speaking, there is a clear break between Gramsci's earlier insistence on the role of the factory councils and his later adherence to the idea that revolution can be conducted only through the agency of a centralised and somewhat authoritarian Leninist Party. This chapter gives an account of these two forms of organisation before suggesting that Gramsci never fully reconciled his faith in autonomous self-development and democracy with the problems of leadership and discipline.

Overall it is hoped that this book will demonstrate that Gramsci's work continues to provide an extremely valuable, although sometimes problematic, perspective for achieving a deeper understanding of social reproduction and social change. If this aim has been fulfilled, this will confirm one of the most fundamental precepts of Marxism, that it is a theory of social evolution which bases itself upon a thorough scrutiny of society as it actually exists. It does not seek to make assumptions and put forward solutions on the basis of a set of ideals and beliefs which may have no actual basis in reality.

1
Central themes and debates

As noted in the Introduction, interest in Gramsci's work has undergone something of an explosion in recent years. In common with all explosions, however, the fall-out has tended to become somewhat dissipated and opaque. For those who are already familiar with Gramsci's work, the task of reconstructing these disparate elements in order to get back to the point of detonation may not pose too much of a problem. For somebody approaching Gramsci for the first time, however, getting a grip on the theoretical and polemical repercussions of Gramsci's work may seem somewhat perplexing. The purpose of this chapter is to help overcome these initial difficulties by outlining two of the most important developments in Marxist theory which are closely associated with Gramsci's writings. This will also provide a context within which the discussion in the following chapters can best be understood. Before doing this, it is useful to look briefly at how interest in Gramsci's work has developed since the initial publication of his writings, and at how Gramsci's influence has coincided with a number of trends in British Marxism.

The development of the Gramsci industry

(i) Gramsci in Italy
The first selections of Gramsci's prison writings were published in Italy between 1947 and 1951 under the watchful eye of the

Communist Party in Moscow. Since becoming Secretary-General of the Italian Communist Party after Gramsci's arrest in 1926, Palmiro Togliatti had depicted Gramsci as being the archetypal working-class hero who had risen from humble origins to lead the Italian revolution. Togliatti insisted that Gramsci had based his theory more or less entirely upon sound Marxist–Leninist principles, and that as a devout and disciplined Bolshevik he had always been one of Stalin's most faithful supporters. Further, Togliatti was keen to show that the Popular Front policy which had been put forward by the Seventh Congress of the Comintern in 1935,[1] and which the Italian Communist Party had endorsed, was closely related to proposals for working-class solidarity which Gramsci had put forward shortly before his imprisonment. In Mouffe and Showstack Sassoon's words:

> The limitation of the discussion of Gramsci in terms of the Italian national heritage was part of the attempt to portray the Italian working-class as the rightful heirs to the Risorgimento, as a new hegemonic national force which could strive to become the fundamental factor in rebuilding Italy on the basis of a wide-ranging alliance of anti-fascist forces. (Mouffe and Showstack Sassoon, 1977: 33)[2]

Because of his senior position within the Communist Party, and because he had been a close companion of Gramsci, Togliatti's interpretation of Gramsci remained largely unchallenged throughout the 1950s. Following Stalin's death in 1953, however, and his subsequent denunciation at the Party Conferences in 1956 and 1961, Togliatti was forced to play down the image of Gramsci the Stalinist in favour of Gramsci the Leninist. At the same time, and as the first publications were being studied more closely, Togliatti began to suggest that although Gramsci had been strongly influenced by Lenin, his prison writings represented a considerable theoretical achievementin their own right: 'Gramsci's writing bears directly upon that of Lenin, but has its own original form, bestowed by the thesis of the party as collective intellectual, and which is virtually a complete theory of politics' (Togliatti, 1979: 155).

Two important issues were raised by this change of view. First, there was some confusion as to how familiar Gramsci actually was with Lenin's writings. Second, questions were raised as to who else might have influenced Gramsci's intellectual development. In answer to the first point, and as Davidson has pointed out, despite his close friendship with Gramsci, Togliatti was forced to concede that 'he had very little concrete evidence to back his thesis about Gramsci's life, his intellectual formation and how his notes should be understood' (Davidson, 1972: 452).[3] On the second point, it became clear that even before going to Turin University in 1911 Gramsci had been strongly influenced not only by the idealist (as opposed to the Marxist or materialist) philosophies of Giovanni Gentile and Benedetto Croce, but also by the distinctly pro-nationalist arguments of Gaetano Salvemini. Following this reassessment from outside the Communist Party, the pendulum swung decisively away from Gramsci the Leninist towards Gramsci the Crocean idealist.

While these disputes continued throughout the late 1950s and early 1960s, more of the original material became available with the publication of Gramsci's early writings and journal articles, a number of important letters between Gramsci and Togliatti, and Giuseppe Fiori's biography. This resulted in a shift of emphasis away from the 'mature' and reflective Gramsci of the prison writings to the 'young' and militant Gramsci of the factory council movement. New disputes then arose over the strategic question of whether the revolution should be conducted on the basis of workplace organisations (factory councils and trade unions) or by the political party. By 1967 both groups of interpreters had more or less agreed that, pending the emergence of a full intellectual biography, 'the meaning of his notes remained an open question, and all earlier interpretations were without value' (Davidson, 1972: 459).

(ii) Gramsci and the New Left in Britain
The first English–language edition of Gramsci's prison writings was published in 1957 (Gramsci, 1957). Aside from two brief articles on Gramsci which appeared in *The Times Literary Supplement* in 1948 and 1952,[4] it was not until the publication of *Selections from the Prison Notebooks* in 1971 (Gramsci, 1971) that Gramsci's absorption into British Marxism began in earnest. Further impetus was provided with the publication of Nairn's (1990) translation of Fiori's biography, together with two editions of Gramsci's letters from prison (Henderson, 1974, and Gramsci, 1973). From this point on, a more or less continuous stream of books has appeared, ranging from the more historical and descriptive accounts of Cammett (1967), Gwyn Williams (1975) and Martin Clark (1977), to the 'intellectual' analyses of Davidson (1977), Adamson (1980) and Femia (1981), and the specifically theoretical treatments of Buci-Glucksmann (1980), Laclau and Mouffe (1985) and Anne Showstack Sassoon (1987).[5] Eley has summarised these developments in terms of three phases:

If 1967–75 was a phase of initiation, when notice of Gramsci was first properly taken, and 1975–7 one of consolidation when a range of essentially biographical studies started to appear, then 1978–82 was the phase of mature Gramsci scholarship, when an adequate basis has finally been laid for a discussion of Gramsci in English. (Eley, 1984: 445)

In Britain, interest in Gramsci's work coincided with a number of important and interconnected trends in the Marxist perspective more generally. First, following the lead of E.P.Thompson, Eric Hobsbawm and others, a strong interest developed in the social history of the working class.[6] The broad rationale behind this research was to develop a sense of historical continuity between the past and present manifestations of working-class struggle, and then to relate this apparently innate predisposition for emancipatory solidarity to the present and future actions of the Communist Party. As Schwarz and Mercer put it:

> The historians' collective project rested on recovering the deep tradition of English popular radicalism, and linking up their own contemporary struggles to this long heritage. . . . the stress of this project fell on the popular as a continuous historical tradition (albeit a tradition unevenly activated) which the Communist Party had to recover and re-present to the people in contemporary times. (Schwarz and Mercer, 1981: 148–9)

Following the Soviet suppression of popular uprisings in Poland and Hungary in June and October 1956, however, Thompson left the Communist Party and decided to pursue the quest for popular radicalism from within a more broadly based 'socialist-humanist' perspective.

A second major development, and one which shared some of Thompson's and Gramsci's concerns, was the emergence of a strongly 'humanist' and 'culturalist' current in the writings of Raymond Williams.[7] Although the definition of 'culture' is not entirely straightforward,[8] and although Williams was initially concerned with refuting earlier distinctions between 'high' and 'low' culture, particularly in the study of English literature, he suggested that understanding the form and nature of society cannot be achieved without also understanding how its various levels or facets come to be joined together. For Williams, this social cement is reflected in and through culture.[9]

Having recognised the interactive and creative character of 'culture', Williams goes on to emphasise that it may be a mistake either to regard some activities as being more important than others, or to assume that some activities are necessarily predetermined by others. He writes that:

> If we find, as often, that a particular activity came radically to change the whole organization, we can still not say that it is to this activity that all the others must be related; we can only study the varying ways in which, within the changing organization, the particular activities and their interrelations were affected. Further, since the particular activities will be serving varying and sometimes conflicting ends, the sort of change we must look for will rarely be of a simple kind: elements of persistence, adjustment, unconscious assimilation, active resistance, alternative effort, will all normally be present in particular activities and in the whole organization. (R. Williams, 1981: 46–7)

The implications of this kind of argument for the Marxist notion that virtually everything is derived from, and is thus determined by, economic activities will be discussed shortly. For the moment, the important point to grasp is that, following Williams, a great deal of Marxist and non-Marxist attention was shifted to the problems of analysing the way that culture is produced and transmitted, the various forms and patterns that it may take, and the ways in which it is absorbed by and affects the behaviour – 'the way of living' – of 'the man in the street'.

Although Thompson subsequently criticised some elements of Williams' culturalism for underplaying what Hall describes as 'the dimensions of struggle and confrontation between opposed *ways* of life', and although they expressed themselves in slightly different terms,[10] the socio-historical and culturalist perspectives became dominant. With regard to Gramsci, and in spite of the fact that neither Williams nor Thompson referred directly to his work, culturalism provided what Forgacs has described as 'a framework, an intellectual space, within which Gramsci, or at least a certain side of Gramsci, could be made visible and readable, a space which his own work would, in turn, begin to illuminate and reconstruct from within' (Forgacs, 1989: 74).

Meanwhile, a third impetus for Gramsci studies began to emerge from the perspectives of the 'second' New Left who had taken over

New Left Review in 1962. Although both Thompson and Williams had been involved in the formation of the 'first' New Left group in England and its journals *Universities and Left Review* and the *New Reasoner*, and had continued to contribute after the fusion of the two in 1960 into the *New Left Review* with Stuart Hall as editor, disagreements emerged when Anderson, Nairn and Blackburn took control of the journal.[11] In a series of articles in 1964,[12] Anderson and Nairn put forward a forthright critique of what they regarded as the self-defeating and inherently *non-revolutionary* position of the British labour movement. As Schwarz and Mercer put it:

> Revolutionary purity was prized in place of the reformist contaminations of popular movements which were invariably viewed as diluting Marxism with a debilitating liberalism. . . . Socialism increasingly came to be presented in terms of leadership – and more often than not, the leadership of a traditionally-organized but 'left' intelligentsia. (Schwarz and Mercer, 1981: 152)[13]

The essence of the critique of 'Labourism' was that, from the beginning, the British trade unions and Labour Party had adopted an economistic perspective which restricted their aims to gaining relatively superficial concessions from the ruling capitalist class: 'A combination of structural and conjunctural factors in the 19th century produced a proletariat distinguished by *an immovable corporate class consciousness and almost no hegemonic ideology*. This paradox is the most important single fact about the English working-class' (Anderson 1964: 41; original emphasis). Having provided what Anderson later called 'a systematic historical explanation of the configuration of class forces in English society and the nature of the present crisis of British capitalism' (Anderson, 1980: 138), Anderson and Nairn argued that, contrary to Thompson's analysis, the English labour movement had never fully realised the potential for revolutionary change.[14] Writing about 'the reactionary consolidation' of the 1950s Anderson argues that:

> Its major idiom was glutinously chauvinist – reverent worship of Westminster, ubiquitous cult of constitutional moderation and common sense, ritualized exaltation of tradition and precedent. The 'left' variant of the political culture of the time descended from the maudlin social patriotism of Orwell: the 'right' variant from the anthems to the wisdom of gradualist 'experience' of thinkers like Oakshott. The bulk of the working

class was passive and integrated into the national 'consensus' – one of the greatest ideological themes of the decade. (Anderson, 1980: 147)

As this quotation shows, a significant part of this critique was directed at the 'cultural nationalism' of the English working class and its intelligentsia. In order to rectify this situation, and assuming the role of intellectual vanguard, the second New Left set out to break the mould of 'wretched cultural provincialism' by introducing British Marxism to a number of theoretical currents which had already become established in Europe. In addition to the work of the Frankfurt School, Lukács, Althusser and Sartre, Gramsci was high on the list of imports. Indeed, Anderson has acknowledged that 'the decisive influence was Gramsci, whose concepts were deployed by the Review in its explorations of English history and politics a decade before they became a vogue elsewhere' (Anderson, 1980: 149–50). To the extent that Anderson's and Nairn's approach adopts a distinctly Gramscian concern with the need to develop a revolutionary hegemony which is untainted by its origins in bourgeois society, and since as Thompson points out 'the Anderson/Nairn positions became the uncontested orthodoxy of the *New Left Review*' (Thompson, 1978: 399), it was clear that a Gramscian perspective would continue to play a leading role in the theoretical development of the British New Left.

A fourth important development associated with the growing interest in Gramsci came with the emergence of a Eurocommunist perspective within the British Left. Eurocommunism developed in continental Europe as a reaction to the perceived excesses of the Communist Party of the Soviet Union during the 1950s and 1960s. The essence of its critique was that, following the disgrace of Stalin and through its treatment of the Poles and Hungarians, and later of the Czechoslovakians, the Soviet Party had demonstrated the inappropriateness not only of its own model for post-war society, but also of its claimed leadership over the other European Communist Parties. Largely at the instigation of the Italian, French and Spanish Communist Parties (all of which had shared the experience of resistance against the Nazis during the Second World War), it was proposed that in the context of advanced capitalist societies the transition to socialism could be achieved only through gradual and democratic means rather than through direct revolution. The Secretary-General of the Spanish Communist Party has summarised the aims of Eurocommunism as:

The need to advance socialism with democracy, a multi-party system, parliaments and representative institutions, sovereignty of the people regularly exercised through universal suffrage, trade unions independent of the State and the parties, freedom for the opposition, human rights, religious freedom, freedom for cultural, scientific and artistic creation, and the development of the broadest forms of popular participation at all levels and in all branches of social activity. (Carrillo, 1977: 110)[15]

As this definition shows, a key feature of Eurocommunism is its recognition of the need to create alliances between different groups, and it was this feature which was particularly attractive to the Communist Party in Britain.

During the 1960s in Britain, support for socialist and other 'left-wing' causes had undergone a process of fragmentation. The Labour Party had alienated large sections of the broad Left, first over its rejection of an anti-nuclear policy during the early 1960s and, second, over the increasingly non-socialist policies of Harold Wilson's Governments in 1964 and 1966. Members of the first New Left, including Williams and Thompson, became disillusioned with both the Communist and Labour Parties and concentrated their attention on the development of popular movements (particularly the Campaign for Nuclear Disarmament, CND, and the Vietnam Solidarity Campaign, VSO), and on trying to resuscitate the ethos of the informal 'Left groups' of the late 1950s.[16] The second New Left, meanwhile, was principally concerned with elaborating upon the problems of social stability and change at the level of theory as a prerequisite for action in the future. To this extent, it concentrated its efforts largely at the level of theoretical discussion and analysis, rather than at the level of immediate organisation and action. In addition, the already faltering progress of the various Left groups was further impeded by deep changes which were taking place in the political milieu more generally. Influential single-issue groups had emerged which were less concerned with the socialist transformation of society as such than with more discrete and immediate concerns for personal rights and freedoms. Women's issues, gay rights and racial equality, for example, created new dimensions and discourses which progressively displaced the paternalistic rhetoric of a fast disappearing manual working class.[17]

Although both the first and second New Lefts and various Trotskyist groupings such as the Socialist Workers' Party had played an important if not exactly leading role in the more militant activities of

CND, VSO and the Anti-Nazi League, and although there were points of overlap between the old popular movements and the new social movements, it was clear that any co-ordination of radical politics would have to recognise the multidimensional nature of contemporary political culture. It was not simply a question, in other words, of trying to apply tried and tested Marxist formulae to what had been a reasonably stable set of circumstances (basic divisions between the manual working class and the rest of society, the assumption that the Labour Party was the 'natural' party of the working class and that the Labour Party was in fact a *socialist* party), but of recognising that since the circumstances had changed, the tools and techniques of analysis would have to change also.

Throughout the 1960s and 1970s, the British Communist Party had already absorbed many of the principles of Eurocommunism. In the 1978 edition of its manifesto *The British Road to Socialism* for example, the Party stated that the socialist revolution 'can be carried through in Britain . . . by a combination of a socialist parliamentary majority and mass struggle outside parliament, ensuring a government that is determined and able to implement a socialist programme', and that 'the need is to develop and unite [the forces for change] in a broad democratic alliance, led by the working class and embracing the majority of the people' (Communist Party of Great Britain, 1978: 3–4). As this reference shows, however, the leading role in this process was given exclusively to the labour movement in general (comprising the Labour Party, the Communist Party and the Co-operative movement, the shop stewards committees and Trades Councils), and the working class in particular: 'The leading force in the alliance will be the working class, whose interests are most directly opposed to those of the capitalist ruling class, and whose strength and capacity for organisation enables it to give leadership to all the democratic forces in society' (p.18). Although the Party recognised that the increase in the number of working women has been 'a significant new feature in the industrial scene' and that 'winning black workers . . . is vital' (p.19), this acknowledgement was framed exclusively in terms of economic disadvantage and class war. The possibility that many of the most pressing social issues were not necessarily *class issues*, and therefore that the people who pursued them might be drawn from a cross-class spectrum of social groups, had not yet been fully realised.[18]

During the 1980s, however, and as awareness of the plural and multidimensional nature of politics increased, the Party gradually acknowledged that the basis of co-ordination and co-operation was, in Forgacs' words, no longer seen 'as being pre-given and cemented by the same objective class interest' but as 'arising out of the subjective consciousness and struggle of groups oppressed on *different* terrains . . . not all of which were directly related to class oppression' (Forgacs, 1989: 85). This change of emphasis was clearly reflected in the 1989 *Manifesto for New Times*, which placed the need for organisational and strategic change at the top of its 'new agenda':

> The social and democratic changes at the heart of the shift to the new times are fracturing many of the old collective sources of identity which the Left was founded upon. Class will be central to politics in the 1990's. But the character of the working class is changing. In addition, other sources of collective identity among women, black people, and other social groups will be central to progressive politics. Progressive politics has to realign itself to the changes in its potential constituencies of support. (Communist Party of Great Britain, 1989: 13)

The Green movement, the growth of 'a new popular international humanism' and 'mounting moral and political opposition', are all acknowledged, while race and gender issues are expressed in terms not only of employment but as 'existing power relations in the home and in our culture' (p.3).

Overall, therefore, interest in Gramsci's work has run parallel with a number of recent trends in Marxist analysis. Among the most important have been: a greater understanding of the deeper social and subjective dimensions of working-class culture; a recognition that achieving radical social change depends upon the formation of a solidaristic hegemony based on *universal* rather than purely *class-based* issues, and that this solidarity necessarily involves the prior formation of sympathetic and democratic alliances throughout society. Although it would be an exaggeration to suggest that Gramsci's writings have directly influenced these trends, it is none the less the case that many of the issues raised coincide with significant aspects of Gramsci's own analysis. However direct or indirect this relationship may have been, it seems certain that from now on Gramsci will remain a central point of reference for Marxian social analysis.

Having given a brief account of Gramsci's assimilation into western Marxism, and having drawn attention to a number of the other developments which nurtured and propagated interest in his work, it will be useful briefly to introduce two of the central problems which have beset Marxist accounts of society.

Themes and debates

As noted in the Introduction, two of the most important issues in Marxist theory centre round the relationship between the economic base and the other 'superstructural' institutions of society, and round the role of ideology as a force acting for or against radical social change. These can be expressed as a question: To what extent do economic structures and circumstances determine all other aspects of activity and social structure? And, following from this, if the institutions of the superstructure (including the parliamentary, legal and education systems, and the mass media and Church) do exercise a degree of independence from the economic base, and if the influence of these latter institutions is primarily intellectual or ideological, then is it not also true that the struggle for radical social change must be at least as much political and ideological as it is economic?

Economic determinism

In its simplest form, exponents of the 'economy determines everything' argument contend that, since human life cannot exist without the production of material goods, the way that these goods are produced and the forms of co-operation which pertain to them must necessarily provide the foundation upon which all other activities are based. As the means of production and the relations of production become more and more complex, it is inevitable that new institutions must be created to regulate and maintain the economic structure. However extensive and interconnected these institutions become, and however autonomous and detached they may appear, it is still the case that they are fundamentally directed towards economic production. In capitalist society, for example, it is argued that the education system may have positive virtues in its own right, but that ultimately its purpose is to provide a suitably educated and disciplined workforce. Similarly, while the legal system provides a framework for the protection of civil liberties and rights of property ownership and control, it also bestows a sense of legitimacy upon various forms of economic exploitation and financial gain. A similar line of argument can be used in the case of non-institutional activities. The production of works of art, for example, may have great intrinsic value, but ultimately it is likely that the artist is at least partly inspired by the possibility that his or her 'products' may acquire value as commodities.

Turning to the political implications of this view, it is argued that although *all societies* depend upon co-operative production for their survival, capitalist society has developed a *particular form* of productive organisation within which a minority enjoys a degree of consumption far in excess of its contribution. The minority is able to maintain this advantage by manipulating the way in which other individuals gain access to the necessities of life. Since this access is overwhelmingly gained through exchanging one's effort and skills for income, and since the minority has effective control over the mechanisms of employment, it inevitably assumes a dominant position within society. Although this control, and the disproportionately large income it yields, provide the dominant group with financial and other resources with which to perpetuate the system, the source of its power originates in its control over the productive process. In order to displace the dominant minority and create a new and more equal distribution of income, it is therefore necessary to gain control over the means of production.

The question then arises as to how this seizure of power can be achieved. This problem can be expressed in terms of three dimensions. First, there is the question of *motivation*. Since all individuals need access to income in order to provide themselves with the necessities of life, it follows that everybody has a vested interest in the productive process. As already noted, however, some individuals gain considerable income and power from the present system and are therefore likely to try to maintain it in its present form. For the majority, however, the present organisation of work is fundamentally exploitative and oppressive since its income bears little relation to the actual 'value' and 'worth' of the products it produces. Clearly, the degree of exploitation varies between different individuals and groups of individuals according to their position in the division of labour. Some individuals in other words *are more exploited* than others. The motivation to achieve a rearrangement of the means of production is therefore related to the degree to which a particular group of individuals is being exploited; the most exploited groups are those which stand to gain the most from revolutionary change.

The second question is one of *organisation*. Since the principal objective of revolution is to take control over the means of production, it follows that those groups who have personal knowledge of the productive process must play a leading role in social transformation. In modern capitalist society the working class in general and the industrial proletariat in particular must therefore develop organisations which will allow them to take control and, most importantly, to supervise the transformation of the means of production *after the revolution*.

The third question relates to *strategy*. Once the working class has developed organisations in preparation for the seizure of power, it must then develop a suitable strategy for bringing it about. Since the present capitalist organisation of the productive forces is based upon the exploitation of one social group by another, its control over society is thus contradictory and highly unstable. Inevitably this instability will give rise to a series of crises culminating in a decisive confrontation between the minority and the majority. A crucial aspect of working-class strategy must therefore be to mobilise its organisations when the final crisis arrives. In anticipation of this confrontation the minority will of course use its resources to defend the economic system in its present form. Since this defence is principally manifest through a series of State agencies such as the police, the army and other paramilitary organisations, the working class will ultimately have to confront these defences and overthrow them by force.

A number of arguments have been raised against this economic determinist view. In the first place it is argued that, by regarding all aspects of society as an elaborate outgrowth of the economic structure, the reductionist approach pays insufficient attention both to the complexity of the institutions of the superstructure, and to the influence they have *in their own right*. It is argued, for example, that although the legal and education systems do play a role in the economy, their continuous development has given them a much more independent and autonomous role in society. The relationship between economic and non-economic institutions should therefore be regarded as one of interaction and mediation than of cause and effect.

In the second place, it is suggested that although the dominant group does exercise power and control through the economy, it also exercises control through a wide range of other institutions which are less explicitly concerned with economic issues. Through contact with the legal, welfare and health bureaucracies, for example, and through participation in the institutions of government and democracy, individuals in modern societies have become integrated into the fabric of society to such an extent that simple economic explanations of social control are insufficient. Most importantly, it is argued that social control is at least partly maintained with the *active consent* of the population. The minority does not so much impose its authority as negotiate for it. Part of this negotiation involves the delegation of rights and responsibilities to other groups, including groups from within the relatively disadvantaged majority. By delegating its authority in this way, the dominant group consolidates its power since a greater proportion of the population has a vested interest in the present organisation of society. To the extent that these latter individuals actively participate in the institutional structure, they contribute to the appearance of legitimacy and consent, as it were *voluntarily*.

With regard to the political implications of economic determinism, it is argued that although gaining control over the means of production is the ultimate aim, control must also be taken of the institutions of the superstructure. In the same way that post-revolutionary society will need to continue to produce goods, it will also have to maintain some form of legal and administrative structure, to provide a democratic system of decision-making, and look after the educational and health needs of the population. To this extent, control over the means of production is *one aspect* of social transformation but not the *only aspect*.

Similar arguments are made regarding motivation, organisation and strategy. First, although exploitation may provide an index of revolutionary motivation, the *realisation* of this potential cannot be taken for granted. Exploitation may be the prerequisite for social change, but it does not guarantee that particular individuals or groups of individuals will make the connection between their circumstances and the nature of society as such. Social transformation, in other words, depends upon the extent to which individuals become *conscious* of this relationship and decide to act; it is an *organic* rather than *mechanical* process. As the processes of meaning-formation and communication become more and more complicated, and as the number of issues and perspectives being discussed continue to multiply, the chances that a radical socialist view will become a majority view are correspondingly reduced.

Second, and closely related to the above, it is suggested that modern methods of production have given rise to such a wide range of occupations and practices that it is no longer possible to allocate a decisive role to any one group. The industrial proletariat of the late nineteenth century has been superseded by a much more diffuse social group, only part of which can be regarded as manual working class in the traditional sense. The production of goods within a complex international division of labour has given considerable influence and control to many groups which are only indirectly concerned with the physical aspects of production as such. To this extent, taking control over the means of production will involve the active consent and organisation of many groups beyond the working class itself. Similarly, in the context of modern societies, the distribution of incomes and therefore of relative exploitation is much broader than it was during the earlier stages of industrialisation. Representing society in terms of simplistic distinctions between broad strata of the population merely disguises the fragmented nature of the contemporary distribution and composition of social groups.

Third, these changes in the nature of society suggest that the expectation of a straightforward seizure of power culminating in direct confrontation with the defensive forces of the State is somewhat unrealistic. In the first place it is argued that although capitalism is fundamentally contradictory, the form and extent of the crises it produces may not lead to an ultimate and sudden crisis. It is more likely that the dominant group will be able to respond to periodic crises such as high levels of unemployment or economic recession in such a way as to avoid or at least postpone any final confrontation. This capacity for flexibility may suggest that capitalism is resilient rather than brittle and fragile. In the second place, given the influence of superstructural institutions and their reciprocal effects on the economic structure, and given the negotiated and consensual nature of modern social control, it is argued that the political and ideological dimensions of social transformation have largely displaced that of revolution through direct conflict and force. Since political and ideological transformation cannot be achieved overnight, the strategy for change must be gradual and persuasive rather than sudden and violent.

(ii) The role of ideology

Two important issues which have arisen in the previous discussion are the extent to which people become *conscious* of their situation in society, and the extent to which social control is maintained through *consent*. Both these issues are bound up with the concept of ideology. From within a bourgeois-liberal perspective, the apparent stability of society is seen as a reflection of the fact that the majority of the population shares a set of coherent beliefs, norms and values. The legitimacy of the social structure is therefore assumed to be demonstrated by the apparent lack of widespread social dissent. A limited degree of social dissent can be regarded as 'functional', as it may ultimately tend to confirm the stability of the structure in the normal course of events. Through institutions such as the democratic process, the education system, the Church and the mass media, individuals participate in an unprejudiced exchange of ideas on the basis of which the dominant group can be seen to be pursuing the goals and priorities which the majority of the population seeks to fulfil. The perceived flexibility and apparent responsiveness of the democratic processes are taken to guarantee that society will continue to develop in accordance with these goals and priorities. Other institutions, including the defensive agencies of the State, are represented as being *subordinate* to these goals and priorities, and as acting on behalf of everyone rather than on behalf of any particular group.

From a Marxist point of view, however, much concern has been expressed over whether these goals and priorities, and the ideas through which they are articulated, are in fact manipulated by some groups to their own advantage. Whether, in other words, bourgeois ideologies create a prejudiced and distorted way of looking at the world which not only encourages support for the status quo, but which also inhibits the development of critical and possibly socialist or revolutionary consciousness. Economistic Marxist accounts of ideology adopt a particularly dismissive critique of the bourgeois-liberal perspective on ideological consensus. They argue that appeals to a process of democratic consent should in fact be seen as a sophisticated means of pseudo-legitimation through which the dominant group seeks to disguise its actual and material control over the productive process. The extent to which individuals are misled by the idea of ideological consensus is merely a measure of the extent to which the dominant group has succeeded in shielding itself from criticism. Drawing on arguments discussed above, it is suggested that the 'consent' of the population is primarily attained through a complex range of structural constraints, which 'physically' locate individuals both in respect to each other and in respect to access to income. Since ideological means of persuasion have relatively little power when measured against these material constraints, they are regarded as secondary and subordinate. When dissent and social conflict emerge, they are taken to be symptomatic of the inherent contradictions which characterise the capitalistic organisation of work. Ultimately, therefore, in order to change society it is necessary to change its *practices* not its *ideologies*.

While sharing some aspects of this view, more recent Marxist accounts of ideological consensus have suggested that it is necessary to develop a much more detailed analysis of the role of ideas and ideologies, and of the ways in which they are articulated and disseminated within society. In line with the trends discussed in above, a great deal of effort has now been invested in providing this kind of analysis. In Britain, for example, the development of cultural studies stimulated great interest in the role of the mass media as the principal mechanism of meaning-formation and transmission within society. This analysis was greatly assisted by the development of structuralist and post-structuralist linguistic and semiotic theory, which provided an important framework within which discourse analysis and media studies could be conducted. In a parallel vein, the work of the early Frankfurt School has drawn attention to the ways in which modern consumer society has anaesthetised the revolutionary potential of the population by stimulating an insatiable desire for consumer goods.

With regard to the implications of these developments for political organisation and strategy, the turn to ideology has had a considerable impact. One of the clearest examples of this new approach has emerged in the critique of Thatcherism in Britain. In the *Manifesto for New Times*, for example, it is argued that through the Conservative Party the dominant minority in Britain has been able to maintain its power 'by articulating a range of strongly felt, and popular, fears, prejudices and aspirations'. It has 'responded to demands for greater autonomy and choice with an ideology of assertive individualism'. This individualism is then combined with 'an authoritarianism aimed at instilling social and economic discipline. Its socially authoritarian and repressive agendas on crime, law and order, immigration and homosexuality, are a response to the so-called permissiveness of the 1960's, which it blames for a collapse of respect for traditional British values' (Communist Party of Great Britain, 1989: 8).

Having characterised Thatcherism as 'a novel, innovative, hegemonic political force', and bearing in mind the non-reductionist perspective outlined above, the business of displacing the dominant group is seen as being principally located within the ideological and political realms. Since 'Thatcherism will only be defeated electorally if it is defeated politically and ideologically', the task of the Left therefore becomes one of developing a novel and innovative hegemony, a 'political and ideological vision' which will not only challenge the current hegemony but will also provide the 'tributaries of opposition' with 'a common centre of gravity' upon which to base its new alliances.

Summary

In summary, then, since Gramsci's work first became available in the early 1950s in Italy, and in the late 1950s in Britain and the United States, interest in his work has grown enormously. This interest has been further stimulated by other developments in Marxist theory which either share Gramsci's concerns directly or run parallel to them. As the discussion in the following chapters will show, the importance of Gramsci's work relates to the contribution he has made to resolving two central weaknesses of Marx's original approach. First, that Marx was mistaken in assuming that social development always originates from, or is determined by, changes in the economic structure. This resulted in a misconceived and rather simplistic understanding of the relationship between economic and non-economic aspects of society. Second, that Marx placed too much faith in the possibility of a spontaneous outburst of revolutionary consciousness among the working class. This resulted in an inadequate recognition of the cultural and ideological forces which help to maintain the power and legitimacy of the dominant group.

Gramsci repeatedly turns his attention to trying to resolve these problems both by reworking a number of traditional precepts of Marxist political theory and by developing a number of new ones. Drawing upon his study of Italian history, for example, Gramsci argued that a social group or class can sustain a dominant position only if it is able to obtain *the conscious consent* of the majority of the population. It must in other words represent, and be seen to represent, the norms values and aspirations of society as a whole. It cannot rule by force alone. These beliefs are not random and arbitrary, but constitute an overarching world-view: a clear and cohesive understanding of the moral, ethical and cultural fabric of the society which its advocates seek to maintain or bring about.

Gramsci then used this new focus on the synthesis of force and consent – a synthesis which he expresses through the notion of 'hegemony' – as a basis for understanding events in his own time. He goes on to argue that the Leninist strategy of mounting a direct military assault or a 'war of manoeuvre' against the ruling group had been successful since the institutions of tsarist Russia were relatively simple and underdeveloped. In the context of more advanced democratic nation-states with complex social structures, however, Gramsci argued that a new, more gradual and sophisticated strategy had to be developed; a 'war of position'. The key to 'revolutionary' social change in modern societies does not therefore depend, as Marx had predicted, on the spontaneous awakening of critical class consciousness but upon the prior formation of a new alliance of interests, an alternative hegemony or 'historical bloc', which has already developed a cohesive world-view of its own. Significantly, this alliance and the conception of reality which it holds, must be based upon a set of attitudes which are not confined within the limitations of *particular* economic aims and 'class' interests, but which are *universal* and appeal to the general aspirations of the population as a whole.

Notes

1. Schwarz and Mercer describe the Popular Front as a strategy

    which was to be broad and popular, aimed not only to safeguard constitutional liberties already won – an immediate priority in the face of fascism and reaction – but also to deepen as far as possible existing democratic rights. Those who supported the Popular Front did not envisage the dismantling of parliamentary democracy and its wholesale replacement by proletarian institutions of direct democracy, or soviets, but a movement intent on expanding and making effective representative democracy, in conjunction with more direct forms. The very logic of this conception emphasised the need to pick up, continue and carry forward into the future the prior traditions of democratic struggle so that the Communist Party would come to represent the culmination of the nation's democratic history. (Schwarz and Mercer, 1981: 147–8)

2. Togliatti writes, for example, that:

    We have already managed to achieve great advances as a party, and to make the working-class movement and all Italian society move forward by following the teaching of Gramsci. We must be able to return continually to this teaching, aware that it is not our private affair alone, but the property of the whole nation, which it is particularly our responsibility to cultivate. (Togliatti, 1979: 159)

3. In a paper prepared for the first conference of Gramscian studies in January 1958, Togliatti writes:

> Philological research into Gramsci's knowledge of Lenin's work presents some difficulties. It is not always possible, in fact, to establish precisely when he could have become acquainted with and studied particular writings of Lenin, and, therefore, one cannot always establish which of these had greatest direct influence on him at particular times. (Togliatti, 1979: 164)

  See also Chapters 5 to 8, below, which give a clear indication of the revised interpretation of Gramsci's originality.
4. These were: 'Marxism and culture in Italy', *The Times Literary Supplement*, 28 August 1948, p.796; and 'More about Gramsci', 5 December 1952, p.492. It is interesting to note that these articles tend to adopt the Crocean interpretation of Gramsci's work. The 1948 article concludes with the suggestion that: 'Unless Marxism can give the Italians everything they look to get from Benedetto Croce, and something more, it can never obtain the "hegemony" of Italy.'
5. Detailed accounts of the development of 'Gramsciology' in western Marxism are given by: Eley (1984); Kaye (1981); and more recently in Forgacs (1989). A more directly 'theoretical' account is given in Mouffe and Showstack Sassoon (1977).
6. Thompson's (1963), *The Making of the English Working Class*, is the best example of this genre. See also Hobsbawm (1968).
7. The best known examples are Williams (1958 and 1961). See also Hoggart (1958).
8. Williams suggests, for example, that:

> We need to distinguish three levels of culture, even in its most general definition. There is the lived culture of a particular time and place, only fully accessible to those living in that time and place. There is the recorded culture, of every kind, from art to the most everyday facts: the culture of a period. There is also, as the factor connecting lived culture and period cultures, the culture of the selective tradition. (Williams, 1981: 49)

9. He writes, for example, that:

> The analysis of culture, in the documentary sense, is of great importance because it can yield specific evidence about the whole organization within which it was expressed. We cannot say that we know a particular form or period of society, and that we will see how its art and theory relate to it, for until we know these, we cannot really claim to know the society. (Williams, 1981: 47)

10. Hall suggests, for example, that: 'The organizing terrain of Thompson's work – classes as relations, popular struggle, and historical forms of consciousness, class cultures in their historical particularity – is foreign to the more reflective and "generalizing" mode in which Williams typically works', and that 'Thompson also operates with a more "classical" distinction than Williams, between "social being" and "social conscious ness" rather than between base and superstructure' (Hall, 1981: 24). For Thompson's critique of Williams' *The Long Revolution* see Thompson (1961).
11. For various accounts of these events compare Williams (1979): 361–83; and Anderson (1980): ch.5.
12. See, in particular, Anderson (1964); and Nairn (1964 a–b).
13. This analysis provoked a very strong response from Thompson (see Thompson, 1965). For Anderson's reply to Thompson, see Anderson (1966). See also Anderson (1980): ch.5.
14. Anderson writes, for example, that:

> In Britain, the working-class has generated over 150 years a massive, administrative class consciousness – but it has never developed into a hegemonic political force. The very name of its traditional political party poignantly underlines this truth. Alone of the major European working-class parties, it is called neither a Social-Democratic nor Socialist nor a Communist Party; it is the *Labour* Party – the name designates, not an ideal society, as do all the others, but simply an existent interest. (Anderson, 1964: 45)

15. For an account of the emergence of Eurocommunism see Claudin (1978).
16. These efforts culminated in the publication by Williams, Thompson, Hall and others of the 'May-Day Manifesto' in 1967. Although the Manifesto attracted some support on the Left and stimulated new discussions over policy and strategy, the movement collapsed over proposals to put forward Left Alliance candidates *against* Labour Party candidates in the 1970 General Election. For Williams' account of the Manifesto group see: Williams (1979): 366 ff.
17. For an introduction to these developments see Rustin (1985): ch.2.
18. This should not be taken to imply that 'traditional' working-class issues such as basic inequalities between employer and employee in terms of income, status and power and so on had been completely displaced or superseded by more universal 'rights' issues. Rather, these latter issues emphasised *other dimensions* of social inequality which could not be adequately expressed within the present parameters of class analysis. A particular individual may for example be exploited at work, but she or he might also be oppressed by the white militaristic male-centredness of modern society. Being a member of the working class is not therefore the *only dimension* of relative social disadvantage.

2

□

The development of modern Italy 1861–1914

During the last decades of the nineteenth century, Europe had entered a period of uneasy stability and growing prosperity. With the end of the Franco-Prussian war and the unification of Germany in 1871, the great powers of Britain, Germany, France, Russia and Austria-Hungary dominated the map of Europe. Although international rivalries spurred on by the rush to establish colonial supremacy, particularly in Africa, continued to dominate foreign policy, each country now turned its attention away from military expansion and concentrated its resources on social and economic development. In the economic sphere, these developments were dominated by the expansion of heavy industries, particularly of iron and steel production, and by the emergence of new products and manufacturing techniques as mainland Europe followed Britain's lead as the most advanced industrial nation. The drive towards modernisation was most marked in Germany and by the turn of the century its industrial and military strength had made it the most powerful of the nation-states.

The power of the leading nation-states inevitably meant that the smaller states had to seek protection from their larger neighbours. The formal recognition of these dependent relationships generated something of a paradox, however, since the treaties and trade concessions which resulted from them amounted to a recognition on the part of the larger powers of the role of the smaller states in maintaining the balance of power. The potential fragility of this diplomatic, military and economic equilibrium was further complicated by the emergence of a general aspiration towards national independence and self-determination both between states and within the larger states themselves. In eastern Europe, for example, Greece, Romania, Bulgaria, Montenegro and then Serbia had each achieved full independence from the Ottoman Empire by 1878, while, in central Europe, the rulers of the Austro-Hungarian Empire were faced with the perplexing task of maintaining some semblance of national solidarity between the very wide range of different races, languages and cultural traditions whose common identity depended upon the increasingly symbolic presence of the Habsburg Emperor Franz Joseph. Similar difficulties arose between France and Germany over the annexation by Germany of the iron-ore rich provinces of Alsace and Lorraine at the end of the Franco–Prussian war in 1871. Although the major powers were largely able to prevent these aspirations for independence from developing into direct military conflict until after the turn of the century, they none the less had to take them into account if stability was to be maintained. One country which qualified for this special attention and one which sought to establish its place as one of the leading powers was the newly united nation-state of Italy.

To a large extent, the process of Italian unification (or the *Risorgimento*), was a direct consequence of these processes of external inter-state rivalries and internal aspirations for nationalistic self-determination. Prior to its formal unification in 1861, the Italian peninsula was made up of a number of large provinces which were under foreign rule. The provinces of Lombardy and Venetia in the north, and of Naples and Sicily (the Kingdom of the Two Sicilies) in the south were under French, Austrian and Bourbon rule, while the Papal States of central Italy were dominated by the Pope in Rome. Within Italy, the desire for national identity was brought about through the efforts of two factions: the Moderate Party led by the enlightened reformist Count Camillo Benso di Cavour, and the strongly republican Action Party led first by Giuseppe Mazzini and then by Giuseppe Garibaldi. In 1859 and having pushed forward an ambitious programme of reform and modernisation in the prosperous northern province of Sardinia-Piedmont and by deliberately nurturing pro-unity sentiments with the equally prosperous neighbouring provinces of Emilia-Romagna and Tuscany, Cavour solicited the help of the French and forced the Austrians out of Lombardy in return for the cession of Nice and Savoy to France. Cavour then formed an uneasy alliance with the Action Party under Garibaldi and the following year the latter led the famous military expedition of the 'red shirts' to liberate the southern provinces. Once Sicily and Naples had been freed, the Piedmontese army marched south and by the spring of 1861 only the Papal States centred on Rome and Venetia in the north blocked the path to complete unification. Despite Garibaldi's two further attempts to defeat the French garrison in 1862 and 1867, it was not until 1870 that Rome was finally liberated when French defeats against Prussia forced the garrison to withdrawal of its own accord. Rome became the new capital of Italy while the Pope retained sovereignty over the Vatican State. Meanwhile, and despite Italy's own defeats against the Austrian army, Venetia was liberated as a result of Prussia's success against the Austrians in 1866.

It should be emphasised that the formal and political unification of Italy did not mean that cultural, economic and social unity had also been achieved. Widely different levels of economic development and prosperity, of literacy and language and of institutional and political complexity presented considerable obstacles to the process of unification. Taken together, these divisions can be characterised in terms of the relative backwardness of the south compared with that of the north, and of a separation between the educated and politically active minority whose organisation had brought about the unification in the first place, and the largely uneducated, disinterested and disorganised majority which were much less convinced of the possible benefits of unification. Italy's development in the decades which followed unification was therefore somewhat precarious and piecemeal as repeated attempts were made to reconcile 'legal' Italy with 'real' Italy.

To begin with, the country was largely agricultural and lacked many of the prerequisites for industrialisation. What little heavy and manufacturing industry there was, was concentrated in the semi-urban areas around Milan, Genoa and Naples and in the silk-producing areas of Lombardy and Piedmont in the north. These industries were very much the exception, however, and the vast majority of the population earned a meagre living through a highly localised and rudimentary subsistence economy whose organisation differed little from that of feudal society. Italy's financial situation was also very weak, making the country vulnerable to the attentions of predatory foreign banks and investors. Despite these difficulties, reforms in the system of inter-regional tariffs and infrastructural improvements, including the expansion of the canal and rail network, and the imposition of a range of heavy agricultural taxes gradually laid the foundation for a growth in domestic industry and an expansion of foreign trade.

Developments in the political field were dominated by the struggle for power between the two broad factions of right-wing Moderates and the left-wing republicans of the Action Party. The respective programmes for reform and modernisation put forward by these factions were, however, quite similar, so that up to the turn of the century the country was governed by a series of shifting alliances and temporary coalitions based more on immediate expediency than on long-term planning. The high point of this programme of Liberal–Moderate compromise was reached following a series of left-wing electoral victories during the late 1870s and 1880s under the premiership of Agostino Depretis. This period, known as the *trasformismo* after Depretis' policy of trying to 'transform' the party rivalries of the *Risorgimento* into a united central bloc, heralded a period of reform in the political, economic and social spheres which brought Italy much more into line with similar developments elsewhere in Europe. The highly restrictive suffrage laws which in 1870 had meant that less than 2 per cent of the population was eligible to vote were reformed, increasing the electorate from 600,000 to over 2 million in 1882 (Seton-Watson, 1967: 51). In 1880, the bitterly resented *macinato* tax on the grinding of corn was abolished, while further financial and monetary reforms boosted the value of the lire and attracted much-needed foreign investment. A standardised compulsory primary education system was introduced along with increased spending on a public works programme aimed at improving infrastructural utilities and housing, particularly in the expanding urban centres. Ambitious rail-building programmes and a somewhat lavish expansion of the army and refit of the navy were also undertaken as Depretis tried to make Italy's dream of becoming a strong international power into a reality.

These developments were accompanied by a gradual modernisation of the economy. In agriculture, programmes of land reclamation and the introduction of modern crops and farming methods throughout northern and central Italy, and a shift towards viniculture and citrus crops in the south, led to a gradual but none the less decisive increase in exports and a decrease in imports. Development in the 'industrial triangle' between Genoa, Milan and Turin in the north also increased as the demand for industrial products, particularly for railway and other construction projects, and for the mechanisation of the textile industry, gathered momentum.

These developments did not, of course, take place in isolation, as Italy became more and more dependent on its neighbours for imports of coal and other raw materials, and for external markets for its own produce. During the *trasformismo* Italy's approach to foreign affairs was therefore largely dictated by these and other economic considerations, and by the re-emergence of rivalries between the European states over their foreign interests.[1] The consequences of Italy's still fragile position were clearly demonstrated following the Congress of Berlin in 1878. The treaty left Italy in a somewhat ambiguous position since it was obliged to accept Austro-Hungarian gains in the Balkans in return for a rather vague promise of support if Italy wished to annex Tripoli on the North African coast. Matters were not quite so straightforward, however, since Germany was already supporting the French claim to the neighbouring province of Tunisia in order to develop friendly relations with France. In 1881 the French invaded from Algeria, occupied the city and declared a protectorate over Tunisia. This gave France a considerable strategic advantage in the region, not least because Tunis itself was only a few miles away from the island of Sicily.

The feeling of national humiliation which followed this diplomatic defeat had a profound and long-lasting effect in Italy. From a psychological point of view, the incident rekindled many of the feelings of republicanism and self-determination upon which the unification itself had been based. In economic and military terms, it emphasised the importance of gaining a strategic foothold on the African coast of the Mediterranean which in turn nurtured a general belief that Italy was destined to relive the glory of its past and become a leading power in the modern industrial age. This growth in nationalistic sentiment and the emergence of a strong sense of self-importance became the dominant feature of Italy's approach to foreign affairs for the next twenty years, culminating in the Italian invasion of Tripoli in 1911.

The second and closely related aspect of Italy's foreign policy during this period was to secure protection for Italian territorial aspirations, particularly in West Africa. Despite continuing reservations over Austrian interests in the Adriatic, Italy therefore joined the alliance between Germany and Austria-Hungary to form the first Triple Alliance in 1882. The renewal of the Alliance in 1887 and 1891, and the establishment of friendly agreements with Britain further consolidated Italy's role as an important player in the European balance of power up to the turn of the century.

Although the period of the *trasformismo* had been one of economic and social consolidation in Italy, Depretis was not able to narrow the considerable divisions which persisted between the north and the south, and between the increasingly prosperous middle-class urban élite and the general mass of the population. Both economic development and social and political reforms tended to favour the north not only in general, but, within this region, the benefits of modernisation and industrialisation were concentrated in the hands of a powerful minority of absentee landowners and industrialists. Broadly speaking, the shortcomings of the *trasformismo* centred round the recurrent problem of trying to allocate limited national resources to an ever-expanding programme of reform.[2] None of the manifestations of the Left–Right coalition was able to solve this problem and inevitably the main financial burden fell upon the still largely disenfranchised rural poor. A series of financial crises during the 1870s and 1880s, and the imposition of stringent tariffs on imports, particularly with France, in 1887 put additional pressure on the rural economy as the balance of trade worsened. This pattern of periods of growth interspersed with periods of economic stagnation and financial chaos set a trend which persisted until well into the twentieth century.

The instability created by this situation also established a pattern of social unrest and rebellion as the poorest strata of Italian society grew increasingly intolerant of their continued oppression. This new perspective was further stimulated as the process of rural and industrial modernisation precipitated important shifts in the character and composition of the working classes themselves. Although the rate of change was slow and varied considerably between different regions, more and more of the landless poor began to move towards the towns and cities to find work in the expanding manufacturing, textiles and engineering industries. Long-established patterns of domestic production were also disrupted when the handicrafts and local produce side of the rural economy began to decline as more and more commodities were imported from abroad. It should be emphasised that this evolution in the economic structure did not herald the wholesale replacement of the rural peasantry by an urban proletariat of the kind which had already emerged in the much more heavily industrialised economies of Britain and Germany. Indeed, as the discussion of Gramsci's childhood in Sardinia in the following chapter will show, the continued deprivation of the casual labourers and tenant farmers of the south highlights the fact that the nature of the *latifundi* estates of central and southern Italy remained relatively unchanged until well into the twentieth century. The point to emphasise is that changes in the methods of production and the organisation of work inevitably had a significant effect upon *the working relationships and outlook* of the workforce as the industrial side of the economy began to displace the agricultural. At the same time, other factors, including the gradual spread of literacy, improved communications and greater geographical mobility, tended to raise *the general level of awareness* as to the causes and consequences of social division. It became more and more obvious, in other words, that the appalling living conditions of the poor were at least as much man-made as God-given. Inevitably, the growing dissatisfaction and frustration which resulted from this new consciousness began to be expressed through increasingly direct demands for improvements in social and economic equality.

During the last decades of the nineteenth century, these aspirations and the social and political policies which developed in response to them, had become a central feature of European domestic politics as a whole. By the mid-1880s for example, Britain, Germany and France had all introduced legislation to limit working hours and establish a minimum working age. Public health issues rose to the top of the agenda as scientific developments in the control of infectious diseases such as cholera, diphtheria and typhoid and improvements in medical treatment, including the use of antiseptics and anaesthetics, began to emerge. Infrastructural improvements, including slum-clearance projects and urban rebuilding, together with the separation of water supply from sewage disposal resulted in significant improvements in housing and access to basic utilities. However, while the living conditions of the propertyless working classes were improving in a gradual and piecemeal way, those of the comfortable middle-class industrialists and landowners improved much more rapidly. In response to their growing prosperity and self-assurance, these classes eagerly developed new tastes as the emergence of shopping arcades and department stores signified the beginnings of a revolution in retailing which would eventually lead to the 'consumer society' of the twentieth century. New opportunities for investment and speculation also multiplied, as the increased demand for ever greater varieties of new and exotic commodities further stimulated an already buoyant entrepreneurialism. In turn, the increased magnitude and diversity of business activity led to the consolidation of new forms of commercial organisation as international conglomerates and joint-stock companies gradually displaced the more paternalistic and localised organisations of an earlier period. Essentially, therefore, despite a *general increase* in the standard of living, the prosperous strata of European society still enjoyed a quality of life that was far better than that of the labouring masses; the gap between the rich and the poor, in other words, was as wide as it had ever been.

The effects of this relative deprivation were thrown into even sharper focus as the European economies entered a period of depression towards the end of the century. Among the most severe consequences of this was a collapse in agricultural prices in the face of cheaper imports from colonies outside Europe. The pressure to preserve the value of domestic products while also maintaining the balance of trade inevitably raised levels of anxiety and frustration among the working classes, as a reduction in wages coincided with a rise in the cost of living. The new policy which emerged to counter the problems of a weakening economy and an increasingly restless working class, centred round a reconsideration of the philosophy of *laissez-faire* first put forward by Richard Cobden and other members of the Manchester School in England during the 1850s. By the latter part of the century this policy, which held that any intervention by the State in matters of trade and commerce would necessarily impede the development of 'enlightened self-interest', was displaced by a more 'interventionist' view of the State as an appropriate and indeed necessary means of maintaining growth and stability by intervening directly in economic and social affairs. New legislation was therefore introduced to manipulate the flow of trade and the value of commodities through stringent tariffs and import controls, and by the end of the century all the major European countries were operating a vigorous protectionist strategy. These changes in the economic sphere were accompanied by changes in the social sphere, as a number of largely middle-class reformist groups, such as the Fabian Society in Britain and the Association for Social Policy in Germany, proposed legislative reform aimed at improving the lot of the working classes. Despite the progressive nature of these reforms and the adoption of a more sympathetic and humanitarian outlook on the part of government, their extent and, more importantly, *the speed* with which they could be brought about fell far short of the demands of the working classes themselves. Spurred on by a growing sense of disillusionment and frustration, new working-class organisations emerged advocating a much more rapid and widespread reorganisation of society based on the socialist principles of common ownership and equality of opportunity.

By the turn of the century, trade union organisations and socialist parties had become widely established throughout Europe. Among the most important were: in Britain, the Trades Union Congress (1868) and the Labour Representative Committee (1869) which became the Independent Labour Party in 1893; in Germany, the Social Democratic Workers' Party of Germany in 1869 under the leadership of Wilhelm Liebknecht and August Bebel, which later became the Social Democratic Party of Germany (SPD) under Karl Kautsky in 1890; in France, the *Confédération Générale du Travail* (CGT) in 1895 and the French Socialist Party (SFIO) in 1905; and in Russia the Social Democratic Workers' Party (1898), which later split in 1903 into the Mensheviks (the minority) under Plekhanov and Trotsky, and the Bolsheviks (the majority) under Lenin. Having established representative organisations of their own, the working classes were still left with the problem of devising *an effective strategy* for gaining power. This was not a new problem, however, and the political upheavals in the mid-nineteenth century, most notably the revolutions of 1848 and the brief but dramatic formation of the Paris Commune in 1871, provided the socialists with a rich variety of strategies from which to choose. Among the leading contenders in this respect were Pierre-Joseph Proudhon (1809–65) who advocated the transition to a decentralised non-authoritarian form of society based on self-supporting local co-operatives; Louis-Auguste Blanqui (1805–81), a leading figure in the Paris Commune who advocated a direct and violent assault on the State; the anarchist Mikhail Bakunin (1814–76) who advocated the spontaneous insurrection of the peasantry; and Ferdinand Lassalle (1825–64), the founder of the General Association of German Workers in 1863, who believed that the key to working-class power lay in the establishment of universal suffrage. However, the person who had the most significant and long-lasting impact on the development of socialist strategy was Karl Marx (1818–83).

Although major theoretical and tactical differences concerning, for example, the respective roles of the urban proletariat and the rural peasantry, and the precise way in which a socialist party should be organised were never fully resolved,[3] Marx's popularity was at least partly due to the fact that his analysis encompassed many of the principles which had already become widely accepted on the Left. First, there was a general recognition that the development and social organisation of society was intimately bound up with the economic practices and institutions of that society. It therefore followed that gaining control over the economic structure was an absolute prerequisite for bringing about fundamental social change. Second, there was general agreement that the interests of the working classes could best be represented not only through the agency of a mass party to which all members of the working class could belong, but that these interests were *international* rather than purely domestic.[4] Third, within this party, *the urban proletariat* were seen as having a particularly significant role because their knowledge of modern industrial processes would be essential to the formation of a new socialist economy. Finally, there was a general feeling, not only among the socialists but also among their opponents, that revolutionary change was very much on the agenda; revolution, in other words, was a *probability* rather than merely a theoretical possibility.

Having established the broad principles of, and theoretical basis for, revolutionary change, and having considered the effectiveness or otherwise of previous attempts at gaining power, the socialists were faced with a choice between two more or less distinct strategies. On the one hand they could adopt a full-blooded *revolutionary* approach involving the complete overthrow of the capitalist system by a direct and violent assault on the institutions of the bourgeois State, or they could adopt a more gradual *reformist* approach involving an acceptance of some aspects of the institutional framework while trying to gain control over them through lawful and peaceful electoral superiority. To a large extent, and with the exception of the Russian Revolution in 1917, it would be true to say that the latter approach has tended to prevail within socialist politics up to the present day, and that the various splits which have occurred within left-wing parties have invariably been caused by a growing sense of disillusionment with the inherently cautious and phlegmatic nature of the reformist strategy. Nowhere was this rivalry between the revolutionary and reformist strategies more evident than in Italy itself. From the foundation of the *Partito Socialista Italiano*, the Italian Socialist Party (PSI), in the early 1890s until the emergence and dictatorship of Mussolini's National Fascist Party twenty years later, these issues dominated the discourse and conduct of the Italian left-wing.

It has already been noted that the *trasformismo* had brought about significant changes in the social and economic character of Italian society, but that, in common with the situation elsewhere, the positive benefits of these changes had largely failed to filter down the social hierarchy. During the 1870s, the animosity caused by this continuing

inequality began to take on a more homogeneous form as the ideas of
Marx and the ideology of the International Movement took root in
Italy.[5] With a growing awareness that concessions could be won
through combined strike action, both rural and urban trade unions
emerged throughout the 1880s, and by 1892 the leading militant
factions on the Left had combined to form the PSI, adopting a
reformist strategy with the anti-*trasformismo* policy that alliances
should not be made with parties of the Right. The importance of the
amalgamation of urban with rural interests brought about by the newly
united Party was further enhanced as it attracted the support of a large
number of young students and intellectuals whose militant enthusiasm
greatly accelerated the spread of the vision of an egalitarian socialist
future. Two individuals who were particularly influential in this
respect were Antonio Labriola and Filippo Turati.

Labriola, a leading Italian philosopher and historian, developed a
strong interest in the ideas of Marx, believing that the 'philosophy of
praxis' represented a highly convincing account of the reciprocal
nature of the relationship between *theory* and *action*, which is to say,
between the analysis and *interpretation* of history and the *practice* of
changing its course. Although Labriola was subsequently criticised
after his death in 1904 for sustaining a somewhat idealistic-Hegelian
position, his influence among the leading intellectuals of the day was
none the less considerable, as he gave a sense of academic
respectability and legitimacy to the Marxist cause in Italy. While
Labriola contributed to the naturalisation of the academic dimension
of Italian Marxism, its development as the basis for a practical socialist
political programme was greatly enhanced by the efforts of Turati. A
law graduate from Bologna University, Turati was convinced that
working-class unity and solidarity went hand in hand with the
development of democracy, and that a combination of these two forces
would inevitably result in the victory of the proletariat. The inherently
reformist character of this approach inevitably attracted considerable
criticism from the more radical components of the Left, but Turati's
influence upon Italian socialism remained strong even after his formal
expulsion from the PSI in 1922.

The emergence and consolidation of a *socialist* left-wing in Italy
during the 1880s and 1890s coincided with continuing social unrest
and a general lack of stability at the level of established national
politics. Depretis had resigned as prime minister in 1887 and was
followed into office by Francesco Crispi who, despite his earlier

criticism while in opposition, continued to exercise the shifting alliance system of *trasformismo* politics. Crispi pursued a broadly-based reformist policy and introduced legislative changes including an extension of the franchise to virtually all literate males, a reform of local government and a general reorganisation and standardisation of the legal system and penal code. However, following a further financial crisis in 1891 Crispi himself was forced to resign and the new leader of the Right, Antonio Di Rudini became prime minister. Unable to secure support for a reduction in military spending aimed at balancing the budget, Rudini also resigned after barely a year in office and was replaced by the lawyer and career civil servant Giovanni Giolitti. The crisis continued, however, as confidence in the new government was undermined first by its inability and apparent unwillingness to deal with a severe outburst of popular unrest and banditry in Sicily, and second as Giolitti and a number of his ministers were implicated in accusations of embezzlement and corruption surrounding the activities of the Banca Romana which had nearly collapsed in 1889. In November 1893 Giolitti resigned and Crispi returned to office at the age of seventy-five. A wave of repression followed in Sicily and on the mainland, and many radical organisations, including the PSI, were temporarily outlawed and their leaders arrested. Stringent financial measures were also introduced including the raising of income tax and duties on basic commodities such as salt, sugar, alcohol and imported wheat. Crispi's heavy-handed and authoritarian measures not only outraged many former supporters of the coalition system, but also tended to polarise public support both round those individuals who had not been tainted by the bank scandals and towards the new ideas which they put forward.

It was a crisis in foreign policy, however, which caused Crispi's final downfall in 1896. Crispi concentrated on trying to consolidate the position of the Italian colonies which had been established along the banks of the Red Sea in West Africa during the 1870s. By 1889 successive military expeditions had succeeded in establishing the colony of Eritrea and the protectorates of Abyssinia (Ethiopia) and Italian Somaliland through a treaty with the Abyssinian King Menelik II. Shortly after Crispi's return to office in 1893, Menelik, with support from Russia and France, cancelled the treaty and forced Italy into a renewed campaign to protect its interests in the region. After some initial success the Italian army was unexpectedly and disastrously defeated by Menelik at Adowa in 1896. Nearly 5,000 Italians were killed and a further 2,000 were taken prisoner. As noted above, a general belief in the country's mission to push forward the frontiers of civilisation and culture meant that Italian popular sentiment was particularly sensitive to defeats of this kind. Crispi was unable to answer the overwhelming public dismay which followed and in March he left office for the last time. Crispi's fall from power, combined with the general feeling of distrust and disillusionment surrounding the banking and fiscal crises, gave rise to a period of extreme uncertainty and instability. During the next five years no less than four government coalitions came and went until a measure of calm was finally achieved when Giolitti returned as prime minister in 1903. Aside from two brief periods between February and May 1906, and between December 1909 and March 1911, Giolitti remained in power until the outbreak of the First World War in 1914.

Prior to Giolitti's return, social unrest and militancy had continued to multiply throughout Italy as the weak state of the economy placed almost unbearable pressure on large sectors of the rural and urban poor. This crisis became particularly acute as mass strikes and demonstrations followed the failed harvest and subsequent rise in the price of bread during 1898. During this period of social and political disarray, the parties of the Left and the socialists in particular grew in strength as successive governments were obliged to solicit their support in parliament.[6] While it would be a mistake to exaggerate the extent to which the organisations of the Left were wholly socialist in nature or were fully in agreement on issues of strategy and policy, they did represent an important development in the formation of Italian working-class consciousness and, to some extent at least, laid the foundations for the revolutionary upsurge of the following decades. It should also be acknowledged, however, that the lack of decisive leadership which resulted in the ultimate failure of radical socialism in Italy can be traced back to the fragmented character and tactical indecisiveness which was so typical of its activities during this formative period.

Important changes in the political milieu were also taking place outside parliament as other organisations began to attract the support of the working classes. In addition to increases in rural and urban trade unionism, members of the Catholic Church became more and more active in political affairs. This amounted to something of a resolution of the rather hostile relationship which had developed between Church and State during the *Risorgimento*. Soon after becoming Pope in 1878, Leo XIII had forbidden any Catholic involvement in politics and a new organisation called Catholic Action had been formed to 'keep the faithful separate from the rest of the nation, free from the contamination of liberalism' (Seton-Watson, 1967: 59). Under the auspices of a new central administrative body, the *Opera dei Congressi*, the Church soon developed a highly organised and efficient network throughout Italy. Although the Vatican's attitude towards party politics remained ambiguous, by 1904 the first Catholic deputies had been elected to parliament, and by 1913 the Catholics held twenty-nine seats. With the election of the much more politically-minded Pope Benedict XV in 1914, the Church lost its remaining scruples and the first independent Catholic Party, the Italian Popular Party (*Partito Popolare Italiano*) was formed in 1919. Catholic working-class representation was given a further boost following the formation of a new Catholic trade union organisation, the Italian Confederation of Labour (*Confederazione Italiana del Lavoro*; CIL) in 1918. Since the vast majority of the population was Catholic, and since the Church already had an effective system of organisation, particularly among the rural poor, these developments constituted an important further step towards universal political awareness and participation.

The position of the radicals and socialists was further consolidated during the first years of the new century as one government after another was forced to adopt a more responsive attitude towards the claims and aspirations of the working class. The switch from repression to liberalism soon gave rise to problems of its own, however, as government tried to steer a course between the powerful interests of the landowners and industrialists on the one hand, and organised labour on the other. This new phase of political negotiation also exacerbated problems *within* the parties of the Left as radical socialists soon became impatient with what they regarded as a betrayal of their fundamental aims, namely the total replacement of bourgeois-liberalism by socialism.

These differences came to a head at the PSI Party Congress in 1904. Following disagreements over the conduct of the general strike which had been called in retaliation to the severe repression of the Sardinian mineworkers at the 'massacre of Bugerru' (see Chapter 3 below), two clear factions emerged representing the reformist and revolutionary positions outlined above. In the centre stood Turati and Leonida Bissolati (who had been instrumental in the formation of peasant co-operatives in the Emilia-Romagna region during the mid–

1880s and had been the first editor of the leading socialist newspaper *Avanti!* in 1896), advocating the reformist policy of gaining concessions for the working class through alliances with Giolitti's government. This group was opposed by Enrico Ferri and Arturo Labriola (not to be confused with Antonio Labriola mentioned above) whose militant syndicalist faction advocated a violent and direct seizure of power. The syndicalists temporarily took control of the Party but, following a series of abortive general strikes in Turin, Ferrara, Milan and Parma City in northern Italy between 1906 and 1908, both Ferria and Labriola adopted an increasingly reformist position, and at the PSI Congress in 1908 Turati and Bissolati regained control of the Party. Further evidence of this turn towards reformism emerged as the PSI began to collaborate with the avowedly non-political and moderate trans-union organisation, the General Confederation of Labour (*Confederazione Generale del Lavoro*; CGL) founded in 1906. The aura of respectability which now surrounded the PSI was also reflected in an increase in public support, and at the election of 1909 the Party increased its number of delegates to forty-one while membership of the CGL steadily increased. Giolitti was similarly impressed with the apparent maturity and moderate attitude of these working-class organisations and a further series of legislative reforms were introduced including the introduction of universal male suffrage which increased the electorate from 3.3 to 8.6 million (Seton-Watson, 1967; 282).

During the first decade of the twentieth century, therefore, Italy had entered a period of general consolidation and political reorientation as government came into a new relationship with the organisations of the working class. From the point of view of the less militant and more tightly organised skilled workers, professionals, civil servants and bureaucrats, evidence of the effectiveness of the reformist strategy was given by the fact that significant improvements in pay and conditions could be achieved through negotiation and compromise. The general improvement in the lot of the working class was not, however, solely the result of the new partnership between conciliatory labour and employers' organisations and a beneficent government. During the next fifteen years the Italian economy entered a period of rapid growth as manufacturing, engineering, textiles and motor vehicle production all expanded. Coal imports more than doubled between 1896 and 1913, annual steel production increased nearly ten-fold and electricity generation grew from 100 million to nearly 2,600 million kilowatt-hours over the same period.[7] The impact of this expansion and the introduction of mass production inevitably led to a greater centralisation of industry as small firms were displaced by large conglomerates and as entirely new industries came into being. By 1914 over 220,000 were employed in the cotton industry, 200,000 in engineering and 12,000 in motor manufacture. Communications and international trade also improved with a further extension of the rail network both within Italy and between Italy and its European neighbours. The population increased from 28.5 million in 1881 to nearly 40 million in 1911 as public health improved and the death rate fell. General prosperity increased as *per capita* income rose by nearly 30 per cent between 1896 and 1915. Illiteracy fell to less than 40 per cent compared with nearly 70 per cent in 1871. New legislation was introduced to restrict hours of work particularly for women and children, and improvements were made to insurance and pension schemes.

Although Italy's economic expansion was very impressive during this period, in fact being matched by only that of Germany, the process of modernisation largely failed to conquer the social problems of inequality and exploitation noted above. Reflecting trends which were very similar to those of the late 1870s and early 1880s, economic expansion was highly concentrated not only towards industry rather than agriculture, but towards the north rather than the south. The unevenness of this development inevitably led to further friction within the working-class organisations. In terms of factory and workplace representation, major differences of opinion and strategy resurfaced between the reformist CGL and the much more militant Chambers of Labour (*Camera del Lavoro*) and National Federation of Landworkers (*Federterra*) which had been established during the early 1890s. These differences stemmed from the fact that the CGL tended to represent the largely conservative and trade-specific interests of the skilled strata of the workforce, 'the aristocracy of labour', while the Chambers and agricultural unions wished to intervene in a more overtly political way on behalf of broader and more disparate groups of urban and rural workers. In addition, although membership of all these organisations continued to increase up to the outbreak of the First World War, they remained a feature of the north rather than of the south and therefore provided formal representation only for a minority of the overall working population.

The perceived prejudice of the labour organisations towards the interests of the relatively affluent and secure strata of the northern industrial workforce inevitably caused problems within the PSI, and at the Party Congress in 1910 Gaetano Salvemini, who was one of the strongest advocates of increased support for the south, denounced the Party and resigned. The backwardness of the south did, however, begin to attract more attention and a number of schemes were introduced aimed at improving the plight of those who lived there. Encouragement was given to industrial development around Naples, expenditure was increased on public works programmes and changes were made in both direct and indirect taxation. Attempts were also made to reorganise farming practices and to reduce the proportion of dependent casual labourers by encouraging a switch to landownership and share-cropping. To a large extent, however, these efforts brought little general improvement and the traditional inequalities and inherent geographical and infrastructural difficulties of the south continued to assert themselves.[8]

Divisions over the acceptability of the reformist contract with Giolitti's government were further heightened by the resurgence of nationalist and imperialist aspirations in Italy during the early part of the twentieth century. As noted above, Italy's position in Europe was largely dictated by changes in the international situation more generally. The Triple Alliance with Germany and Austria-Hungary had been renewed in 1902 and, following the signing of a new *Entente Cordiale* between Britain and France, relations between Italy and France improved considerably. Tensions in West Africa had been temporarily settled with the signing of an agreement with Britain and France in 1906. By 1910 the European balance of power rested between the two great alliances of Britain, France and Russia on the one hand, and Germany and Austria-Hungary on the other. Italy occupied a somewhat complicated position in that it was on more or less friendly terms with both these blocs. Colonial and other territorial rivalries persisted, however, and the first part of the century was marked by a series of diplomatic and military crises as continued economic prosperity became increasingly dependent upon the exploitation of new sources of raw materials and foreign markets.

Italy's direct involvement in these affairs came to a head in 1911 following a second attempt by Germany to break up the Franco–British alliance by staking a claim to Morocco on the North African coast. Although the German expedition failed, a new agreement was made between Germany and France granting the latter yet more territory in North Africa. In Italy, these events stimulated renewed appeals by the nationalists[9] to avenge the defeats at Adowa and the French annexation of Tunisia in 1881. The idea of a military operation against the Turks in Libya was widely welcomed by liberals, Catholics and nationalists alike, drawing as it did upon the deeply-held and romanticised sense of national destiny which had been so bitterly undermined by the failures of the recent past. At the end of September 1911 the Turks were sent an ultimatum demanding that Italian troops should be allowed to operate freely in Tripoli. The ultimatum was rejected and a force of 1,600 Italian marines, shortly followed by a further 35,000 troops, were duly dispatched to occupy Tripoli and a number of other major ports along the Libyan coast. Despite a further 50,000 reinforcements, the offensive soon faltered as joint Turkish and Arab resistance hampered the Italian advance. Giolitti's government then decided to weaken Turkish morale and resources by launching a second attack against a number of Turkish-held islands in the Aegean. This move was successful and Turkey capitulated in October 1912.

Although this victory temporarily distracted attention from domestic problems, the cost of the war was high and caused more problems than it solved. In the international sphere, the Aegean campaign aggravated the situation in the Balkans, leading to the outbreak of war in 1912.[10] At home, the passification of Libya continued to impose a major financial and military burden on the country, and this in turn led to a further polarisation of the political atmosphere. On the Right, the nationalists, who felt that Giolitti had not been sufficiently vigorous or patriotic in his conduct of the war, began to put forward an anti-liberal philosophy based on military power and authoritarianism. On the Left, where enthusiasm for the war had been much more restrained from the outset, the Libyan expedition caused general disarray. On the reformist wing of the Party two factions emerged, led by Bissolati and Turati respectively. The former advocated continued support for the government, largely on the grounds that the proletariat had a legitimate role in spreading civilisation abroad. Against this Turati argued that the government had betrayed the support of the PSI by behaving in a barbaric and undemocratic way, and that the Party should therefore withdraw its support forthwith. This crisis came to a head at the PSI's conference in July 1912. Benito Mussolini, who had become Secretary of the Trento Chamber of Labour in 1909, argued forcibly for the expulsion of the reformist right-wing and Bissolati's faction duly resigned from the Party. Despite the popular support which the government still received, and despite the resistance of the reformist CGL, the PSI had made a decisive move to the left and reiterated the principles of class war and political independence set out at its founding conference of 1892.

The new belligerence of the PSI was accompanied by a growing sense of restlessness and dissatisfaction with *Giolittismo* among the population at large, and at the General Election of 1913 the combined strength of the Left grew to 169 deputies out of a total of 508.[11] Giolitti was unable to maintain a majority and Antonio Salandra became prime minister in March 1914. Under Mussolini, who had become a member of the PSI executive and editor of *Avanti!* in 1912, the Left continued to grow in confidence; a general strike was called when the police intervened against anti-government demonstrators in Ancona. The spontaneous outburst of near anarchy and violence which followed throughout the Emilia and Marche districts along the Adriatic coast during the 'red week' of June 1914 provided the government with ample warning of the potential for revolution in Italy. The localised and rather fragmentary nature of the uprisings also showed, however, that the organisations of the Left were still a very long way away from developing an effective leadership capable of molding these disparate elements into a co-ordinated whole.

While the respective challenges of the Left and Right continued to dominate domestic politics in Italy, the international situation grew steadily worse as the underlying tensions of the previous decades reached crisis point. While on a visit to Bosnia in June 1914, the heir to the Austro-Hungarian throne, the Archduke Franz Ferdinand had been assassinated. Although there was no direct proof of involvement by the Serbian government, Austria took advantage of the crisis to pursue its policy against the growth of Serbian nationalism. Once they had secured support from Germany, the Austrians issued an ultimatum which effectively demanded the submission of Serbia to Austrian rule. The Serbs refused, mobilised their army and approached Russia for help. Austria then declared war on Serbia. The Russian government, which had recently renewed its alliance with France, declared support for Serbia and mobilised its army along both the German and Austro-Hungarian boarders. In response, Germany demanded that Russia withdraw its forces, and sought an assurance from France that it would remain neutral in the event of war with Russia. Neither of these demands was met and in August 1914 Germany declared war on both Russia and France. When Belgium refused to allow the passage of German troops against France,

Germany invaded Belgium which then invoked its guarantee of neutrality with Britain. Germany refused to withdraw and Britain immediately declared war. By November, Turkey had entered the war on the side of Germany and was duly presented with declarations of war by Russia, France and Britain.

Summary

By the outbreak of war in 1914, Italy had come a long way since its formal unification in 1861. In the economic sphere, the industrialisation of the north laid the foundation for a modern manufacturing economy which was soon to receive a further boost during the war itself. In agriculture, significant changes had taken place as more modern farming methods gradually overcame the limitations of the feudal economy of the recent past. In the political sphere, the extension of the franchise and the establishment of more or less homogeneous political parties with recognisably different policies and outlooks gradually displaced the élitism and unaccountability which had been such a central feature of the *trasformismo*. Although successive governments continued to operate with a fair degree of corrupt self-interest, the relative stability of the parliamentary system had none the less brought about considerable improvements in the functioning of the executive and legislature. The overall administration of the country took on a much more cohesive and structured character as a modern civil service, state bureaucracy and standardised legal system were introduced. In the social sphere, major advances in public health and education, and in housing and domestic utilities, had brought about a substantial raising of the average standard of living and quality of life. These improvements, along with the emergence of new industries and employment opportunities, helped to create a forward-looking and optimistic view of the future.

This new anticipation of what the future might hold was not, however, limited to members of the prosperous middle classes and cultural intelligentsia. Despite the emergence of a more enlightened attitude towards social development, and despite a general rise in the standard of living, considerable differences still existed between the north and south and between rich and poor. This division was largely due to the fact that the new industries were heavily concentrated in the north. As the modernisation of the economy gathered pace, this unevenness became more and more apparent as large sectors of the rural poor were effectively excluded from Italy's new prosperity. At the same time, changes in the economic structure had been accompanied by significant changes in the relationships both between and within different sectors of the working population. Most significantly, the spread of centralised factory production and the subsequent concentration of the urban industrial workforce had brought large numbers of individuals into contact with new ways of understanding the form and content of capitalist society. In common with developments elsewhere in Europe, the Italian working classes soon acquired a taste for the socialist perspective and created trade unions and political parties to represent their views.

By the outbreak of the First World War, the international dimension of socialism had taken root as large sectors of the working class extended the principles of common experience and common cause across national boundaries. Although considerable problems still persisted over the correctness or otherwise of the social-democratic reformist approach, governments and employers throughout Europe were forced to acknowledge not only that the material circumstances of the working class had to be improved, but that the political parties of the Left had a legitimate right to participate in government. As the working classes grew more confident in their ability to gain concessions from their capitalist employers, their overall aims became increasingly ambitious. Rather than simply trying to change capitalist society from within, it was necessary to replace it altogether. While the reformists could point to their success in terms of legislative changes, the brief but dramatic seizure of power by the St Petersburg Soviet in 1905, which had forced the Tsar to set up the first elected State Parliament or *Duma* in Russia, provided the revolutionaries with a clear demonstration of what could be achieved by direct action in even the most autocratic and politically backward of the modern nation-states.

The above discussion has also given an impression of the complex international and domestic circumstances which accompanied Italy's emergence into the modern industrial age. It has been shown that, during this crucial phase of its development, Italy was obliged to solicit support and protection from its larger European neighbours and, consequently, to frame its own foreign policy in the context of long-standing and in some cases bitter international rivalry. In turn, this necessity gave rise to a strong sense of national identity and purpose which among at least some sectors of the population established a taste for nationalism. Although, in other words, a significant part of the working population found its aspirations reflected in the doctrines and practices of socialism, this perspective did not have a monopoly over popular demands for reform and progress.

Finally, the discussion has also shown that the Italian political milieu was extremely volatile. From the shifting alliance system of the *trasformismo*, to the liberal-moderate compromises of the Giolitti era, the government of the country seemed to falter from one crisis to another as a stream of coalitions and ministers followed each other in quick succession. Although the socialists steadily gained popular support and thus influence over the trajectories of national policy, deep divisions continually resurfaced over both long-term aims and appropriate strategy. In common with the socialist parties elsewhere in Europe, these difficulties seriously undermined the decision-making and leadership abilities of the PSI, a failing which was to have disastrous consequences in the post-war period.

This chapter has given a brief account of the principal events which surrounded and moulded Italy's development up to the outbreak of the First World War. As might be expected, the war set in motion a new train of events in Italy's political life, not least among the parties of the Left whose previous approach to the problem of military intervention had not been entirely convincing. In the same way that the invasion of Libya had led to a polarisation of views a few years earlier, the new conflict immediately generated much discussion and debate. In addition to the more established members of the Left, the war attracted the attention of a younger generation of intellectuals and provided them with an important opportunity to express their views. Among those who came to the fore during this time was Antonio Gramsci.

Notes

1. For example, Britain was concerned with the possibility that Russian expansion into central Asia might adversely affect its access to India and Egypt. Similarly, Germany was concerned with Russia's increasing intervention in the affairs of the Balkan states and with the possibility of a Franco-Russian alliance.
2. Seton-Watson (1967:65) points out that between 1880 and 1890 expenditure increased by 58 per cent while revenue grew only by 18 per cent, and

that between 1876 and 1887 the national debt had grown from 8.5 to 11.5 million lire.
3. It was these differences which led to a split between Marx and Bakunin in 1876, and subsequently caused the collapse of the First International. For more details see Karabel (1976).
4. The international dimension of the class struggle, which suggested that the working classes in one country had much more in common with their fellow workers abroad than with the bourgeois middle classes of their own country, was formally established by Marx with the foundation of the First International Working Men's Association in 1864. Although the First International largely failed in its aim of uniting 'the workers of the world', it none the less established an ideological and practical framework upon which the First Communist International or Comintern was built in 1919.
5. For Bakunin, in particular, the large rural population seemed to offer fertile ground for a spontaneous revolutionary outburst and he began to attract a number of recruits from the more militant wing of the Action Party. However, after a brief interlude of insurrection in the Emilia-Romagna region, Bakunin was forced to flee to Switzerland where he died in 1878.
6. A measure of this changing balance of power is given by increases in formal representation among the representatives of the Left. The number of socialist deputies grew steadily from five in 1892, fifteen in 1895, to thirty-three in 1900. To this can be added sixty-three radical and republican deputies representing an extreme left-wing point of view, and a further 116 deputies representing a more moderate social-democratic position. It should also be noted that although the government had a majority of eighty-four deputies (296 against 212 of the combined Left), the actual number of votes cast were split more or less equally between the two blocs, and that the extreme Left's share of the vote was around 25 per cent of the total (334,000 out of 1.27 million) (Seton-Watson, 1967: 195).
7. These and the following figures are taken from Seton-Watson (1967): 284–97.
8. A clear indication of the continued backwardness of the south is given by Seton-Watson. He reports, for example, that:

> Its *per capita* income in 1900 was just under one-half that of the north. It contained 40% of the population of Italy, yet in 1911 its total consumption of industrial power was only just larger than Piedmont's. . . . In 1910–14 the national death rate was 19.2 per thousand inhabitants; but for the south the lowest rate was 19.7 in Calabria, the highest 22.6 in Basilicata. Whereas in 1911 less than 1% of the population of Genoa, Florence and Leghorn lived in one room, in Bari the figure was 42% and in Foggia 70.5%. The illiteracy rate increased steadily from north to south. In 1911 (compared with a national average of 37.6%) it was 11% in Piedmont, 37% in Tuscany, 54% in

Campania, 65% in Basilicata and 70% in Calabria, Sicily showing some improvement with 58%. (Seton-Watson, 1967: 307)

One important consequence of rural poverty was that it gave rise to very high levels of emigration. Seton-Watson (1967) reports that between 1891 and 1913 the official number of people seeking economic salvation elsewhere in Europe and America rose from 129,000 to 873,000 by which time nearly two-thirds came from the south (p.313, n.4). It is particularly ironic that this out-flow not only acted as a kind of safety valve as it offered an avenue of escape to large numbers of people who might otherwise have rebelled against the State, it also provided an important source of finance as emigrants sent a large proportion of their earnings back to their families in Italy. For further details see Seton-Watson, 1967: 316.

9. Seton-Watson (1967) describes the first congress of the Nationalist Party in 1910 as: 'a heterogeneous gathering of imperialists and irredentisists, republicans and monarchists, democrats and ex-syndicalists, ex-socialists and reactionaries' (p.364).
10. Put briefly, the First and Second Balkan Wars were caused by continuing Turkish aggression in response to which Bulgaria, Serbia, Greece and Montenegro formed the First Balkan League in 1912. Turkey, which had been weakened by its war with Italy in Libya and the Aegean, was quickly defeated. In the confusion which followed, Bulgaria tried to annex Serbia itself. Romania entered the conflict on the side of the three remaining members of the League and Bulgaria was defeated in 1913. As a result Turkey lost all its territory west of the Dardanelles, Greece gained large parts of southern Macedonia including the provinces of Salonika and Thrace which effectively gave it control of the northern Aegean coast. Albania became an independent country.
11. This total was made up of fifty-two from the PSI, nineteen members of the Reformist Socialist Party which had been set up by Bissolati following his resignation from the PSI in 1912, eight independent socialists and ninety radicals and republicans. Remaining deputies were made up of 382 liberals and twenty-nine Catholics (Seton-Watson, 1967: 388, n.1).

3
Gramsci's life and work: 1891–1937

In describing the circumstances of Gramsci's life and work, one impression which emerges time and again is of a man constantly struggling against adversity. The struggle against physical deformity and recurrent illness, the struggle against material hardship and poverty, the struggle against political adversaries and finally the psychological struggle for survival in prison. Looked at objectively, and with the partial exception of the months spent with his wife Julia in Russia during the summer of 1922, the circumstances of Gramsci's life were particularly inauspicious and lonely. At the same time, however, there is the impression of a man who, by drawing upon his profound inner resolve and tenacity, is determined to overcome the material circumstances of his own life and to play an active part in the emancipation of the working class. While imprisonment effectively put an end to his practical involvement in the working-class movement in Italy, Gramsci's great determination allowed him to produce a large body of writing which has had a lasting effect upon our understanding of the processes of social change.

Throughout his adult life Gramsci was primarily concerned with the practical means by which the working class could come to power. In order to achieve this goal, Gramsci emphasised that it is necessary to develop a clear understanding of the historical circumstances and events which have given rise to or created the present. As the influences of past events are as important for individuals as they are for whole societies, it is inevitable that the circumstances of Gramsci's own early life and experiences had a lasting influence upon the man and his thoughts. Since, as noted in Chapter 1, Gramsci's writings are now widely accepted as occupying a central position in the evolution of Marxism, and since Gramsci was as much a practical politician as he was a theoretician, it is particularly important to consider the context within which he lived and worked.

This chapter divides into four parts. The first describes Gramsci's family background and the circumstances of his early life and education on the island of Sardinia up to his enrolment as a scholarship student at Turin University in November 1911 at the age of twenty. It was during this period that Gramsci first became aware of the severe hardship which faced the urban and rural poor of Italy, an awareness which stimulated his interest in the causes of social inequality and brought him into contact with socialist thinking for the first time. The second part follows Gramsci's university career during the First World War and his formal initiation as a political activist in Turin between the end of the war in 1918 and the formation of the *Partito Communista Italiano*, the Communist Party of Italy (PCI), in January 1921. This was the period of the *bienno rosso*, the 'red years' of the soviet-style factory council movement which represented the high point of revolutionary activity in Italy. Gramsci played a leading role in the council movement, and was instrumental in founding the highly influential socialist weekly newspaper *L'Ordine Nuovo* in 1919. The third part covers the period up to Gramsci's arrest by the fascists in November 1926. This includes an account of the practical and theoretical disputes between Gramsci and other members of the PCI over how the Party should be organised. Other disputes also arose regarding the relationship between both the PCI and the PSI, and between the PCI and the Soviet-led Communist International at a time when the Comintern itself was entering a period of transition. The final part describes the period of Gramsci's detention on the island of Ustica, his trial in Rome and long imprisonment at Turi until his death in April 1937 at the age of forty-six. It was during this time that Gramsci compiled the now famous *Quaderni del Carcere*, the Prison Notebooks, which have since received such close attention.

Gramsci's early life and education, 1891–1911

Gramsci's father, Francesco Gramsci, was born at Gaeta on the southern coast of mainland Italy in March 1860, the fifth child of a colonel in the local police force. Although he had begun training as a lawyer, Francesco Gramsci was forced to give up his studies on the death of his father, and accepted a job as director of the Registrar's office at the small town of Ghilarza in Sardinia. Gramsci's mother, Giuseppina Marcias, was born at Ghilarza in 1861. Her father was a local tax-collector and her mother was a member of a relatively prosperous landowning family in the Ghilarza district. Despite the reservations of Francesco's mother, Francesco and Guiseppina were married in 1883. At a time when the vast majority of Sardinians worked their own small plots of land or were intermittently employed as day-labourers in the precarious semi-feudal economy which was so typical of southern Italy, the Gramsci family occupied a relatively prosperous and prestigious position in the social hierarchy: they were clear members of the southern petty bourgeoisie. After their marriage, the family moved south to the town of Ales where their first three children Gennaro, Grazia and Emma were born in 1883, 1887 and 1889. Antonio Gramsci was born on 22 January 1891. Francesco was transferred briefly to Sorgona where three more children, Mario, Teresina and Carlo were born in 1893, 1895 and 1897.

Following the arrival of the younger children, Antonio, now aged three, was looked after by a local nursemaid and it was during this time that an accident occurred which led to his becoming a hunchback. The exact circumstances remain something of a mystery, but Davidson suggests that a spinal injury occurred when the young child 'slipped and fell down some stairs' (Davidson, 1977: 22). A swelling developed and, despite the efforts of his mother, the local doctor and a number of specialists who prescribed suspending the child from the ceiling in a leather harness, the deformity became permanent. At about the same time as this injury, Antonio fell seriously ill with internal haemorrhaging. Fiori reports how Gramsci later recalled this crisis:

> When I was a child of four I had haemorrhages lasting three days at a stretch which left me quite bloodless and were accompanied by convulsions. The doctors had given me up for dead, and until about 1914 my mother kept the small coffin and little dress I was supposed to be buried in. (Fiori, 1990: 17)

During the next few years, it also become apparent that the young Gramsci was no longer growing at the normal rate; not only was he a hunchback, he was always to remain abnormally short.

The great anxiety caused by these developments was further exacerbated by a calamity which befell the family as a whole. Francesco

Gramsci had become involved in local politics, and during the election of 1897 had unfortunately supported the losing candidate. In the context of a corrupt political system where patronage and retribution played a major part, those on the losing side were inevitably subjected to reprisals. A report was sent to Cagliari, the capital of Sardinia, suggesting an investigation of the Registry at Sorgono and the conduct of Francesco Gramsci in particular. While the investigation was being carried out, Francesco was suspended from his job and the family moved back to Ghilarza in 1898. In August Francesco was arrested, eventually tried and sentenced to five and a half years in prison. Unwilling to seek financial help from other members of the family, Gramsci's mother Giuseppina realised what assets she could and set about earning a living as a seamstress. Gramsci later wrote: 'Her life was a great lesson to us, it showed us how important staying-power can be in overcoming difficulties which looked insuperable even to men of great courage' (Fiori, 1990: 17).

Although his mother's courage kept the family from absolute poverty and starvation, the domestic circumstances of Gramsci's early childhood were certainly harsh. Neither was this harshness relieved by his entry into the primary school at Ghilarza in 1898 at the age of seven. As Davidson points out, the fall in family status inevitably resulted in greater exposure to the vagaries of ordinary village life – a situation which was particularly difficult for the sickly and eccentric-looking Antonio:

> He met extreme cruelty and persecution born both of the social culture itself and realities such as class and the concomitant class hatreds, and of the natural cruelty of children towards the abnormal. As a result he had become by 1900 a desperately lonely child, whose withdrawal from the normal life of his peers resulted in a sensitivity and capacity for fantasy which made him very socially aware of cruelty and injustice. (Davidson, 1977: 27)

As a result of close attention and encouragement from his mother, and because he could speak Italian (in addition to the local Sardinian dialect), Gramsci did well during the five years he spent at primary school, often finishing top of the class. At the end of his fifth year in school in 1903, however, and despite working long hours during the summer holidays at the Land Registry office where his eldest brother Gennaro was now working, he was forced to suspend his education as the family could not afford to send him away to secondary school.

Clearly the physical hardship and isolation of his childhood also had a marked effect on his psychological development. He later recalled:

> For a very long time, I have believed it was absolutely, fatally impossible that I should ever be loved . . . . When I was a ten-year old boy I began to feel this way about my own parents. My physical condition was so feeble, I was forced to make so many sacrifices, that I became convinced I was a burden, an intruder in my own family. These are things one doesn't forget easily, they leave far deeper marks than one would suspect. (Fiori, 1990: 26)

And later in a letter to his wife:

> Because of the isolated existence I have led since childhood, I have become used to hiding my feelings behind a mask of hardness, or an ironic smile . . . . For long this did me great damage; for long, it made my relations to other people enormously complicated. (Fiori, 1990: 27)

Following Francesco's release from prison in January 1904 circumstances improved sufficiently for Gramsci to continue his education. Late in 1905 he enrolled at the communal secondary school at Santu Lussurgiu. Because of his age (he was nearly fifteen years old), and because he had persevered with his studies during the intervening two years, Gramsci was allowed to enter straight into the third year. Although teaching standards at the school were far from ideal and despite the rather menial accommodation and frugal circumstances of his lodgings which did not suit his poor health, Gramsci was awarded his secondary school certificate in September 1908.

While Gramsci was persevering with his education, significant events were taking place elsewhere in Sardinia. As noted in the previous chapter, the unification of Italy during the 1860s and 1870s had done little to improve the chronic economic situation in southern Italy. The situation in Sardinia was even more acute as its geographical separation from the mainland and the particularly backward nature of its economy further impeded the process of modernisation. Such progress as there was, was virtually thrown into reverse during the 1880s and 1890s as the collapse of the major banks on the island coincided with the lapsing of favourable trade agreements with France as protectionism spread through Europe. In addition to a chronic rise in unemployment and bankruptcy, two important developments took place: an expansion of mining activities at Sulcis-Iglesiente on the south-west of the island which was rich in mineral ore, and an increase in rural banditry. Of the latter Gramsci later wrote:

> The class struggle used to be mixed up with banditry: it was scarcely distinguishable from taking ransom, from burning down woods and hamstringing animals, from the abduction of women and children, from attacks on town halls. It was a kind of primitive terrorism, with no lasting or effective results. (Fiori, 1990: 31)

Although these manifestations of economic desperation were largely ineffective in themselves as a means of achieving economic and social reform, they were important in the more general sense of attracting popular attention and support to social and political issues. The instigation of a land survey at Ghilarza, and the arrival of officials from mainland Italy to carry it out, contributed to this general increase in popular awareness and gave a more cohesive form to the discussion of the underlying causes of the Sardinian situation.

At Sulcis-Iglesiente, resistance to the appalling working conditions in the mines had become more and more outspoken, and by 1904 a federation of mineworkers had been formed at Iglesias. In September 1904 the miners at Bugerru went on strike over changes in working hours. Fiori gives the following account of the outcome:

> The troops arrived in the middle of the negotiations . . . . When [they] had taken up position all round the company offices, some workers were ordered to get a warehouse ready for them to camp in. They obeyed the order; but to other workers this looked like scabbing. Stones began to fly. The soldiers fired, killing three of the miners and wounding eleven. This was the first blood drawn by organised class struggle on the island. It led to a general strike throughout Italy, the largest yet in the history of the Italian working-class movement. (Fiori, 1990: 36)

The following year, public discontent reached new levels as both agricultural workers and workers in the towns were subject to reduced wages and increasing prices. In Cagliari strikes broke out among dock workers, shop assistants, bakery workers and tobacco factory workers culminating in a bloody confrontation with the troops stationed in the town. More troops were sent as disorder spread throughout the island.

Although Gramsci was only thirteen at the time of the 'Bugerru Massacre', he would have been aware of these events and of the socialist diagnosis of them, both from conversations with his brother Gennaro, and later by reading newspaper reports of the strikes. It is very probable that these experiences and the harshness of his own circumstances led Gramsci to develop an early sense of identity with other individuals and groups of individuals who suffered the consequences of injustice and oppression. Similarly, both banditry and strike action provided him with two clear examples of the kind of practical action which individuals could use to express their grievances.

In the autumn of 1908, the two brothers moved to Cagliari so that Gramsci, now aged seventeen, could continue his studies at the Dettori state *liceo* (broadly equivalent to a high school or grammar school). Gennaro, who had been transferred to the Land Registry office, soon changed jobs and began work as an accountant in an ice factory. Their living conditions were still frugal, and Gramsci frequently wrote to his parents asking for money to buy food and clothes:

> Dearest Dad, you seem to be under the impression that I can live off nothing at all. Nannaro [Gennaro] is doing too much for me already, because you really must grasp the fact that one cannot live in Cagliari with what you are sending every month, unless one eats nothing but bread – and little enough of that at 50 centimes a kilo. (Fiori, 1990: 54)

By working hard and living a rather solitary existence he made up for the poor teaching he had received at Santu Lussurgiu, and began to make an impression as a very able student. During his second year he was befriended by the school's Italian master, Raffa Garzia, editor of the radical Sardinian nationalist newspaper *L'Unione sarda*, who introduced him to other militant socialists. At the end of his second year, Garzia agreed to adopt Gramsci as a journalist for the paper, and his first article was published on 26 July 1910.

Having completed his studies at the *liceo* the following year, Gramsci decided to try and win one of the thirty-nine scholarships available to deserving Sardinian students to attend Turin University. He travelled to Turin in October, passed the entry examinations and enrolled on the Modern Philosophy course at the university on 16 November 1911.

As regards Gramsci's intellectual and political attitudes at this time, it is clear that he had developed a strong sense of identity with the plight of the rural poor in Sardinia. It was inevitable, therefore, that he would take a particular interest in those writers who addressed this problem. Among the various journals and newspapers he read while living with his brother in Cagliari, and in addition to *L'Unione sarda*, were the journals *La Voce del Popolo* and *Il Marzocco* which published articles by the radical socialist Gaetano Salvemini and the influential philosopher Benedetto Croce. Salvemini argued that the relative stagnation and poverty of the south was the direct result of economic exploitation and political manipulation in the north. Among other things, he argued that the PSI should campaign vigorously for the introduction of universal suffrage to give the peasantry an opportunity to alter this blatant imbalance of power. Unfortunately, however, the PSI was much more interested in soliciting the support of the expanding urban proletariat in the industrial north, and following a series of bitter disputes with Turati, Salvemini left the Party in 1910.

Gramsci's interest in this issue, and consequently in the radical socialist solution proposed by Salvemini and others, was further stimulated by his brother's participation in the socialist movement in Cagliari. Gennaro gives a vivid account of Gramsci's early contact with radical politics:

> I came back from my military service in Turin a militant socialist, and at the beginning of 1911 I got a job as treasurer of the Chamber of Labour and secretary of the local Socialist Party. So I used to meet frequently with Cavallera, Battelli [who had been instrumental in organising the Sardinian mineworkers], and Pesci, the young leaders of the Sardinian socialist movement, and occasionally Nino [Antonio] would be there too. We had a great quantity of books, papers, tracts, and propaganda material in the house. Nino most often spent his evenings at home . . . and made short work of reading the books and newspapers. (Fiori, 1990: 56)

By the time that Gramsci was preparing to leave Cagliari for Turin in 1911, he had clearly adopted a forthright and radical Sardinian nationalism or *Sardism*, some elements of which remained with him throughout his political career.[1]

Gramsci and the '*bienno rosso*' in Turin, 1911–21

Any excitement which Gramsci may have felt at making the transition from the distinctly provincial environment in Cagliari to the busy metropolis of Turin seems to have been short-lived. In terms of his educational achievements he had certainly done very well by Sardinian standards, and a university education offered the possibility of a comfortable career perhaps as a teacher or member of the civil bureaucracy. Once again, however, his poor physical condition and his somewhat reclusive personality dictated that the next phase of his life would be no less difficult than the previous one. The seventy lire a month provided by the scholarship was barely enough to live on and after only a few weeks he was forced to ask his parents for more money:

> I find myself compelled to beg you to send me the 20 lire you promised, without fail, before the end of the month. I only got 62 lire from the college this month, of which I've given 40 to my landlady, and must let her have another 40 shortly. Christmas is going to be a very thin time anyway. I don't want to make it still more depressing by trailing round Turin in the cold looking for another hole to hide in. I had hoped to get an overcoat made this month, with the 10 lire Nannaro sent me. Now God knows how long it'll take me. Think how nice it is to go out and across the city shivering with cold, then come back to a cold room and sit shivering for hours, unable to warm oneself up. (Fiori, 1990: 73)

This pattern of isolation and material hardship continued throughout Gramsci's first two years at university, where one physical or psychological crisis after another severely affected his ability either to study or to sit examinations. By the end of 1913 he was writing to his father:

> Dear Dad, after a whole month's most intensive study I've only managed to make myself dizzy with fatigue and get my old headaches back, more excruciating than ever, and in addition a kind of cerebral anaemia which blots out my memory and ravages my brain, and makes me feel positively insane. I can't get away from it and find peace anywhere, neither walking nor lying on the bed nor (as I do sometimes) rolling to and fro on the floor like a maniac. (Fiori, 1990: 90)

At the end of his third year in November 1914 he was again unable to sit any of the examinations and the following April his education at the university came to an end.

Although Gramsci's formal efforts within the university ended in failure, his early years in Turin were highly significant in other respects. In the same way that personal contact and reading had made him aware of political developments and intellectual trends in Sardinia, a similar pattern of awareness and involvement had begun to emerge in Turin. During his first year at university, for example, he came into contact with Professor Matteo Bartoli whose keen interest in the peculiarities of the Sardinian dialect further stimulated Gramsci's interest in the distinctive culture of the island. The friendship which developed between them must have reassured Gramsci of the profound inaccuracy of the then common belief put forward by the economist Francesco Saverio Nitti and the sociologist Alfredo Nicefero, that the people of the north were genetically superior to those of the south. Gramsci was deeply angered by what he later described as the 'scientific truth' of the 'sociologists of positivism'. He writes:

> It is well known what kind of ideology has been disseminated in myriad ways among the masses in the North, by the propagandists of the bourgeoisie: the South is the ball and chain which prevents the social development of Italy from progressing more rapidly; the Southerners are biologically inferior beings, semi-barbarians or total barbarians, by natural destiny; if the South is backward, the fault does not lie with the capitalist system or with any other historical cause, but with Nature, which has made the Southerners lazy, incapable, criminal and barbaric – only tempering this harsh fate with the purely individual explosion of a few great geniuses, like isolated palm-trees in an arid and barren desert. (Gramsci, 1978: 444; henceforth *SPWII*)[2]

Against this view, however, and from within his Sardist perspective, Gramsci argued that the south was not only full of natural potential, but that the realisation of these riches was directly related to the vested interests of the wealthier industrialists in the north:

> You must picture Sardinia as a fertile and abundant field, whose fertility is nourished by an underground spring rising from a far-off hill. Suddenly you see that the field's fertility has vanished. Where once there were rich harvests there is now only grass burnt brown by the sun. You look for the cause of the disaster, but you can find it only by looking beyond the limits of your own small field, only by looking as far as the hill the water came from and understanding that kilometres away a wicked egoist has cut off the fertility of your field at its source. (Fiori, 1990: 77–8)

In addition to his studies in phonology and linguistics, Gramsci also attended lectures by Umberto Cosmo, Arturo Farinelli and Annibale Pastore who introduced him to the work of Machiavelli, De Sanctis, Marx, Antonio Labriola and most importantly to Benedetto Croce.

Although Gramsci had already become familiar with the work of these authors through his reading, the experience of studying them more formally certainly brought him into contact with what Adamson has described as the 'cultural rejuvenation movement' (Adamson, 1980: 20) which dominated the intellectual climate of this period. Gramsci later recalled that:

> It seemed to me that I and Cosmo, and many other intellectuals at this time (say the first fifteen years of the century) occupied a certain common ground: we were all to some degree part of the movement of moral and intellectual reform which in Italy stemmed from Benedetto Croce, and whose first premise was that modern man can and should live without the help of religion – I mean of course, without revealed religion, positivist religion, mythological religion, or whatever other brand one cares to name. (Fiori, 1990: 74)[3]

Within the university he also came into contact with a number of fellow students who advocated an overtly socialist diagnosis of Italian society. In particular he met Palmiro Togliatti (who had sat the university scholarship exams at the same time as Gramsci), Angelo Tasca and Umberto Terracini who were active members of the Socialist Youth Organisation. It was largely through these contacts that Gramsci eventually became involved in practical left-wing politics, and he eventually joined the PSI at the end of 1913.[4] In terms of his political development, therefore, it would be true to say that by the time Gramsci had concluded his university studies, he had moved decisively away from the *Sardism* of Cagliari to the socialism of Turin.

As noted in the previous chapter, by 1914 the likely outbreak of war in Europe had come to dominate political discussion in Italy. On the Left, the PSI was faced with a dilemma very similar to that which had faced the Party during the Italian invasion of Libya in 1911 over whether to support or oppose the war. This crisis had come to a head at the PSI's conference at Reggio Emilia in July 1912 when Mussolini had forced the expulsion of Bissolati's reformists from the PSI. While the Libyan expedition had been a relatively minor affair, the crisis of 1914 was on an altogether different scale.

The outbreak of war placed the Italian government in a very awkward position. On the one hand they faced the possibility of further Austrian gains in the Adriatic, while on the other Italy's military strength was much weaker than that of its Triple Alliance partners.

Under Antonio Salandra, who had replaced Giolitti as prime minister in March 1914, the government decided to await further developments and remain neutral. This position was generally welcomed by the parties of the Left and Right alike, most of whom agreed that the disadvantages of war far outnumbered the potential advantages to Italy. In effect, however, neutrality amounted to a betrayal of the Triple Alliance since France was able to make its own preparations for war against Germany without having to divert scarce resources to its border with Italy. By the autumn of 1914, the war in central Europe had reached stalemate and the central powers (Austria-Hungary, Germany, Bulgaria and Turkey) as well as the Entente (France, Britain, Russia, Serbia, Montenegro and Belgium, and later Romania and Greece) were approaching Italy for support. While these various negotiations were taking place, largely in secret, popular opinion within Italy became less unanimous. On the Right, support for intervention in the war grew as first the republicans and nationalists, and then a number of radicals and reformist socialists, began to argue that neutrality and passivity were a betrayal not only of those populations and territories currently held by Austria, but of the whole idea of Italy's destiny as a leading world power. On the Left, a split developed between the pacifist position of the PSI, who were also supported by the syndicalist *Unione Sindicale Italiana* (USI; founded as a breakaway group from the reformist CGL in 1912), and a growing number of pro-interventionists.

As in 1911, one of the key figures on the Left was Mussolini. Initially a supporter of neutrality, Mussolini unexpectedly changed his position and published a pro-interventionist article which advocated that the PSI should move from a position of 'absolute neutrality' to one of 'active neutrality'. In effect this meant placing national goals above those of both the domestic working-class movement and of the International. In November 1914, Mussolini resigned as editor of *Avanti!* and launched a new paper, *Il Popolo d'Italia* which rapidly became the main journal of the pro-war lobby. The PSI immediately expelled Mussolini, who reacted by forming a new group or 'fascio' with support from a new pro-interventionist union organisation, the *Unione Italiana di Lavoro* (UIL) which had just broken from the anti-war USI.

In addition to these public repercussions, Mussolini's dramatic behaviour had an unfortunate effect upon Gramsci's own embryonic position within the PSI. Mussolini's article in *Avanti!* had inevitably caused something of a stir in the socialist press and in October Gramsci had written an article for *Il Grido del Popolo* on 'The War and Socialist Opinion' which, superficially at least, supported Mussolini's position. Although Gramsci was in fact supporting the view that the PSI had a duty to remain open to the changes which were taking place, and to be willing to become actively involved if and when the need should arise: 'we must make it clear that we are not questioning the concept of neutrality as such (neutrality of the proletariat, it goes without saying), but *how* this neutrality should be expressed' (Gramsci, 1977: 7; henceforth *SPWI*), and although he was unfortunate that his first foray into public debate was greeted by a particularly sensitive audience, Gramsci was none the less branded an interventionist.

Throughout the winter and following spring, both pro- and anti-war factions became more and more outspoken in their demands. In February and again in April mass meetings and demonstrations in Milan, Reggio Emilia and Rome soon degenerated into a series of violent confrontations between the two groups. In Turin, where Gramsci had withdrawn to the relative seclusion of the university, the PSI and CGL were successful in organising a general strike and over 100,000 workers demonstrated against the war. Elsewhere, however, similar efforts became less successful as popular support for the war increased. By the end of April 1915 the government had completed its negotiations and at the Treaty of London the decision was made to go to war on the side of the Entente. In the event of victory, Italy was promised the Italian-speaking territories of Trentino together with Istria and part of Dalmatia.

The first two years of the war did not go well for Italy. The mobilisation was slow to get under way, and the Italian army faced better armed and better supplied Austrian forces across its northern frontier. Italy's relations with its new allies remained cool while disagreements between government and military command over how the war should be conducted caused much friction. In addition, public support fluctuated as a series of Austrian offensives presented the Italian public with a stark reminder that war in the twentieth century was not simply some great civilising mission or Garibaldian adventure, but that it could just as easily result in invasion and a return to foreign occupation. Although the Italian army was eventually able to force the Austrians back across the frontier, discontent with Salandra's government continued to grow and in June 1916 he finally lost his majority and was replaced by the seventy-eight-year-old Paolo Boselli. For the rest of 1916 and into 1917 the military position first improved and then deteriorated in the face of strong Austrian resistance and as successful German submarine attacks began to disrupt the import of essential food supplies and raw materials. Italy's relations with the Entente gradually improved, however, and France and Britain agreed to send reinforcements and equipment to help the Italian war effort.

With the entry of the United Sates into the war in April 1917, the general character of the conflict began to change. Apart from the provision of considerable material support, the intervention of President Wilson stimulated a wide-ranging discussion of the overall meaning and purpose of the war. He suggested that if the two blocs explained their war aims, the war could be ended by diplomatic rather than military means. Although there was a strong suggestion that both Austria-Hungary and Germany would be willing to negotiate on the basis of the gains they had already made, it soon became clear that the Entente powers not only wanted to see the restoration of all the territories which had been invaded by the central powers, including the return of Alsace-Lorraine to France, but also that the Austro-Hungarian Empire should effectively dismantle itself by recognising the independence of its Romanian, Slav, Czech and Slovak peoples.

Although Wilson's initiative failed and the war continued, this glimpse of peace had an important psychological effect upon the populations involved and did lead to a general discussion of both the causes and possible outcomes of the war, and of the much more profound questions about the kind of society which could be built once peace had been restored. As the war dragged on, it soon became clear that large sections of the European populations were beginning to form very different answers to these questions. In Britain and France, for example, both Lloyd George and Georges Clemenceau were forced to construct new government coalitions to avoid the complete collapse of their respective domestic war-efforts, while in Germany the inability of the High Command to bring a quick victory caused much friction within the Reichstag and led to formation of an anti-war Independent Social Democratic Party (USPD; formerly part of the pro-war SPD). The Reichstag even went so far as to pass a motion to end the war.

A similar pattern of disillusionment and frustration was also beginning to emerge in Italy as the economic situation continued to deteriorate. In the towns and cities large increases in taxation and working hours further undermined industrial relations, while a 50 per cent decline in the number of male agricultural workers made food production extremely arduous. In the political arena, the majority of the PSI tried to balance itself on the rather ambiguous policy of 'neither support nor sabotage' for the government's war measures and continued to argue that the cost of the war let alone the prospect of defeat amply demonstrated the futility of being at war at all. Fresh divisions were, however, beginning to emerge within the PSI as Turati's 'right' argued that the Party should adopt a more conciliatory attitude towards the government on the grounds that victory would lead to improvements in the situation of the working class.

It is important to emphasise that the position of the PSI and the revolutionary Left in Italy at this time did not exist in a kind of domestic political vacuum but was strongly influenced by the international socialist movement more generally. As noted in the previous chapter, one of the central tenets of the Marxist approach to radical social change was its insistence upon the need for supranational working-class solidarity. Although the principle of the Second International of 1889 was carried forward at a number of conferences in the years leading up to the war, the outbreak of conflict plunged the organisation into crisis as the mass of the working class demonstrated their apparent preference for national rather than international solidarity by joining their respective armed forces. Despite this, and partly helped by the discussion of war aims noted above, the international dimension continued to provide an important underlying rationale for the substantial minority of socialists and revolutionaries who not only opposed the war, but who continued to look forward to a time when their contacts abroad might form the basis for a new international revolutionary organisation. These ideas were most clearly expressed at the Zimmerwald and Kienthal Conferences of the International held in September 1915 and April 1916, where Lenin argued that the Second International should be replaced by a new Third International which, among other things, would purge the organisation of its reformist social-democratic tendencies. As elsewhere, these ideas continued to circulate among the anti-war factions of the Italian Left, and provided them with a new horizon beyond that of the immediate and temporary perspective of the war itself. Within a year Lenin and the Russian Bolsheviks had given the new horizon a definite shape by demonstrating what could be achieved by revolutionary action.

In Russia, growing opposition to the war had even more dramatic and immediate consequences than it did elsewhere in Europe. There were a number of reasons for this, but one of the most important was the fact that the relationship between the autocratic Tsar Nicholas II and the *Duma*, and between these centres of authority and the population as a whole, were particularly weak and therefore fragile. The extreme reluctance of the Tsar and his court to come to terms with the demands of the population for radical reform, and particularly for a redistribution of landownership, together with the *Duma*'s perceived lack of accountability, gave rise to very strong feelings of resentment and near desperation among the population. As noted at the end of the previous chapter, the St Petersburg Revolution of 1905 had forced the Tsar to concede some of his power to the *Duma*. Although the Russian army had reoccupied Poland and substantial areas in eastern Germany during 1914, by 1917 the army was largely in retreat. As morale declined, and as the severe effects of the war upon the economic structure of the country increased, social tension reached breaking point. Mass strikes broke out and a number of 'soviets' or 'workers' councils' were formed to synchronise the activities of the revolutionary workers, and to establish what amounted to a semi-centralised counter-administration. As in 1905, these developments were most advanced in the then Russian capital St Petersburg (subsequently renamed Petrograd and Leningrad), where a Provisional Executive Committee of the Soviet of Workers' and Soldiers' Deputies was formed which promptly took control of the city. The Soviet itself was largely made up of members of the Social-Revolutionaries (formed in 1901) who represented the demands of the peasantry for land reform, and the 'reformist' Menshevik faction of the Social Democrats (who had split from the Bolsheviks in 1903), who broadly represented the industrial proletariat. The Executive Committee itself was made up of 104 Mensheviks, 99 Social-Revolutionaries and 35 Bolsheviks.

Between the 'February Revolution' in March and the 'October Revolution' in November events unfolded very rapidly. In March the Tsar abdicated and the *Duma* formed a Provisional Government under Prince Lvov offering a compromise policy of ending the war if this could be done without conceding territory to Germany or Austria-Hungary. The same month, Lenin returned from exile in Switzerland, assumed leadership of the Bolshevik Party and in his 'April Theses' put forward a number of proposals to the effect that the Soviets should immediately take full control over the country, introduce a radical programme of nationalisation and declare the foundation of a Soviet

Republic. In July, the provisional government sanctioned one further offensive along its south-western front which precipitated a further wave of strikes in Petrograd. A new provisional government was formed under Alexander Kerensky which now included a number of Mensheviks and Social-Revolutionaries. The Bolsheviks were blamed for the July insurrections and Lenin fled to Finland, while Trotsky, who had recently returned from exile in New York and joined the Bolsheviks, was arrested. The Bolsheviks continued to gain support, however, and by the autumn Lenin returned to Petrograd and decided that the time had come for a direct seizure of power. The headquarters of the government were seized and most of the deputies arrested. On the 25 October, the Second Congress of the All-Russian Congress of Soviets met and a new executive body, the Council of People's Commissars, was formed. The following month elections were held to form the first Constituent Assembly. It soon became clear that the Bolsheviks, whose majority on the Central Executive Committee had allowed them to impose their own members on the Council, did not have anything like a majority of support among the electorate as a whole. Of the 36 million votes cast the Bolsheviks secured less than a quarter which gave them 168 seats compared with 299 for the Social-Revolutionaries and other parties. This outcome did not alter the fact that the Bolsheviks were still the most powerful party by virtue of their effective control over the Executive Committee, the Council and over what was soon to become the Red Army. The Bolsheviks remained unwilling to accept any challenge to their executive authority and in January the Constituent Assembly was forcibly dissolved and the Soviet Socialist Republic declared. Within two months, Trotsky, who had become Peoples' Commissar for Foreign Affairs, fulfilled the Bolsheviks' promise of taking Russia out of the war by signing the Treaty of Brest-Litovsk with Germany.

By the time that Italy had entered the war, Gramsci's personal circumstances had reached a particularly low point. His university career had come to an end and the disastrous reception of his article on the neutrality question had forced him to withdraw more or less completely from political life. For someone as physically weak and psychologically sensitive as Gramsci, these setbacks must have been almost unbearable. By the end of 1915, however, Gramsci seems to have decided that his depressed state of mind was at least partly due to the solitary nature of his life. He also began to recognise that the practical and active dimension of the revolutionary struggle was as important as the intellectual. These reflections and changes of mood are clearly shown in a letter to his eldest sister Grazia:

> In two years, I don't think I either laughed or cried once. I attempted to conquer physical weakness through work, and only made myself weaker than before . . . . I should never have detached myself so far from life in the way I did. I've lived right out of this world for a couple of years: it was like a long dream. I allowed the links which bound me to the world of men to snap off, one by one. I lived entirely by the brain, and not at all by the heart . . . . It was as if the whole of humanity had ceased to exist for me, and I was a wolf alone in its den. (Fiori, 1990: 98–9)

Buoyed up by this new sense of purpose, Gramsci cast off his melancholia and embarked on a new life of political agitation. By 1916 his political participation began to increase as he started giving lectures and attending meetings of various socialist groups. He also began writing articles on contemporary issues for *Il Grido del Popolo* and *Avanti!* where he was soon employed as a full-time journalist. As noted above, Gramsci's experiences at university and during the war led him beyond the arguments of *Sardism* towards a more overtly socialist understanding of social change. Partly because of his long-standing interest in theatre and the arts more generally, and partly through the influence of his intellectual contemporaries, Gramsci developed a strong interest in the relationship between political awareness and culture. This theme, which subsequently came to play an important part in his discussion of the development of political consciousness in the *Prison Notebooks*, became the dominant feature of his writing and political activity at this time as he tried to establish what amounted to a proletarian counter-culture.

Although this new quest ran parallel to more profound changes in Gramsci's intellectual approach – for example, that a correct understanding of the world is something which comes from experience rather than from learning about 'facts' – it had important practical consequences since it implied a criticism of what the young Turinese intellectuals regarded as the somewhat conservative tactics of the older members of the PSI. As the war continued, Gramsci and his circle began to argue more and more forcibly for a complete renovation of the socialist approach to the education and organisation of the working-class movement. In a much-quoted article written for *Il Grido del Popolo* in January 1916 under the title 'Socialism and Culture', Gramsci expresses these new ideas in the following way:

> We need to free ourselves from the habit of seeing culture as encyclopaedic knowledge, and men as mere receptacles to be stuffed full of empirical data and a mass of unconnected raw facts . . . . Culture is something quite different. It is organisation, discipline of one's inner self, a coming to terms with one's own personality; it is the attainment of a higher awareness, with the aid of which one succeeds in understanding one's own historical value, one's own function in life, one's own rights and obligations . . . . The fact is that only by degrees, one stage at a time, has humanity acquired consciousness of its own value and won for itself the right to throw off patterns of organisation imposed on it by minorities at a previous period in history. And this consciousness was formed not under the brutal goad of physiological necessity, but as a result of intelligent reflection, at first by just a few people and later by a whole class, on why certain conditions exist and how best to convert the facts of vassalage into the signals of rebellion and social reconstruction. (*SPWI*, pp.11–12)

It is important to emphasise that, for Gramsci, this belief in the value of personal experience as the basis for knowledge in general, and for the development of political consciousness in particular, was not simply a convenient device for philosophical reflection but provided a basis for a series of practical experiments in political education. In December 1917, for example, Gramsci formed the *Club di Vita Morale* as a cultural discussion group for young workers and intellectuals. Similarly, in December 1919, the *Ordine* group established a number of 'Labour schools' and a 'School of Culture and Socialist Propaganda' as part of the wider programme of worker education. The need for this kind of guidance was still very much in Gramsci's mind when in 1925 he suggested that, in order to carry out the 'ideological struggle' (in addition to the economic and political struggles), the PCI should establish a Party School. As the discussion in the following chapters will show, these experiments and the philosophy which lay behind them remained central to Gramsci's analysis of social change throughout his life.

As news of the Russian Revolution gradually reached Italy, it was inevitable that Gramsci would take a particularly keen interest in these events and seek to understand their implications for the Italian working class. Because of the difficulty of communications during the war, news of the Revolution reached Italy in a slow and somewhat distorted way. The right-wing press was very wary of presenting the Revolution as a victory of the Russian working class for the obvious reason that this might stir up similar aspirations in Italy itself. In addition, *Avanti!* based its own reports on the eyewitness account of a member of the Social-Revolutionaries who deliberately played down the role of Lenin and the Bolsheviks. Initially, therefore, there was some confusion both as to whether the revolution was primarily 'bourgeois' along the lines of the French Revolution, or whether it was a genuinely proletarian or at least working-class event, and as to who were the actual leaders of the Revolution. By July some of the confusion had cleared and Gramsci was writing in praise of Lenin and the Bolsheviks:

> [Lenin] has been able to convert his thought into a meaningful historical force. He has released energies that will never die. He and his Bolshevik comrades are convinced that socialism can be achieved at any time. They are nourished on Marxist thought. They are revolutionaries not evolutionaries. And revolutionary thought does not see time as a progressive factor. It denies that all intermediate stages between the conception of socialism and its achievement must have absolute and complete confirmation in time and place.... Their conviction has not remained audacious in thought alone. It has been embodied in individuals, in many individuals; it has borne fruit in activities. It has created the very group that was necessary to oppose any final compromises, any settlement which could have become definitive. And the revolution is continuing. (*SPWI*, p.32)

As this article shows, Gramsci was also beginning to interpret the Revolution as representing a major transition in the conduct of Marxist revolutionary practice itself. By emphasising that 'revolutionary thought does not see time as a progressive factor', and that socialism can be achieved directly without having to pass through 'intermediate stages', Gramsci argues that, contrary to the 'evolutionist' and 'mechanicist' interpretation of Marx put forward by the Second International, proletarian revolution 'can be achieved at any time'. Most significantly, and again in contradiction to previous interpreters of Marx, he argues that the 'intermediate stages' through which it had been assumed that society must pass before revolution could occur can be realised '*in thought*'. Revolutionary practice, in other words, need not necessarily follow the evolutionary path apparently mapped out by Marx. By December, in an article significantly entitled 'The Revolution Against "Capital" ', Gramsci writes that:

The Bolsheviks reject Karl Marx, and their explicit actions and conquests bear witness that the canons of historical materialism are not so rigid as one might have thought and has been believed. And yet there is a fatality even in these events, and if the Bolsheviks reject some of the statements in *Capital*, they do not reject its invigorating, immanent thought. These people are not "Marxists", that is all; they have not used the works of the Master to compile a rigid doctrine of dogmatic utterances never to be questioned. They live Marxist thought . . . [and] this thought sees as the dominant factor in history, not raw economic facts, but man, men in societies, men in relation to one another . . . men coming to understand economic facts, judging them and adapting them to their will until this becomes the driving force of the economy and moulds objective reality, which lives and moves and comes to resemble a current of volcanic lava that can be channelled wherever and in whatever way men's will determines. (*SPWI*, pp.34–5)

This reading of the Revolution and its implications was soon absorbed by the Turinese workers as a whole, and when a largely reformist delegation from the Petrograd Soviet visited the city on behalf of Kerenski's provisional government in August, the large and militant crowd shouted in support of Lenin and against the war. Within a few days, the mass demonstration had escalated into a major riot and the government was forced to respond with military force.

Although it is not clear what role Gramsci played in these demonstrations, they were certainly instrumental in accelerating his transition from culture-critic and journalist to practising revolutionary. The wave of repression and arrests which followed the Turin uprising effectively deprived the PSI of its local leadership. A new committee was formed and Gramsci became Secretary of the Turin section of the Party. His involvement with the Party at the national level soon followed when he represented the Turin section at a secret meeting of the Party at Florence in November 1917. The aim of this meeting was to try and reunite the reformist and revolutionary factions whose different positions had become increasingly entrenched during the course of the war. With the lessons of the Russian Revolution fresh in their minds, the left-wing of the PSI led by Giacinto Serrati, a militant socialist who had taken over as editor of *Avanti!* after Mussolini's defection and who had attended the Kienthal Conference in 1916, combined with the Youth Federation led by the militant 'orthodox' Marxist revolutionary Amadeo Bordiga and adopted an explicitly revolutionary position based upon the Bolshevik model. Although

Gramsci's relationship with Bordiga was always to remain awkward, and although both Gramsci and Bordiga soon grew impatient with the somewhat less than revolutionary position of the 'maximalists', Gramsci nevertheless joined Serrati in opposition to Turati's reformists. He therefore became a leading figure in the socialist movement at a particularly crucial time in its history.

While Gramsci and the PSI were engaged in these debates the war continued. It has already been noted that by the end of 1917 the military and economic situation in Italy had deteriorated. In October, Boselli had lost his majority and was replaced by Vittorio Orlando. In November, the Germans inflicted a very heavy defeat on the Italians at the battle of Caporetto where nearly 340,000 Italians had either been killed, wounded or taken prisoner. Following a change of command and with further help from the British and French, the Italians just managed to prevent any further loss of territory and by the end of the year the German forces had begun to withdraw. The defeat at Caporetto and the indignity of occupation had a powerful sanitising effect on the Italian population, and support for the war effort took on a more urgent character. With the help of very substantial loans from its allies and through the introduction of stringent austerity measures, the new government were able to pull the economy back from the brink of collapse. Imports of food and raw materials stabilised and industrial output increased. The welfare and morale of the army became a top priority, and a new force of specially trained shock troops, the *arditi*, was created. On the domestic political front, the activities of anti-war groups were forcibly suppressed and many of their leaders imprisoned.

As the war entered its fourth and final year in 1918, events on the Italian front were soon overshadowed by those in occupied France. Russia's withdrawal from the war together with separate peace treaties between the central powers and the Ukraine in February, and with Romania in May, effectively ended the war in the East and allowed Germany to concentrate its efforts on the western front. In June a final offensive was launched against the French and British forces. German supplies and morale could not keep pace with this advance, however, and by September the Entente had once again forced the Germans into full retreat. In Austria-Hungary the situation had become equally bad as the empire began to disintegrate in the face of fresh demands for independence from its Yugoslav and Czech populations. The final Austrian attack was launched in June, but by November the Italian army was advancing north virtually unhindered. By the autumn, and faced with the virtual collapse of its own and the Austrian army abroad, and with the very real possibility of a soviet-style revolution at home, the German High Command accepted defeat and offered an armistice based on the conditions of President Wilson's earlier peace initiatives. By the end of October, Austria-Hungary, Bulgaria and Turkey had accepted the same terms and 'the war to end all wars' came to an end.

The cessation of formal hostilities did not, of course, mean that Europe was at peace in the more general sense, and it soon became apparent that many of the underlying resentments and conflicts of the continent remained unresolved. In addition to having to come to terms with the physical and psychological effects of the war and its huge financial and human costs (more than 8.5 million had been killed), the populations of Europe became increasingly preoccupied with fundamental questions about the nature of post-war industrial society itself. Two issues which were particularly important in this respect were a resurgence of the already well-established demands for independence and self-determination, and the more recent emergence of popular and well-organised working-class parties. With regard to the first issue, a number of new states quickly emerged, particularly in central and eastern Europe, following the collapse of the Austro-Hungarian Empire.[5] The second issue, the demands of the working classes, posed an even more fundamental challenge to the structures of western society. From a radical socialist perspective, and quite apart from the inspirational activities of the Russian Bolsheviks, the traumatic experience of the war had placed considerable pressure upon the already strained worker–employer relationship, and the economic fatigue and general disarray which accompanied the switch from war-time to peace-time production seemed to offer an ideal opportunity for revolution. Although very similar conditions existed in Britain, France, Italy and elsewhere, it was in Germany that a truly revolutionary situation began to emerge.

As noted above, the formation of the anti-war USPD in 1917 had clearly demonstrated the extent of working-class militancy in Germany. During November 1918 and as part of the demands of the victorious Entente, the Kaiser and his military leadership resigned and the SPD leader Friedrich Ebert formed a new government with an interim Council composed of equal numbers of SPD and USPD deputies. At the same time, a rash of workers' and soldiers' councils emerged throughout Germany as activists attempted to establish a new German socialist republic along the lines of the Russian model. When in December the Berlin Council accepted a resolution to elect a new National Assembly, the USPD left in protest, and by January 1919 its radical left-wing, the Spartakus League led by Rosa Luxemburg and Karl Liebknecht, had broken away to form the German Communist Party (KPD). The same month the KPD and other revolutionary factions organised a series of uprisings in Berlin. Within a few days, however, the demonstrations were suppressed and Luxemburg and Liebknecht had been murdered with the complicity of the government. The National Assembly met for the first time in February and by August the constitution of the Weimer Republic had been established.

Despite the evident failure of the German Revolution and of other communist uprisings in Austria and Hungary in the months immediately after the war,[6] the Russian Bolsheviks remained hopeful that the tide of post-war unrest throughout Europe was still running in their favour. Partly to forestall what he saw as the unwelcome influence of a resuscitated Second International (a conference of socialist delegates had met in Bern in February), and partly in order to defend the revolution in Russia itself, Lenin decided that the time was now right to establish the new Third International. The First Congress of what soon came to be known as the Comintern was duly held in Moscow in March 1919. Although the conference lacked any formal structure, and although many of the delegates expressed views which may not have been truly representative of their respective domestic parties, the Comintern succeeded in providing a new forum for debate among the various European socialist and communist parties. While the German and French communists did not formally join the Comintern until after its Second Congress in July 1920, one party which immediately declared itself in favour of the Bolshevik programme was the Italian Socialists.

Although Italy's international position had been secured under the terms of the Treaty of London, the domestic situation remained very tense. The war had left the economy in a precarious state and circumstances soon deteriorated as the armistice put an end to supplies of raw materials, food and foreign credit. Heavy borrowing and increasing national debt brought inflation which in turn resulted in a general fall in the standard of living.[7] As in previous periods of hardship many workers, peasants and now ex-servicemen began to look towards the organisations of the working class as a means of expressing their grievances and of improving their situation. By the end of 1920, CGL membership had passed 2 million; that of the Catholic CIL had risen to nearly 1.5 million; the Chambers of Labour and the metalworkers' union, FIOM (*Federazione Impriegati Operai Metallurgici*), were up to 90,000 and 22,500 strong respectively; while the USI and UIL claimed a further 1 million members between them (Seton-Watson, 1967: 520–1). This growth in radicalism was confirmed by the results of the 1919 General Election, where the liberal-democratic bloc of Francesco Nitti (who had replaced Orlando as prime minister in June) secured only 252 seats compared with 156 for the Socialists and 100 for the Catholic Popular Party.

With regard to the position of the PSI itself, it was noted above that, by the end of the war, Turati's moderate position within the Party had been largely overshadowed by the more radical position of Serrati in the 'centre' and Bordiga on the 'left'. In Turin, the end of the war inevitably affected Gramsci's position within the PSI as the old leadership returned to active political life. Gramsci temporarily lost his place on the Executive Committee elected in November 1918 before being re-elected the following May. Within Gramsci's own intellectual circle, Tasca, Togliatti and Terracini also returned to the city, and within a few months they had decided to start a new journal aimed at consolidating the links between different factions of the Turinese working class. As Gramsci put it: 'We wanted to *do* something. We felt desperate, disoriented, immersed in the excitement of life in those months after the Armistice, when the cataclysm in Italian society appeared so imminent' (*SPWI*, p.291). The first edition of *L'Ordine Nuovo* ('The New Order') appeared in May 1919. Although it was originally intended to be 'a weekly review of Socialist culture', Gramsci and Togliatti soon became impatient with the somewhat literary and aesthetic tone of the journal and by the end of June they had displaced Tasca as editor. From this time on, *L'Ordine Nuovo* adopted a much more radical position aimed specifically at creating a new socialist state:

> How are the immense social forces unleashed by the war to be harnessed? How are they to be disciplined and given a political form which has the potential to develop normally and continuously into the skeleton of the socialist State in which the dictatorship of the proletariat will be embodied? ... The formula 'dictatorship of the proletariat' must cease to be a mere formula, a flourish of revolutionary rhetoric. Whoever wills the end, must

will the means. The dictatorship of the proletariat represents the establishment of a new, proletarian State, which channels the institutional experiences of the oppressed class and transforms the social activity of the working class and peasantry into a widespread and powerfully organised system. (*SPWI*, pp.65, 68)

It is important to emphasise that the analysis put forward by the *Ordine* group went well beyond an 'abstract' Marxian diagnosis of the revolutionary potential of the Italian working class and peasantry. What Gramsci and his followers really wanted to do was to develop a new and highly practical working-class structure which would not only lead and direct the revolution, but would also become the actual basis of the socialist state in Italy. As we have seen, Gramsci had followed the development of the Russian Soviets with great interest. As the war drew to an end he extended his knowledge of trade union and other working-class organisations and methods including those of the British unions and shop stewards, and the American Industrial Workers of the World (IWW) led by Daniel De Leon. In the same way that the Turin intellectuals had criticised the PSI leadership for its lack of a progressive intellectual and cultural programme during the war, the *Ordine* group now suggested that the Party and the reformist CGL no longer provided a suitable structure within which the revolution could be organised.

The reasons for these deficiencies largely stemmed from the particular characteristics of the Turinese working class itself. It has already been noted in the previous chapter that the development of heavy manufacturing industries in Italy had been highly concentrated in the northern centres of Milan, Turin and Genoa. With the increased national dependence on industrial products and income, successive governments had allowed the development of a number of highly concentrated and powerful conglomerates. Of particular note were the giant Ilva steel combine and the Ansaldo shipping company, both of which were closely associated with major Italian banks, and the giant engineering and motor-manufacturer FIAT based in Turin. The development of the industrial sector and of the skilled and semi-skilled workforce had received a further boost during the war as the demand for armaments and machines quickly outstripped supply. This expansion was matched by a growth in organisations which represented the industrialists and the workers respectively and by a general aura of compromise and negotiation between the two blocs. This situation tended to favour the skilled workers whose privileged status within the production process placed them in a strong bargaining position. For the unskilled and casual workers who moved to the towns and cities during the war, however, and for the mass of agricultural workers and peasants who remained in the countryside, the craft-based urban unions and their leadership seemed increasingly remote and unrepresentative. This left the FIOM and the CGL in a somewhat paradoxical position since the élitism which had brought concessions from the employers during the war now constituted a barrier to the expansion of their organisation at precisely the moment when their potential membership was expanding. This situation also cast a shadow over the relationship between the unions and the PSI, whose long-standing reformism made it extremely sensitive to the idea of a mass party whose membership might force it to abandon the tried and tested methods of negotiation in favour of direct action.

Through his personal contacts with the workers, Gramsci had become very much aware of this growing dissatisfaction and of the problems of organisation which any solution required. In June 1919 it was proposed that a new form of 'workers' democracy' and a new structure of *consigli di fabbrica* or factory councils should be established centred round the *commissioni interne* or internal shop stewards' committees:

> Today the internal commissions limit the power of the capitalist in the factory and perform functions of arbitration and discipline. Tomorrow, developed and enriched, they must be the organs of proletarian power, replacing the capitalist in all his useful functions of management and administration. The workers should proceed at once to the election of vast assemblies of delegates, chosen from their best and most conscious comrades, under the slogan: 'All power in the workshop to the workshop committees' together with its complement: 'All State power to the Workers' and Peasants' Councils.' (*SPWI*, pp.66–7)

The ideas put forward in *L'Ordine Nuovo* were particularly appealing to the expanding proletariat precisely because they offered a highly democratic and universal programme for revolutionary action. Clearly, this proposal of an alternative means of actually conducting the revolution represented a further important transition in Gramsci's intellectual and political development. (Detailed discussions of this transition and of the underlying critique of the PSI and the CGL are given in Chapter 8.)

The activities and influence of the 'council movement' coincided with a further wave of strikes, factory occupations and civil unrest throughout Italy during the summer of 1919. At the PSI Congress held at Bologna in October the programme put forward by the *Ordine* group was largely ignored as Serrati's maximalist centre held sway over Turati's marginalised reformism and Bordiga's recommendation that the Party should *abstain* from the forthcoming General Election on the grounds that participation would merely serve to legitimise the bourgeois political process. Outside the formal structure, however, the new programme was attracting growing support and by the end of the year factory councils had been set up in each of the FIAT works, representing over 30,000 workers, while the leadership of the FIOM also became more radical.

The following spring, the employers' organisations Confindustria and the Industrial League had decided that something would have to be done to challenge the growing power and influence of the new councils even if this meant provoking all-out confrontation. In March a minor dispute soon escalated into a a full-scale confrontation and the entire FIAT works had ground to a halt. By April the whole organised Piedmont workforce of over 500,000 had stopped work. Although the Turinese workforce occupied a central position in the industrial economy, it soon became clear that their success ultimately depended upon the support of the whole Italian working class. Their victory, in other words, required the escalation of the dispute into a full-scale *national* strike. At the crucial moment, however, neither the CGL nor the PSI could bring itself to take the plunge. At its National Congress held in Milan (the Congress was originally planned for Turin) on 19–20 April, a majority of delegates 'refused to authorise the extension of the strike beyond Piedmont', because it considered the actions of the metalworkers to be 'impetuous and irresponsible'. Now isolated from both the PSI and the CGL, and threatened by a very large military force in Turin,[8] the strike collapsed.

In the light of the bitter disappointment and sense of betrayal which surrounded these events, Gramsci immediately turned his attention to an aggressive critique of the PSI itself. Suspicions about the fundamental unwillingness of the Party leadership even to consider, let alone to engage in, revolutionary activity had been evident since the Bologna Conference in October 1919 where, despite voting to join the Third International, Serrati had refused to expel Turati and the other reformists. In May 1920, while the strike was still going on, *L'Ordine*

Nuovo published a detailed critique of the PSI under the heading 'Towards a Renewal of the Socialist Party'. It accused the Party of effectively relinquishing its responsibility to the working classes:

> The worker and peasant forces lack revolutionary co-ordination and concentration because the leading organs of the Socialist party have shown no understanding at all of the stage of development that national and international history is currently passing through. . . . The Socialist Party watches the course of events like a spectator; it never has an opinion of its own to express, based on the revolutionary theses of Marxism and the Communist International. . . . [It] has continued to be merely a parliamentary party, immobilising itself within the narrow limits of bourgeois democracy, and concerning itself only with the superficial political declarations of the governing caste.

The article went on to suggest that the Party should expel the reformists and concentrate exclusively on the task of organisation:

> As political expression of the vanguard section of the working class, the Socialist Party should develop a comprehensive action designed to put the whole of the working class in a position to win the revolution, and win it permanently. . . . Nothing was done by the central Party organs to give the masses a communist political education, to induce the masses to eliminate the reformists and opportunists from the leadership of the trade unions and the co-operative institutions, or to give individual sections and the most active groups of comrades a unified line and tactics. . . . The Party must acquire its own precise and distinct character. From a petty-bourgeois parliamentary party it must become the party of the revolutionary proletariat in its struggle to achieve a communist society by way of the workers' State – a homogeneous, cohesive party, with a doctrine and tactics of its own, and a rigid and implacable discipline. (*SPWI*, pp.191–2,194)

While Gramsci attacked the Party from the perspective of the council movement, Bordiga attacked it through the pages of his revolutionary journal *Il Soviet*, and in his direct correspondence with the Comintern in Moscow:

> The Italian party [PSI] is not a communist party; *it is not even a revolutionary party* . . . in all likelihood, although we have maintained discipline within the PSI and upheld its tactics until now, before long . . . our fraction will break away from the party that seems set on retaining many anti-communists in

its ranks, to form the Italian Communist Party, whose first act will be to affiliate to the Communist International. (Letter to Central Committee of the Comintern, November 1920; *SPWI*, pp.210, 213; original emphasis)

Although Gramsci and Bordiga were moving closer to the idea of establishing a separate communist party, it would be a mistake to assume that they were developing identical ideas as to how the revolution should be conducted and organised. Most importantly, they disagreed over the nature of the relationship between the new party and the factory councils. Bordiga argued that the correct, and more limited, role of the councils should be to represent the particular 'economic functions' and 'technical' concerns of the workers *as workers*, while the political dimension of the revolution should be conducted by an organisation of 'political soviets' and a communist party representing the interests of the proletariat '*as a whole class over and above sectional interests*' (*SPWI*, p.200). For his part, Gramsci argued that although the political aspect of the struggle should indeed be conducted by the new party, the eventual success of the revolution and the establishment of a socialist state would ultimately depend upon control over the production process itself. The party should therefore be *subordinate* to the councils:

> The relations that should link the political party and the Factory Council, the trade union and the Factory Council, are implicitly contained in the argument presented above. The Party and trade unions should not project themselves as tutors or as ready-made superstructures for this new institution, in which the historical process of the revolution takes a controllable historical form. They should project themselves as the conscious agents of its liberation from the restrictive forces concentrated in the bourgeois State. (*SPWI*, p.264)

While these debates were taking place, Gramsci was becoming increasingly marginalised within the *Ordine* group itself. Tasca, Togliatti and Terracini began to argue that the collapse of the recent strike in Turin was chiefly caused by the fact that the councils had not developed sufficiently close links with the traditional unions and the CGL. They therefore proposed that the councils and internal committees should align themselves much more closely with the latter and, most importantly, adopt their strategy and tactics *including* participation in local elections. This rift coincided with further disagreements *within* the communist left of the Turin section of the

Party between Bordiga's 'abstentionists' and other Communists including Gramsci, who argued for the formation of an non-abstentionist faction. When a new Executive Committee was elected in August, Gramsci received only thirty-one votes compared with 466 for Togliatti's group and 186 for Bordiga's abstentionists.

Although these debates within the PSI had forced Gramsci into a somewhat isolated position, events outside the Party soon brought him back to the centre of attention. At the Second Congress of the Comintern held in Moscow during July and August 1920, and much to the dismay of both Serrati and Bordiga who attended the Congress, Lenin gave explicit approval for the *L'Ordine Nuovo* critique of the PSI as set out in the article on 'renewal' quoted above. Lenin also put forward the 'Twenty-one Conditions' which all affiliated parties would have to meet before being admitted to the Comintern. Among other things, this meant that Serrati had to agree to expel all remaining reformists from the PSI:

> To the Italian comrades we must say simply that it is the outlook of the *Ordine Nuovo* militants which corresponds to the principles of the Communist International, and not the outlook of the present majority among the leaders of their parliamentary group. . . . Hence, we must say to the Italian comrades and to all parties which have a right wing: the reformist tendency has nothing in common with communists. (Davidson, 1977: 140ff.)

Although Serrati's refusal and subsequent loss of favour with the Comintern tended to support Bordiga's wish to establish a separate Communist Party, Bordiga was himself criticised for his anti-parliamentary attitude. Repeating arguments put forward in *Left-wing Communism, an Infantile Disorder*, Lenin explained that although the revolution would ultimately destroy the institutions of bourgeois democracy, it was still important to gain control over them during the early phase of the revolution.

In summary, therefore, during the summer of 1920 the right-wing of the PSI, represented by Serrati, continued to argue that under Italian conditions the best chance of a successful working-class accession to power still lay in maintaining close links with the CGL in order to sustain a strong negotiating position against the employers' organisations. Within the majority faction of the Turin section of the Party, Tasca, Togliatti and Terracini tended to agreed with this policy, but emphasised that the development of the factory councils added a new and more direct means of working-class resistance and action. On the radical revolutionary wing, Gramsci and Bordiga had become increasingly dismayed with the reformist character of the Party and argued that it would either have to be completely renewed from within or that a separate and 'pure' Communist Party would have to be formed outside the PSI.

As noted above, post-war fatigue and political instability had resulted in a general governmental crisis as Nitti had failed to gain a majority at the 1919 General Election. By the summer of 1920, the April strike and other disorder had weakened his position even further, and in June he resigned in favour of Giolitti. Giolitti was very well aware of the militancy of the working class and decided that, if at all possible, the government should combat the growing threat to its own authority either by avoiding industrial disputes altogether, or by encouraging reconciliation and negotiation. Following the April strike, the FIOM had entered negotiations with the industrialists over improvements in pay and conditions. By August the situation deteriorated and in order to avoid an employers' lock out the union ordered an occupation of the Alfa Romeo plant in Milan. This action soon spread throughout the industrial sector including Turin, and by the end of the month over 500,000 workers were involved throughout Italy. With this second glimpse of a possible revolution, the Turin factions reunited and turned their attention to organising the factory occupations. Most significantly, and unlike the earlier strike, the councils encouraged the workers to continue production. Gramsci hoped that this new tactic would not only demonstrate that the councils could run the factories without the help of management or the white-collar technical staff, but also, as noted above, that this would provide a practical demonstration of how a workers' state might operate.

As the occupations spread and the tempo of events increased, the PSI leadership once again found itself in the very awkward position of having to decide whether to assume responsibility for, and thus leadership of, the strike, or to do as they had done in April and declare that the strike was an economic rather than a political event and as such was not their responsibility. For their part, the CGL leadership still believed that arbitration was preferable to revolution, and they too refused to take on the leadership role. Indecision inevitably led to paralysis and when the two organisations met on 10 September a resolution calling for an escalation of the dispute into a full-scale offensive against the State was defeated. With the effective decapitation of the working class the crisis passed and Giolitti proposed a resumption of negotiations. By the end of the month a pay rise had been agreed along with a vague promise of a new contract for 'industrial co-partnership', and control of the factories passed back to the employers. As later events soon demonstrated, this second major defeat signalled the end not only of Italy's socialist revolution, but also seriously undermined support for the socialist organisations of the working class as a whole.

In terms of its immediate effects, the rift between the PSI and the Turin radicals was now complete. Faced with the evident failure of the council movement, Gramsci reluctantly agreed to join Bordiga, Terracini and others in forming a new communist fraction. In December and under the suggestive title 'Split or Ruin?', the *Ordine* group made its future plans quite explicit:

> It would be ridiculous to whine about what has happened and what is irremediable. Communists are cold and calm reasoners – they have to be. If everything lies in ruins, then everything has to be done again. The Party has to be rebuilt, and henceforth the communist fraction must be considered and esteemed as a party in its own right, as the solid framework of the Italian Communist Party. (*SPWI*, p.364)

At the Livorno Congress of the PSI in January 1921, and under continuing pressure from the Comintern to accept the 'Twenty-one Conditions' unconditionally, Serrati tried in vain to hold the Party together. Despite gaining 98,000 votes for his 'unitary' policy, the communists won a substantial minority of nearly 60,000 and so split the Party. The following day, the inaugural meeting of the Italian Communist Party (PCI) was held in a theatre adjacent to the PSI conference building. Bordiga became the first leader of the new Party, while Terracini and Gramsci represented the views of the *Ordine* group as members of the first Central Committee.

Gramsci and the PCI, 1921–6

As the foregoing account has shown, the activities of the PSI and of the Italian Left more generally did not take place in a vacuum but were constantly mitigated by developments in Italian society as a whole.

Since the turn of the century the balance of social and political power had tended to settle on the side of reformist liberalism, while socialism took root among the newly created urban industrial proletariat whose interests rose to the top of the political agenda. After the defeat of the socialists during 1919–20, however, this balance began to move back in favour of the vested interests of capitalism as the 'red years' gave way to the 'black reaction' of fascism.

To some extent, the psychological origins of Italian fascism can be traced back to the period of the *Risorgimento* and the imperialist adventures in Libya and West Africa, when the Italian population clearly nurtured a deep sense of national self-importance and destiny. There was also a strong tradition, particularly in the rural south and in Sicily, of local syndicates and co-operatives which operated outside the control of central authority. From a psychological and practical point of view in other words, a large proportion of the population was *at least potentially* both willing and able to provide the basis for a nationalistic mass movement. A more immediate source of support came at the end of the war in 1918, when large numbers of servicemen returned home. As noted above, many of these people were attracted to the working-class movement and the vision it offered of a new form of society. For the majority, however, the aggressive anti-war attitudes of the PSI and the Catholic Popular Party were seen as a betrayal of the feelings of patriotism and national pride which had sustained them for the past three years. In addition, the misunderstandings between government and military command during the war had made many of the returnees deeply suspicious about the motives of government and big business.

This sense of disaffection added to the already widespread feeling that the institutions of Italy's liberal State and the structures of the parliamentary system were in crisis. In effect, therefore, a gap had emerged in the centre of the political spectrum which none of the established parties could claim for itself. By the end of the war two figures had emerged whose nationalistic credentials were very much in tune with these mixed sentiments of disillusionment and desire for action. The first was the internationally renowned poet and dramatist Gabriele d'Annunzio who had developed a colourful reputation during the war for his daring exploits as a propagandist and agitator behind enemy lines. This reputation was greatly enhanced when in September 1919, and in direct defiance of Nitti's government, he led a force of 8,000 army deserters and patriots to occupy and liberate the disputed Adriatic port of Fiume.[9] Aside from the general excitement caused by d'Annunzio's larger-than-life behaviour, he provided the nationalists and patriots with a practical demonstration of what could be achieved by direct action. This lesson was not lost on the second putative leader of the reactionary upsurge, Benito Mussolini.

After leaving the PSI in November 1914, and aside from a brief spell of active service, Mussolini had devoted himself to spreading pro-war propaganda through his interventionist journal *Il Popolo d'Italia*. When the war ended, and sensitive to the growing number of potential recruits for his radical anti-socialist, anti-clerical and anti-parliamentary perspective, he turned his attention to establishing a new organisation. In March 1919 the *Fasci Italiani di Combattimento* was formally set up in Milan. A key feature of the new fascist organisation was its strongly militaristic orientation, and within a few months armed groups of largely middle-class *arditi* (including many ex-members of the élite corps formed in the last year of the war) began to emerge in Milan and a number of other large cities in the north. It is important to emphasise that the early fascist movement attracted support from a wide variety of sources ranging from the radical syndicalist trade unions of the UIL to the artistic avant-garde including such well known personalities as the leader and mentor of the Futurists Filippo Marinetti, and the composer Arturo Toscanini. This eclecticism and willingness to alter its dogma and sources of support was a central ingredient in the movement's early success, as Mussolini was prepared to consider more or less any practical means of widening its appeal. In particular, he was well aware that Italy's economy had undergone a period of intense modernisation and that any new movement could survive only if it gained the confidence and support of the powerful industrialists and landowners. He therefore began to argue that the new movement could satisfy the radical yearnings of the working class without turning the country over to socialism; a fascist revolution, in other words, would transform society without doing away with industrial capitalism. Although many industrialists and landowners remained deeply suspicious of Mussolini's true motives, they none the less began to provide him with substantial financial backing.

In terms of attracting more general popular support, it soon became clear that the fascists were quite prepared to take matters into their own hands and to use whatever means were necessary to 'convince' people of the correctness of their views. From early 1920 onwards the *arditi* began a concerted campaign of attacking anything and anyone who either supported, or were in any way associated with, the socialists and their organisations. Meetings were disrupted, Party offices and presses were wrecked, private houses were burnt and many individuals were terrorised or simply beaten up. In the autumn of 1919, the movement received a further boost as sympathy for d'Annunzio's adventures gripped the public's imagination and confirmed that radical nationalism was not only alive and well, but capable of fulfilling its promises. By the beginning of 1921, the movement turned its attention to the rural areas and new fascist gangs or *squadre* effectively took control of many regions in northern and central Italy. As popular support increased the organisation gradually took on the character of a mass party and moved its allegiance away from the UIL and the intellectual élite towards the expanding lower middle-class white-collar workforce in the towns and the property-owning peasants in the countryside. In effect, the fascists had now filled the post-war political vacuum and established themselves as the representatives of a new and highly reactionary petty-bourgeoisie.

It was no coincidence that the apparent freedom of action enjoyed by the *arditi* coincided with the defeat of the socialists. In the first place, the economic situation had worsened as the post-war boom turned from slump into depression. Unemployment and inflation increased and output fell at precisely the same moment that the militant working classes were at their most vulnerable. Having regained control over the labour process, the employers immediately took advantage of their very strong position and dismissed most of the radical socialists and their leaders. By the end of 1921 CGL membership and strike activity had both declined by 50 per cent. As long as the fascists' counter-revolutionary behaviour contributed to the demise of organised labour, the industrialists, and consequently the local authorities that were under their influence, were quite happy for them to do more or less anything they wished. In the second place, ever since the war the socialists had tended to undermine their own popular base by alienating many individuals who might otherwise have supported them. Seton-Watson suggests, for example, that their blanket condemnation of patriotism *per se* and their total rejection of alliances with other groups made them vulnerable to precisely the kind of reactionary backlash which was now taking place. In addition, and aside from the fact that the PSI's evident and catastrophic unwillingness to take on a national leadership role had undermined the whole idea of a socialist transformation of society, many other groups such as the urban petty-bourgeoisie and sections of the aforementioned conservative-minded peasantry felt distinctly uneasy about what a socialist revolution would do for them. Thirdly, each of the post-war governments, including the current one under Giolitti, were unwilling to take the risk of exacerbating an already tense situation by throwing in their lot with either group. It quite suited Giolitti's non-interventionist policy, in other words, to allow the right- and left-wing militants to work off their energies against each other rather than against the State.

By the summer of 1921 Giolitti decided that the PSI leadership was now in such a vulnerable position that it might be persuaded to join him in a new coalition, and a General Election was called for May. Ever since the 1919 election which had been a complete failure for the fascists (in Milan, Mussolini had polled less than 2 per cent of the vote), Mussolini had been very much aware that the long-term success of fascism depended upon formal representation in parliament. He therefore decided, for the time being at least, to support Giolitti's National Bloc (made up largely of liberals and democrats) against the PSI and the Popular Party. Unfortunately for Giolitti, the results of the election left him in a rather more vulnerable position than he had anticipated. Although his National Bloc gained 105 seats compared with 123 and 108 for the Socialists and Popular Party respectively, neither of the latter was prepared to form a coalition. In addition, none of the smaller groups of democrats, right-wing liberals and left-wing republicans (who had gained some 173 seats between them) was prepared to forget its deep-seated hatred of Giolitti. The PCI, standing for the first time as an independent party gained fifteen seats. Finally, the fascists, who had gained thirty-five seats, almost immediately threatened to withdraw their support. After barely a month in office, Giolitti conceded defeat and resigned for the last time.

While Ivanoe Bonomi hurriedly tried to assemble a new government, the fascists underwent yet another metamorphosis. Although it suited Mussolini that the movement had now gained a degree of formal respectability within parliament, many of the still largely autonomous *squadristi* felt that 'respectability' was exactly what the movement did not need. As the prospect of dissent and collapse within the movement increased, and as it became more and more obvious that his personal support was insufficient to rebuff a challenge from the grass roots, Mussolini was forced to compromise. By the autumn he had rejected appeals he had made during the election for a reduction in the paramilitary activities of the *squadristi*, while the latter, now to be regulated by a new central command, agreed that the movement should become the National Fascist Party (*Partito Nazionale Fascista*; PNF) with a revised and distinctively right-wing political programme.

For the remainder of 1921 and into 1922, the functions of government, administration and law-and-order each began to disintegrate as first Bonomi and then Luigi Facta tried in vain to establish an anti-fascist coalition. On the Left, a series of new alliances came and went as first the CGL, UIL and USI, and then the PSI and the Popular Party desperately tried put up some kind of organised resistance to fascism. The final crisis came in October. While negotiations continued with Giolitti and others to form a government, Facta decided that the only chance of averting a final fascist assault lay in organising a rival nationalist demonstration in Rome with the support of d'Annunzio and the remnants of his legionaries. The army was still loyal to the king and constitution, and he hoped that a show of strength would force Mussolini to opt for compromise rather than a direct military confrontation. However, at their Party Congress on the 24 October, the PNF decided to mobilise the *squadristi* for a combined march on Rome without further delay. Facta declared a state of emergency and the army took up defensive positions at strategic points on the approaches to the city with orders to prevent the fascists from entering the capital. On the morning of 28 October, and much to Facta's dismay, the king refused to sign the formal declaration of a state of siege which would in effect have sanctioned immediate military action against the *squadristi*. Facta resigned. The situation had reached stalemate; the army and the *squadistri* stood facing each other on the outskirts of the city; the king went through the motions of looking for a new prime minister, and Mussolini awaited developments in Milan. Finally, the king made the only choice still open to him and invited Mussolini to form a government. The following day the fascist columns marched peacefully into the city to celebrate their bloodless victory.

The rise of Mussolini and the disintegration of the working-class movement left Gramsci and the other leaders of the newly-formed PCI in a very isolated if not totally desperate situation. Membership of all left-wing organisations, including the PCI and the various socialist trade union groups, declined sharply, while communist influence upon what remained of the factory councils also fell away. The activities of the *squadristi* made communication and organisation difficult even within Turin itself, and the threat of violence was never very far away.

About the only good things to come out of the situation were a new sense of solidarity in the face of dire adversity, and a feeling that the Comintern could be relied upon for encouragement and support. Before long, however, both of these sources of optimism had also faded.

As regards Gramsci's personal situation, the trauma of defeat caused him to revert to the kind of bad-tempered reclusiveness which had characterised his behaviour before the rise of the council movement. The intense activity and concentration of energy which had brought him to the forefront of events in Turin during the *bienno rosso* now ebbed away leaving him weak and ill. In addition to this physical regression he also had to contend with the intellectual stress of understanding why the revolution had failed and of trying to gloss over the deep differences which still existed between himself and Bordiga's majority faction within the PCI. With these problems on his mind, Gramsci became less active during the first months of 1921 and concentrated on the job of editing a new daily edition of *L'Ordine Nuovo*. Even here, however, Gramsci lost his former control as the paper fell under Bordiga's influence. With the holding of the Third Congress of the Comintern in Moscow during July, however, this situation began to change.

As in Italy, the likelihood of revolution elsewhere in Europe had now passed as the German, Hungarian and Bulgarian communists all suffered major set-backs.[10] In the Soviet Republic itself, the communists faced considerable problems as the civil war and war against Poland threatened the very survival of the Revolution. For Lenin and the other leaders of the Comintern, it now seemed that a new policy of consolidation was needed. In order to stimulate the faltering economy of the Republic and to offset further internal dissent, Lenin put forward a 'new economic policy', which among other things allowed a partial revival of private commerce and enterprise outside the direct control of the Sate. This adoption of 'state-capitalism' and a 'mixed economy' was generally welcomed abroad and by 1922 valuable trade agreements had been reached with Britain and Germany. In order to revive the Revolution outside the Republic, the Comintern proposed a new policy of reconciliation between the various communist and socialist parties in Europe. It was hoped that by establishing a new 'united front', the working class would attract further support, improve its organisation and be in a much stronger position to mount a final and decisive assault against capitalism.

For Terracini and the other delegates from the PCI, adherence to the united front policy would mean reopening contacts with the very same socialists from whom they had split at Livorno barely six months earlier. For their part, the PSI delegation led by Costantino Lazzari, still hoped that the Comintern would give them more time to expel Turati's right-wing and thus avoid a complete split between the Comintern and the PSI. In the event, Terracini was severely reprimanded by Lenin for sustaining what was now regarded as an outdated separatist position, while Lazzari was persuaded that a split with the reformists had to be made in the very near future. At the Milan Congress of the PSI in October 1921, Serrati and the maximalists continued to argue that although they sympathised with Comintern policy, circumstances in Italy were such that the expulsion of the reformist right-wing would weaken rather than strengthen the position of the working class. In effect, the PSI had hardly moved at all from the position it had adopted when the Comintern was originally founded in March 1919. The following month the PSI was formally expelled from the Comintern.

Throughout the summer of 1921, both Bordiga and Gramsci continued to support Terracini's position that collaboration with the PSI was entirely out of the question, and that a 'pure' Communist Party of dedicated activists was much more important than a new 'mass' party which could lead only to a repeat of the failures of 1920. By the autumn this dissent culminated in the publication of what soon came to be known as the 'Rome Theses'. Largely written by Bordiga and Terracini, this policy, which was subsequently ratified at the PCI Congress held at Rome in March 1922, restated that a successful revolution in Italy could be achieved only by a direct assault on the State (rather than by gradual reforms), that this assault would have to be led by a disciplined Communist Party acting as the genuine vanguard of the working class (rather than by a coalition of separate organisations which tended to have competing interests), and that the business of recruiting new members should be undertaken in strict isolation from all other discredited organisations.[11] Each of these points ran directly against the united front policy, and not surprisingly the Comintern rejected it as a yet another manifestation of Italian extremism and lack of realism. What was important from Gramsci's point of view, however, was that although he supported the Rome Theses, the Comintern's criticism was largely directed at Bordiga and Terracini. Less stigma was therefore attached to Gramsci himself and this offerred the possibility that his future relations with the Comintern might be more successful than those of the present leadership of the PCI. In early 1922, however, there was little real indication that Gramsci might begin to move away from Bordiga's line and in May the PCI Central Committee elected him as their next representative on the Comintern's Executive Committee in Moscow at the age of thirty-one.

The two years which Gramsci spent outside Italy between May 1922 and May 1924 marked a further turning point in both his political and personal life. Gramsci reached Moscow in a particularly miserable and depressed state of mind and it was suggested that he should spend some time recuperating at a sanatorium outside Moscow. During his six months at 'Silvery Wood', Gramsci met and fell deeply in love with the twenty-six-year-old younger sister of a fellow patient, Julia Schucht. Although Gramsci found this encounter rather awkward and was somewhat taken aback by this reflection of his own affections, he was soon immersed in the kind of physical and emotional attachment which he had not experienced since childhood. His duties in Moscow prevented them from spending long periods of time together, but they met as often as they could and kept in touch by letter. After a somewhat hectic and euphoric courtship, the couple were married in 1922 and their first son Delio was born in August 1924. In retrospect, it is rather tragic that a relationship which clearly meant a great deal to Gramsci, and which demonstrated the deeply emotional personality which underlay the professional revolutionary and intellectual, was always to remain fragmented and unfulfilled. As Gramsci's later correspondence with Julia from prison shows, his lack of contact with her and their children tormented him quite as much if not more than his removal from active political life.

While this relationship with Julia stirred new passions and opened fresh horizons, familiar political debates and entrenched positions continued to undermine the PCI's relations with the Comintern. With Mussolini now in power, the Comintern was more concerned than ever with how to reunite what remained of the socialist and communist factions in Italy. The PSI had finally expelled the reformists at its Rome Congress in October 1922 (who subsequently reformed as the Unitary Socialist Party), while a new group emerged on the left of the PSI, the *terzinternazionalisti* or *terzini* led by Serrati, who wished to follow the third internationalist line of the Comintern. At the Fourth Congress of the Comintern in November 1922, and encouraged by these new developments, the Soviet leadership continued to press for reconciliation. For their part, Bordiga and Terracini argued that although Mussolini's intervention had changed the situation, fascism should be regarded as merely the latest if not final manifestation of a desperate bourgeoisie and, consequently, that there was no substantive reason why they should reject their earlier arguments for maintaining a 'pure' Communist Party. Gramsci, whose personal contact with the Comintern had evidently made him much more familiar with the intricacies of their position, at last began to make his criticisms of Bordiga more public and recommended that negotiations should be started to unite with the terzinian faction of the PSI, albeit on very strict terms. For the first time it was privately suggested that Gramsci should consider replacing Bordiga as leader of the PCI.

It is important to emphasise that the differences between the Italian comrades were partly due to the fact that Gramsci had started to develop a much more sophisticated interpretation of the significance of fascism. While still in Turin, he had agreed with Bordiga that fascism could be accurately understood as the latest phase of the class struggle. In an article under the title 'The Monkey-People' published in January 1921 Gramsci writes:

> In this its latest political incarnation of 'fascism', the petty bourgeoisie has once again shown its true colours as the servant of capitalism and landed property, as the agent of counter-revolution. But it has also shown itself to be fundamentally incapable of accomplishing any historical task whatsoever. The Monkey-People [meaning the fascists] make news, not history. They leave their mark in newspapers, but provide no material for books. Having ruined Parliament, the petty bourgeoisie is currently ruining the bourgeois State. On an ever increasing scale, it is replacing the 'authority' of the law by private violence. It practices this violence in a chaotic and brutal fashion (and cannot help but do so), and in the process it is causing ever broader sections of the population to revolt against the State and against capitalism. (*SPWI*, p.374)

By April 1921, however, he had refined this view and suggested that fascism was a cross-class phenomenon which attracted mass 'popular' support from a variety of sources including the peasantry and the Church. Its development was, in other words, much more to do with the *particular* characteristics of Italian psychology and culture than with the international development of capitalism as such:

> It has now become obvious that fascism can only be partially interpreted as a class phenomenon, as a movement of political forces conscious of a real

aim. It has spread, it has broken every possible organizational framework, it is above the wishes and proposals of any central or regional Committee, it has become an unchaining of elemental forces which cannot be restrained under the bourgeois system of economic and political government. Fascism is the name of the far-reaching decomposition of the State, and which today can only be explained by reference to the low level of civilization which the Italian nation has been able to attain in these last sixty years of unitary administration. (*SPWII*, p.38)

This fresh interpretation automatically implied that the Left would have to adopt new tactics in its own defence, and it was on this point that Gramsci moved decisively away from Bordiga.

Back in Italy, it soon became clear that all attempts at fusion between the PCI and either the PSI as a whole or its terzinian minority were doomed to failure. In February 1923, the fascists carried out a further purge of the socialists and communists and many of their supporters and leaders including Bordiga and the greater part of his anti-fusion majority within the PCI were arrested. With most of its leaders already in prison, and with the remainder under the threat of arrest, the Comintern Executive persuaded Terracini, who had become the acting leader of the PCI in Italy, to form a new Central Committee with representatives of Bordiga's majority and Tasca's minority. Within a few months, the PCI leadership was operating almost entirely outside Italy as Tasca went to Paris and Terracini to Moscow. Togliatti remained to organise the Party at home and requested that Gramsci should now leave Moscow to help him.

The Comintern ratified the new leadership in June and for the rest of the summer disputes came and went as the rival factions within and outside Italy continued to put forward alternative views as to how the Party should develop. For Gramsci, the immediate problem was to re-establish the links between the leadership and the grass roots who were becoming increasingly disillusioned with the seemingly endless round of theoretical squabblings. In essence, he was suggesting that the disputes with Bordiga were distracting the Party from its actual task of supporting the Italian working class:

> I am absolutely convinced that today any discussion on our part that is limited to the organizational and juridical aspects of the Italian question can have no useful result. It could only make things worse and make our task more difficult and dangerous. Instead, it is necessary to work concretely and show, through a general party activity and political work that is

adequate to the Italian situation, that we are what we claim to be, instead of continuing any longer with the attitude of 'misunderstood geniuses' which we have adopted hitherto. (Letter to Togliatti and others, July 1923; *SPWII*, p.159)

Gramsci continued with this line of argument throughout the autumn and into the following spring and gradually a new strategy began to emerge. He proposed that the basic organisational structure of the factory councils and internal committees should be revived to re-establish not only the links between the mass movement and its leadership, but also to differentiate their revolutionary aims more clearly from the capitulatory reformism of the CGL. In terms of mounting a counter-offensive to fascism, he suggested that special attention should be given to incorporating the interests and support of the southern peasantry. In order to propagate a new sense of direction and purpose within the movement, a new journal called *L'Unita* should be produced together with a revised fortnightly edition of *L'Ordine Nuovo*.

Having outlined a plan of action, the next major problem was to settle the question of who should lead the next phase of the struggle; or to put it another way, would it be possible to establish a new leadership without Bordiga? As already noted, Gramsci's relationship with Bordiga had always been somewhat strained, but throughout his appointment in Moscow he had tended to agree with Bordiga that at least some aspects of the Comintern's intervention in the affairs of the PCI were unnecessarily divisive. In addition, Gramsci clearly felt that despite his 'stubborn and inflexible nature' Bordiga's energy and personal following were such that excluding him from the new leadership would inevitably weaken the Party:

> My attitudes on the question were not my own, they were always influenced by my concern over what Amadeo [Bordiga] might do if I became an opponent: he would have withdrawn, provoked a crisis, he would never have adapted himself to any compromise.... I said that I would do all in my power to help the International solve the Italian problem, but that I did not believe it possible to replace Amadeo without much preparatory work inside the Party. Replacing Amadeo, in the Italian situation, meant much more than finding one cadre to take his place; in terms of general capacity for work, he is worth three at least. (Fiori, 1990: 160; cf. *SPWII* pp.417–23, n. 63)

However, by the time he had moved from Moscow to Vienna in December 1923, and bearing in mind that relations with the Comintern had reached crisis point, Gramsci had come to accept that a new leadership could perhaps be established around the old *Ordine* group. In March 1924 he responded to a suggestion to this effect from Togliatti:

> For a time I was lacking in capacity and will-power and felt unable in the circumstances to take on the responsibility of deciding what form the new political situation should assume. Today after getting your letter, I've changed my mind: it is possible to get together a group capable of hard work and determined action. I am prepared to put all I can into this group, to the limits of my powers, such as they are. (Fiori, 1990: 169)

While the PCI debated these issues, Mussolini decided to dissolve parliament and call a General Election for April 1924. The fascists had now been in power for over a year and, having rendered all opposition parties either ineffective or completely inoperative, Mussolini wished to make his position 'legal' as well as total. The PCI decided to contest the election and approached the *terzini*, the PSI and the Unitary Socialist Party to form an electoral pact. As might be expected, the latter groups declined the offer and the communists put up their own list of candidates. Mussolini got his mandate with a total of 374 deputies (275 were members of the PNF) as against 161 for the combined opposition. The PCI improved on their 1921 result with nineteen seats while the Unitary Socialists and the PSI had twenty-four and twenty-two respectively. Gramsci, who had been nominated as a candidate in Veneto won the seat and so became a member of the Italian Parliament at the age of thirty-three.

The six months which Gramsci spent in Vienna between December 1923 and May 1924 must have seemed very reminiscent of his early years in Turin. Although he was very busy producing articles for *L'Unita* and *L'Ordine Nuovo* and constantly writing letters to Togliatti and others about the new strategy and leadership, his health was still poor and his frugal lodgings and unfamiliar surroundings left him feeling depressed and isolated. In particular, he was very upset that Julia seemed unwilling to leave her family in Moscow to join him:

> I'm leading a very isolated existence, and it can hardly be otherwise, at least for a while. I feel your absence physically, like a great emptiness all around

me. Today I understand better than yesterday, and yesterday I understood better than the day before, how much I love you and how it's possible to love someone more each day. . . . I have thought about your family too:, but couldn't you come for a few months? (Fiori, 1990: 164-5)

This sense of separation became even more acute when Gramsci discovered that his wife was expecting their first child:

I felt a shock of emotion reading your letter. You know the reason. But your words were very vague, and left me overcome with desire to hold you in my arms and feel for myself the new life uniting our two lives even closer than before. (Fiori, 1990: 165-6)

As it turned out, their separation was to continue until Gramsci returned to Moscow over a year later in March 1925.

Gramsci's election to parliament gave him immunity from arrest, and so he returned to Italy after an absence of two years. Within a few days of his arrival, the PCI held a secret conference at Como in May 1924 to decide the leadership issue once and for all. Three proposals were put forward representing the contrasting views of Tasca's 'right' who argued for compliance with the Comintern, Bordiga's 'left' who repeated the arguments of the Rome Theses of March 1922, and Togliatti's 'centre' (which included Gramsci), who argued that the PCI should remain within the Comintern so long as it was recognised that Italian circumstances required the development of a new revolutionary strategy which was not the same as that used in Russia. (The details of this new strategy or 'war of position' are discussed in Chapter 5 below.) The upshot of the meeting was that the right and the centre had roughly equivalent support among the Central Committee, while Bordiga still had a majority among the mass membership. During the months which followed, however, the centre gradually gained support from both right and left and by the end of the year Gramsci's strategy had effectively become official policy within the PCI.

It should be emphasised that Gramsci's supremacy was at least to some extent made easier by the bitter power struggle which had developed within the CPSU in Moscow. Lenin had died in January 1924 and the question of succession brought Stalin and Bukharin into direct conflict with Trotsky. Trotsky argued that the revolutionary momentum could be maintained through the action of militant communists and socialist workers within non-socialist countries. Since capitalism had evidently regained its balance following the war, the survival of the Revolution now depended on accumulating technical and material support from putative socialist states in the advanced industrial societies of the West. The Comintern therefore had an important role to play in the international co-ordination of this strategy without as it were, dictating precisely what form it should take. Stalin and Bukharin, on the other hand, began to develop the concept of 'socialism in one country' where the ultimate success of the Revolution was dependent upon the preservation of the Soviet Union itself. The material resources necessary for this were seen as lying *within* rather than *outside* the country. The activities of other national communist parties were therefore regarded as sources of support for, and thus subordinate to, the directives of the Soviet Party.[12]

For several years to come, but particularly between 1924 and 1926, the disputes within the CPSU tended to become virtually indistinguishable from debates over Comintern policy and appropriate strategy for communist parties in other countries. It was this uncertainty and subsequent confusion between policy and practice which allowed several different positions, including those of Gramsci and Bordiga, to co-exist. At the Fifth Congress of the Comintern in Moscow in June 1924, Bordiga was somewhat caught out by the manoeuvrings within the CPSU and by his apparent support for Trotsky's opposition, and it was Gramsci's centre faction which took control of the PCI. Within a few months Gramsci had become Secretary-General of the PCI.

While the Italian delegation was busy in Moscow, Gramsci was confronted by yet another fascist atrocity. At the opening session of the new parliament in May 1924, the Secretary of the Unitary Socialist Party, Giacomo Matteotti, launched a bitter attack on the way the PNF had conducted its campaign and called for the immediate dissolution of parliament. Within a few days Matteotti had been kidnapped and murdered by a group of PNF agents. Under considerable popular and parliamentary pressure, Mussolini declared that a full investigation would take place and a number of officials who had been implicated in the murder were arrested. He also made conciliatory gestures by offering a number of government posts to members of the opposition. These attempts to restore legitimacy were largely ineffective, however, and in June about one hundred opposition deputies, including the socialists and communists, formed a rival 'parliament' known as the Aventine Secession. Once again, however, the long-standing friction between the opposition parties prevented them from developing a united plan of action. Gramsci suggested, for example, that a general strike should be called which would give the proletariat and peasantry an opportunity to express their outrage and might lead to a general mass counter-attack against fascism. Neither the socialists nor the Popular Party were prepared to support such spontaneous behaviour, and the PCI threatened to leave the Aventine and fight the fascists within parliament proper.

At the time of the 1924 election there were reasonable grounds for thinking that, under the right conditions, the revolution in Italy could be revived. PCI membership had grown considerably from the low point of around 5,000 in 1923 to around 12,000, and by the end of the year membership had approximately doubled. The Party could rely on the support of a further 5,000 in the youth organisation and about 20,000 communist trade unionists. In addition, the continued interest in the communist press (*L'Unita* and *L'Ordine Nuovo* had circulations of around 25,000 and 6,000 respectively) suggested that fascism had not totally expunged the idea of a socialist alternative. Against this background, Gramsci clearly felt that Matteotti's murder and the crisis which followed provided an ideal opportunity for mounting the counter-offensive. In June he wrote to his wife Julia:

> We are walking along the edge of a volcano on the point of eruption. Then suddenly, when no one expected it – certainly not the fascists, complacent in their absolute power – the volcano erupted, releasing an immense torrent of burning lava which has spread across the whole country, carrying the fascists bag and baggage before it. Events succeeded one another like lightening with unheard-of rapidity. . . . The regime found itself under attack from every angle, and fascism was isolated in the country to the point where its leaders became panic-stricken and the hangers-on were deserting its ranks. We worked feverishly, taking decisions, issuing orders, trying to give aim and direction to this flood of popular feeling which had burst its banks. (Fiori, 1990: 173–4)

Throughout the summer, Gramsci threw himself headlong into a new burst of activity. He travelled from one town to another holding meetings, listening to new ideas and suggesting how the Party could organise the counter-offensive. In addition to boosting morale, these discussions gave Gramsci a valuable opportunity to disseminate the new direction of the Party which not only included a revival of the themes of the old *Ordine* group, but also included the idea of extending the popular base of the Party to the peasantry and southern population more generally.

Unfortunately, however, the collapse of the PCI after 1921 and the highly disruptive tactics of the fascists in the intervening years had weakened the organisation to such an extent that the process of reconstruction was more arduous and time-consuming than expected. In addition, the continuing friction between the leadership and the mass membership caused interminable misunderstandings and delays with the result that they were simply unable to respond to the new situation quickly enough. Gramsci himself was also becoming weaker as the activity of the summer and the tension caused by negotiations with the Comintern took their toll. As in Vienna, this fatigue was made worse by Julia's absence. In July he writes that:

> Thinking tires me out, work reduces me to being a limp rag in no time. How many things I should be doing, and just cannot do. I think of you, and the sweetness of loving you, and knowing that you are very close as well as far away . . . but my life can never become normal again as long as we're separated; loving you has become too much part of my personality for me to feel normal again without your presence. (Fiori, 1990: 177)

By the autumn Mussolini had recovered his nerve as first his own party and then other groups including the king, the Pope, the military and the industrialists, realised that the Aventine opposition was incapable of agreement let alone action. When parliament met in January 1925, Mussolini denounced the Aventine and declared that he would 'clarify' the problem of two parliaments 'within forty-eight hours'. Almost immediately the opposition press was crushed, many clubs and organisations were banned and its members arrested as the militia once again began to terrorise anyone they regarded as anti-fascist. This signalled the beginning of the end of Italy's liberal state; over the next two years Mussolini concentrated the roles of Chief Minister, Leader of the Fascists, President of the Grand Council and Party Secretary into his own hands and Italy became a one-party dictatorship.

In March 1925 the Executive of the Comintern met in Moscow and at last Gramsci was able to see Julia again and meet their son Delio who had been born the previous August. It is difficult to tell how much Gramsci enjoyed the reunion since Delio was suffering from whooping-cough while Julia's elder sister Eugenie (who had been a patient with Gramsci at Silvery Wood) was on the verge of a second nervous breakdown. If the family situation was less than ideal, then the discussions of the Executive may not have been particularly inspiring either. The criticism of Trotsky continued while the PCI restricted itself to a somewhat tame discussion of the appropriateness or otherwise of the tactics of the Russian Revolution to the Italian situation. Gramsci repeated that the PCI would continue to build on the basis of the factory councils and 'committees of workers and peasants', and that while accepting that Leninism provided an indispensable framework for understanding the form and role of the Party, the PCI would act in the light of particular circumstances and not on the basis of theoretical precedent and Soviet dictat alone.

Gramsci returned to Rome in May just in time to take part in a debate on a new law which would effectively outlaw all non-fascist organisations including the PCI. In what was to be his only parliamentary speech, he gave a detailed and highly critical analysis of fascism. Although Gramsci neither enjoyed nor was very effective at speaking to large audiences, the speech made an impression and certainly confirmed Mussolini's view that Gramsci did indeed have 'a brain of undeniable power'. From this time on Gramsci had to be especially careful whom he met and where he went since clearly the State was particularly interested in the activities of the leader of the Communist Party. Julia, Delio and Eugenie finally came to Rome in October and Gramsci rented a flat for them to live in. With Gramsci under close supervision it was clearly very difficult for them to live anything like the 'normal life' of which Gramsci had spoken in his letters, but at least he could spend time with his son. Julia's elder sister Tatiana, who had been living in Rome for some time and was already a close friend of Gramsci's, was a frequent visitor and this too must have helped to create the kind of family atmosphere for which Gramsci had waited so long.

For the rest of the year, Gramsci continued his activities as well as circumstances would allow and prepared for the forthcoming Congress of the PCI to be held at Lyons in January 1926.[13] He had become increasingly preoccupied with how successive governments had been able to establish and impose their own world-view on the population as a whole. How, in other words, they had produced bourgeois 'hegemony'. As noted above, Gramsci had always been particularly interested in the relationship between the north and the south, and had emphasised the importance of building strong links between the industrial proletariat and the rural working class and peasantry. In a well-known article on the 'Southern Question', written in October 1926, Gramsci suggests for example that:

> The Turin communists posed correctly the question of the 'hegemony of the proletariat': i.e. of the social basis of the proletarian dictatorship and of the workers' State. The proletariat can become the leading [*dirigente*] and the dominant class to the extent that it succeeds in creating a system of alliances which allows it to mobilize the majority of the working population against capitalism and the bourgeois State. In Italy, in the real class relations which exist there, this means to the extent that it succeeds in gaining the consent of the broad peasant masses. . . . Winning the majority of the peasant masses thus means, for the Italian proletariat, making these two questions [the Southern question and the Vatican] its own from the social point of view; understanding the class demands which they represent; incorporating these demands into its revolutionary transitional programme; placing these demands among the objectives for which it struggles. (*SPWII*, p.443)

He went on to argue that the processes of building hegemony and of neutralising competing views and aspirations were intimately bound up with the activities of different strata of 'intellectuals'. (A detailed discussion of the importance of establishing new working-class intellectuals and their role in constructing an 'alternative hegemony' is given in Chapter 7.)

After the Lyons Congress which overwhelmingly accepted Gramsci's analysis and proposals, Gramsci returned to his wife and family in Rome. With the collapse of the Aventine Secession in the spring, it soon became clear that all political opponents to fascism were likely to be arrested or worse, and the family made plans to leave Italy. In July, Julia, Eugenie and Tatiana went to Trafoi on the Swiss border and Gramsci joined them briefly in August before again returning to Rome. As expected, it was not long before the fascists had gathered sufficient evidence against the PCI leadership, and on 8 November Gramsci was arrested.

Prison 1926–37

While the State was preparing its case against him, Gramsci was first sent to the small penal island of Usticia off the north coast of Sicily, and then, at the end of January 1927, to the San Vittore prison in Milan. While conditions on the island had been relatively comfortable, the journey to Milan gave Gramsci his first glimpse of what prison life might be like: 'One collapses on palliasses of unimaginable age, keeping on all one's clothes to avoid contact with the filth, covering face and hands with towels and the rest with blankets to avoid being frozen' (Fiori, 1990: 222). He also became aware how imprisonment would make contact with his friends and family very difficult. In April 1927 he complained to Tatiana:

> You write to me and say a letter is coming from Julia; then you write again saying that another is on the way; then I receive still another letter from you (and your letters are very dear to me) but nothing from Julia, none of hers have arrived. You simply cannot imagine what existence is like here in prison. You cannot imagine how, when one is told something is coming, one expects it each day, and each day becomes a fresh deception which affects every hour, every minute of the day. (Fiori, 1990: 225)

By the end of January the authorities had failed to find sufficient evidence to prosecute Gramsci under the terms of the first warrant of arrest, and in June a second warrant was issued which, in Fiori's words, accused Gramsci of 'provoking civil war and destroying property and life'. Despite not being able to find any concrete evidence against him, Gramsci's trial was eventually fixed to take place in Rome in May 1928.

Always keen to make an impression, the fascist leadership took the opportunity of turning the trial into a demonstration of its power, and so Gramsci was tried along with twenty-one other political prisoners. It soon became clear that the outcome of the trial was a foregone conclusion, and after an eight-day hearing all the defendants were given maximum sentences. Gramsci now faced the prospect of twenty years in prison.[14] After the trial, Gramsci was sent to the prison in the isolated town of Turi on the south-east coast of the mainland. By now he had spent some eighteen months in custody, and his health was fast deteriorating: 'He was suffering from skin eruptions caused by a urinary disorder, his digestive system was completely upset, he was breathing with great difficulty, and unable to walk more than a step at a time without leaning on someone' (Fiori, 1990: 233, quoting Giuseppe Ceresa). Although the prison authorities were well aware of his condition they made no real effort to help him, and this indifference to

Gramsci's physical well-being set a trend which was to last for the rest of his time at Turi.

While he had been awaiting trial at San Vittore, Gramsci had decided to devote his energies to reading and further study. Although conditions were less than ideal, he did have access to a number of books and writing materials supplied by his friends outside prison. In a letter to Tatiana in March 1927 he explained his intentions:

> I am spurred on by this idea: that I ought to do something *für ewig* [for ever] ... that is, I would like to work intensively and systematically, according to a predetermined plan, on certain subjects which could absorb me totally and give focus and direction to my inner life. (Fiori, 1990: 235)

Although he had to wait for two years at Turi before being allowed access to books and 'the wherewithal for writing', Gramsci was at last able to begin work. By the time he left Turi at the end of 1933 he had already filled over twenty exercise books with highly condensed notes and translations. In addition to his original plan of studying the history of the Italian intellectuals, language and linguistics, and essays on popular literature and popular culture, he also took up many of the themes which he had begun to develop in the years immediately before his arrest. Questions of hegemony and working-class culture, of the particular role of the southern peasantry in the class struggle and the 'Southern Question' more generally, and the nature of political leadership and organisation are all discussed, together with notes on the *Risorgimento*, 'Americanism and Fordism' and many other aspects of philosophy and political theory.[15]

While recognising that the notebooks represent a considerable achievement in intellectual terms, it is important not to forget the personal suffering and anguish which Gramsci must have experienced while writing them. For a man who had until recently been at the centre of the communist movement in Italy and in Moscow, who was suffering from acute physical illness, and who must have felt that he would never see his wife and children again (his second son Giuliano had been born shortly after his final return to Rome in August 1926), the isolation of prison must have been a living nightmare.

With regard to political events, and apart from some access to the fascist press, news from other inmates and visits from his brother Gennaro and Tatiana, Gramsci received very little information. Stalin had become Secretary-General of the CPSU in February 1922, and by

1930 his chief opponents, Trotsky, Kamenev, Zinoviev and Bukharin had all been expelled from the Executive of the Party. (Kamenev and Zinoviev were executed in 1936, Bukharin in 1938 and Trotsky was murdered in 1940.) With the new leadership came a new policy and, after the Sixth Congress of the Comintern in 1928, the united front policy was abandoned in favour of a new 'left-turn' which claimed that as the Revolution was now imminent, there was no longer any need to seek alliances with other socialist or social-democratic parties. Similarly, the idea that the Revolution would be preceded by a 'transitional phase', perhaps including the temporary restoration of some form of democratic or semi-republican state, was replaced by the idea that the 'dictatorship proletariat' would assume power directly.[16] This change of policy and tactics inevitably caused problems for the PCI since, as Gramsci had argued, the chances of a direct working-class overthrow of fascism without the prior formation of alliances with other groups seemed somewhat unlikely. By 1931, Bordiga and a further six members of the PCI's Executive, including Tasca who had openly opposed the new line, were expelled. Togliatti, who had become Secretary-General of the PCI after Gramsci's arrest, and was to remain so until his own death in 1964, did what he could to reorganise the Party, but to all intents and purposes the PCI was to remain a party of opposition in exile until the end of the Second World War.[17]

As time went by Gramsci also began to lose contact with his wife. Since the beginning of their relationship in 1922, it had been clear that the nervous complaints and mental fragility which afflicted Eugenie were a common feature of the family as a whole. Both Julia and Tatiana had suffered periods of illness in the past, and it is likely that the strain of Gramsci's imprisonment may have contributed to Julia's apparent unwillingness to answer his letters. In any event, it is clear that this loss of contact caused him much pain. In July 1930 he writes to Tatiana:

> There is the prison regime which consists of four walls, the grating, the spy-hole, etc., etc.; I foresaw all this and indeed discounted it, since from 1921 up to November 1926 the strongest probability was not even prison, it was losing one's life. What I did not foresee was this other prison added to the first, which consists of being cut off not only from social life in general, but even from one's own family, etc., etc. I was able to foresee the blows of the enemies I was fighting against, but not these blows struck from a

different direction altogether, from where I had least reason to expect them. (Fiori, 1990: 248)

This enforced separation from political and family life together with the harshness of the prison regime inevitably had serious consequences for Gramsci's physical and psychological health. Restlessness, insomnia and periods of absent-mindedness, combined with coughing fits and haemorrhages all indicated that he was unlikely to survive for very much longer without urgent medical treatment. At the end of 1932 and the beginning of 1933 a brief glimmer of hope came and went as Mussolini announced that a number of remissions might be granted to political prisoners to celebrate the tenth anniversary of the March on Rome. There was also the possibility that he might be included in an exchange of prisoners between the Soviet Union and the Vatican. Although his sentence was reduced from twenty to ten years, it was clear that Mussolini had no intention of granting him an early release.

Finally, in March 1933 Gramsci collapsed in his cell. It was clear that the intellectual resolve and sense of purpose which had kept him going for so long could not make up for his almost complete physical deterioration. A doctor was called who confirmed how desperate the situation really was:

> Antonio Gramsci is suffering from Pott's Disease. He has tubercular lesions in the upper lobe of the right lung, which have given rise to two discharges of blood, one of which was serious and accompanied by fever lasting several days. He is also suffering from arterio-sclerosis, with hypertension of the arteries. He has suffered several collapses, with loss of consciousness and partial aphasia lasting several days. Since October 1932 he has lost seven kilos in weight. (Report by Prof. Umberto Arcangeli, March 1933; Fiori 1990: 278)

After a further delay of six months, and following public pressure from outside Italy, Gramsci was moved to a private clinic at Formia on the coast north of Naples. He had been at Turi for over five years. He arrived at the clinic early in December 1933, and almost immediately his health and confidence began to return. Unfortunately, however, these improvements proved to be too little too late. Further appeals were made and, having been granted 'provisional freedom' on the grounds of ill health in October, he was moved to the Quisisana clinic in Rome in August 1935.

For the next eighteen months Gramsci grew steadily weaker. Then, finally, on 27 April 1937 he suffered a final brain haemorrhage and died. He had survived his prison sentence by just six days. The notebooks, which Tatiana had managed to smuggle out of Gramsci's room at the clinic, were eventually passed to Togliatti for safe-keeping in Moscow.

This chapter has outlined some of the national and international circumstances within which Gramsci developed his intellectual and political career. It has emerged that for a large part of his life Gramsci suffered from a series of physical and psychological weaknesses which, during his early career at least, made it difficult for him to relate to others and forced him to withdraw within himself for strength and consolation. Between illnesses, however, and despite his personal inhibitions, he engaged in intensive bouts of activity on behalf of the Italian working classes and their struggle for revolutionary change. His journal articles, many of which were composed under very difficult circumstances, show a capacity for polemical analysis and detailed understanding which was barely surpassed by any of his contemporaries. His personal involvement in the council movement and later in the PCI demonstrate a capacity not only to theorise about the problems of social transformation, but also to develop and explore the practical means by which it can be brought about. It is reasonable to speculate that if he had not been so determined to prosecute the struggle against fascism from within Italy, he would have continued to play an active part in the development of the PCI, and would have provided an important point of opposition to Stalin. Given his somewhat reclusive and introspective nature, and given that he had witnessed the rise and fall of the first communist movement in Italy, it is perhaps not surprising that he used the isolation of prison life to write an account of his thoughts and experiences. The scope of the *Prison Notebooks* and the originality they express clearly demonstrate a willingness to engage in intellectual struggle with at least as much vigour and determination as he had previously devoted to active political struggle.

Despite these capacities, however, it must be recognised that, up until the time of his arrest, neither the council movement nor the PCI achieved their ultimate aims. Despite the efforts of Gramsci and other members of the *Ordine* group, the strikes in 1920 did not raise the consciousness of the Italian working class sufficiently to generate revolution. Following the final split with the PSI in 1921, the leadership of the PCI remained deeply divided and never received the kind of popular support they needed to play a decisive role in Italian politics. Although Gramsci had made an important contribution to the formation of PCI policy before becoming Party leader in 1924, it was not until after the Lyons Congress in 1926 that his views and suggestions for strategy took a genuinely leading role. His arrest in November of the same year meant that his actual and direct control over the Party was extremely short-lived. It is a sobering thought that, for all their polemics and attempts at innovation and organisation, the Italian communists of the 1920s were, in a number of important respects, far less successful than Mussolini's PNF. Given these failures it is tragic that, in terms of practical outcomes at least, Gramsci's influence was far less decisive in his own time than it has been in ours.

Having outlined the background against which Gramsci developed his ideas, it is now possible to consider some of his conclusions and theoretical propositions in more detail.

Notes

1. Fiori reports Togliatti's recollection that:

   > at that time, as a very young man, [Gramsci's] outlook was frankly and proudly pro-Sardinian, even Sardinian nationalist. He felt very deeply the common resentment of all Sardinians at the wrongs suffered by the island; and for him, too, such resentment turned easily against continentals, and against the Continent itself. (Fiori, 1990: 77).

   A discussion of Gramsci's belief in the importance of the peasantry as a potential source of resistance to fascism is given in the final part of this chapter and in Chapter 8 below.
2. For a more detailed discussion of the 'Southern Question' see *SPN*, pp.70–4.
3. For an introduction to this topic and a discussion of Gramsci's intellectual development at university see: Adamson (1980): ch.1; and Davidson (1977): ch.2.
4. In a letter to Alfonso Leonetti, Togliatti wrote:

   > As you know, I met Antonio in the autumn of 1911, at the University. For months and months we did nothing but meet and discuss – you remember well what he was like. From all these talks it was quite clear, beyond any possible doubt, that he already had firm socialist

convictions. These convictions went back to his Cagliari period, when Gramsci had been in contact with the Chamber of Labour there. What I am not clear about is the year in which he first acquired a PSI card. . . . I did so in 1914; but Gramsci already had one at that time. (Fiori, 1990: 91–2)

5. By the end of 1918, for example, its north-eastern populations had declared the independent state of Czechoslovakia, while its south-eastern populations had combined with Serbia to form the new state of Yugoslavia. Hungary formed an independent government in Budapest and ceded the eastern province of Transylvania to Romania. Following the acquisition of territory both from Russia and Germany a new Polish Republic was also declared.
6. The German uprisings have already been discussed briefly above. For a more detailed account see Ryder (1967). In Hungary, a Social Democratic government had been formed under the leadership of Count Michael Karolyi. By the spring of 1919 social unrest had escalated and, following a series of riots in Budapest, the leadership of the recently formed Communist Party was arrested. The riots continued, however, and in March 1919 Karolyi resigned. The Communists' leader, Bela Kun, took control and formed a Soviet government. In the face of continuing hostilities with the Czechoslovakians, Romanians and Yugoslavians abroad, and with growing opposition at home, however, the Soviet regime collapsed and Kun fled to Moscow. For a detailed account see Jaszi (1969).
7. Seton-Watson reports that by June 1919

    industrial production had still not reached the pre-war level. Exports in 1919 paid for only 36% of imports (compared with 68% in 1913). Inflation was rampant. The cost of living had more than quadrupled since 1913 and was still rising. The budget deficit had grown from 214 million lire in 1913–14 to 23,345 million in 1918–19, with revenue covering only 24% of expenditure. (Seton-Watson, 1967: 520)

8. In *Avanti!* Gramsci reported:

    Today Turin is a garrisoned fortress. It is said that there are 50,000 soldiers in the city, that artillery is drawn up on the hills, that reinforcements are waiting on the outskirts of the town and armoured cars in the city. Machine-guns are positioned on private houses, in those districts which are considered to be most eager to revolt, at bridge-heads, by cross-roads and factories. ('Turin and Italy', *Avanti!*, 3 April 1920; *SPWI*, p.183)

9. D'Annunzio and his 'legionaries' continued to occupy Fiume until January 1921 when he was eventually forced to withdraw by the Italian army. For a detailed account see Seton-Watson (1967): 536–47.

10. In March 1921 the KPD had started a series of insurrections in the Mansfeld-Merseburg district of central Germany which they hoped would lead to revolution throughout the country. In the event the offensive failed and the KPD was forcibly repressed. For more information see note 6 above.
11. The text of the 'Rome Theses' is reproduced in *SPWII*, pp.73–117. The view of the Party it puts forward is discussed in Chapter 8 below.
12. For an account of the evolution of Marxism-Leninism during the Stalinist period see Kolakowski, 1978: vol.3, *The Breakdown*, esp. chs 1–3.
13. The text of Gramsci's and Togliatti's 'Lyons Theses' is reproduced in *SPWII*, pp.340–75. The view of the Party it puts forward is discussed in Chapter 8 below.
14. For a detailed discussion of the trial and Gramsci's defence see Fiori (1990): 230–2; and Zucaro, (ed.) (1961).
15. For more detailed discussion of the order and content of the *Prison Notebooks*, see Davidson (1977): 232–71.
16. For a discussion of Stalin's policy during this period see: Colletti (1971).
17. For a discussion of the activities of the PCI under Togliatti see Davidson (1982). On the role of the factory councils after 1926 see: Clark (1977): 227–38.

4

Ideology and the concept hegemony

It was noted in Chapter 1, that Marx has been much criticised for placing too much faith in the ability of the industrial proletariat to become 'conscious' of its exploitation by the capitalist class, and of the likelihood that this awareness will be expressed through a spontaneous outburst of revolutionary activity. It has been suggested that by concentrating on the influence of material economic experience as the source of beliefs about society, Marx both underestimated the influence of other non-economic experiences and consequently assumed a rather simplistic cause-and-effect model of the development of political consciousness that exploitation at work = alienation = revolution. In response to this criticism, a number of Marxist thinkers have paid particular attention to the ways in which ideas and their combination into 'ideologies' may have a profound impact upon our understanding and interpretation of society and subsequently upon how we might go about changing it. It is important to emphasise, however, that stressing the role of ideologies has not *replaced* the need for understanding the powerful influence of material or 'real' social phenomena. The debate, in other words, now turns on the question of the *relative importance* of ideological and material forces in producing or resisting social change. In many respects, Gramsci's concept of hegemony represents one of the most useful analyses of how different world-views or ideological explanations of society may have an important bearing upon both the perception of society and of the processes by which it evolves. In order to understand the evolution of hegemony as a concept of ideology, it is useful to trace its development from Marx through the work of Lenin and Georg Lukács.

Marx: the pejorative use of the concept ideology

A particularly lucid account of Marx's analysis of the concept of ideology has been put forward by Jorge Larrain.[1] Larrain suggests that Marx's analysis of ideology developed through three stages, corresponding to the more general development of his thought:

> The first philosophical stage comprises Marx's early writings and continues until 1844. The second stage begins with the break with Feuerbach in 1845, which finds its most coherent expression in the 'Theses on Feuerbach' and *The German Ideology*, and lasts until 1857. The start of the third stage is marked by Marx's re-reading of Hegel's *Science and Logic* in 1858 and encompasses his mature writings from the *Grundrisse* onwards. (Larrain, 1983: 100)[2]

During the first stage Marx developed his critique of Hegelian idealism which he felt made the critical error of 'inverting' the real world by making physical being subordinate to intellectual thought: 'real human practice was transformed into a mere manifestation, a finite phase of this idea' (Larrain, 1983: 11–12.). Hegel, in other words, made the mistake of attributing greater significance to the metaphysical 'idea' than to the physical 'real' world. Secondly, by assigning responsibility to the State for resolving the imperfections and contradictions of society, he made the further mistake of arguing that conflicts between capitalists and workers could be resolved *by the State*, rather than by changes in the labour process itself. Hegel therefore reversed the relationship between political State and civil society (which includes all the economic institutions of society) so that the latter was held to be determined by the former. Marx was particularly critical of this second inversion since he believed that the resolution of class conflict necessarily had to take place within the economic structure of civil society rather than within the institutions of the superstructure.

Marx's early critique of Hegel's 'inversions' has three important implications for the Marxist concept of ideology. First, by assigning ideas priority over physical being, and of State over civil society, Hegel's analysis tends to disguise the true nature of reality and so gives rise to a *distorted and inaccurate* awareness or consciousness of the nature of that society. Because, in other words, the order of analysis is

IDEOLOGY AND THE CONCEPT HEGEMONY

reversed, any conclusions reached as to the character of society will also be inverted. Second, and although mistaken, *the inverted perspective itself* should not be regarded simply as an innocent or convenient methodological tool, *but is itself* a symptom of the contradictions to be found in capitalist society. Third, a resolution or demystification of distorted consciousness (and therefore of the contradictions which give rise to it) cannot be achieved at the level of theoretical or philosophical critique but must be achieved in the 'real' material world through practical action: 'Clearly the weapon of criticism cannot replace the criticism of weapons, and material force must be overthrown by material force' (Marx, 1975: 251).

> (Historical materialism) does not explain practice from the idea but explains the formation of ideas from material practice; and accordingly it comes to the conclusion that all forms and products of consciousness cannot be dissolved by mental criticism . . . but only by the practical overthrow of the actual social relations which gave rise to this idealistic humbug. (Marx and Engels, 1977b: 172)

It should also be noted that ideas themselves constitute a form of practice. Thinking, in other words, is no less of an actual human activity than building a house or chopping wood. Indeed, any human activity *necessarily involves* a combination of intellectual and muscular effort.

The significance of practical action or 'practice', and in this context that ideas are themselves a form of practice, is further developed in the second stage. Marx criticises the essentially 'static or mechanical materialism' of Feuerbach as, through his approach, 'the thing, reality, sensuousness, is conceived only in the form of contemplation, but not as sensuous human activity, practice, not subjectively' (Marx, 'Theses on Feuerbach'; McLellan, 1977: 156). Again Marx wishes to emphasise that 'mistaken consciousness' is not the result of faulty thinking or the idiosyncrasies of the intellectual process, but rather is a direct consequence of *actual social contradictions* in the real world. 'Reality' therefore is understood as a subjective process arising out of 'sensuous activity' or felt experience, and not merely as a result of dispassionate and 'objective' observation. Since for Marx all ideas should be explained from practice, it follows that all collections of ideas or 'ideologies' should be explained in the same way:

Morality, religion, metaphysics, all the rest of ideology and their corresponding forms of consciousness, thus no longer retain the semblance of independence. They have no history, no development; but men, developing their material intercourse, alter along with this their real existence, their thinking and the products of their thinking. Life is not determined by consciousness, but consciousness by life. (Marx and Engels, 1977b: 164)

Within capitalism, however, human productive practice becomes contradictory:

> For as soon as the distribution of labour comes into being, each man has a particular, exclusive sphere of activity, which is forced upon him and from which he cannot escape . . . . This fixation of social activity, this consolidation of what we ourselves produce into an objective power above us, growing out of our control, thwarting our expectations, bringing to naught our calculations, is one of the chief factors in historical development up till now. (Marx and Engels, 1977b: 169)

The capitalist division of labour, in other words, gives rise to a contradictory reality in which individuals are confronted by a set of methods or means of production which turns the business of providing for their needs into a form of repression and domination. Since, within capitalism, access to necessary resources can be achieved only via the medium of money, and since the earning of money can be achieved only by participating in the mechanisms of formal employment, individuals are forced to accept a particular organisation of work on unequal terms. Ironically, by participating in the capitalist labour process, individuals constantly re-create the contradictory reality which oppresses them.

Having recognised that ideas and ideologies are a consequence of material practice, it follows that overcoming the contradictions and 'alienation' of 'reproductive practice' cannot be achieved through an intellectual reinterpretation of these circumstances, but requires a different kind of practice, namely *revolutionary practice*: 'The coincidence of the changing of circumstances and of human activity or self-changing can be conceived and rationally understood only as revolutionary practice' (Marx, 'Theses on Feuerbach'; McLellan, 1977: 156). Marx believed therefore that revolutionary practice will emerge when the evident and felt contradiction of living in a world of 'wealth and culture' in which capitalism has 'rendered the great mass of humanity "propertyless"' reaches crisis point (Marx and Engels, 1977b: 170). This point will be reached when human 'productive powers', including technological development and inventiveness, have made it at least technically possible for everyone to satisfy their needs. Marx believed that, by the end of the nineteenth century, the industrial societies had reached this point. Because the 'propertyless' industrial proletariat occupied the most exploited and thus most contradictory position in those societies, he argued that they would develop revolutionary practice without further ado.

Returning to the problems of consciousness and ideology, if consciousness is determined by practice (reproductive or revolutionary), *limited* or contradictory practice will result in *limited* or distorted forms of consciousness. If ideas are the means by which consciousness is represented, then ideas can either represent a truthful and 'real' representation of reality or a distorted and 'illusory' representation. Two problems arise here, however. In the first place, since all individuals inherently construct intellectual interpretations of their physical actions and experiences, it is necessary to distinguish between ideas and combinations of ideas *in general*, and ideas and combinations which *are ideological* (unless one wants to claim that *all ideas* are ideological). In order to make this distinction, Larrain suggests that:

> If one wants to uphold both a negative concept of ideology and the idea of an all-encompassing level of consciousness, then the solution is to propose a superstructure of ideas or 'ideational superstructure' which contains both non-ideological and ideological forms of consciousness. The superstructure of ideas refers to a global societal level of consciousness, whereas ideology is only a restricted part of the superstructure which includes specific forms of distorted consciousness. (Larrain, 1983: 172–3)

On this understanding, 'ideology' can be defined as that subset of the overall level of 'ideational' understanding which is based upon *a mistaken interpretation of how the world actually is*. Following Marx's argument, the most effective way of determining whether an idea is ideological or not is by referring back to the material world from where the idea originally came. If the idea represents an *accurate* representation of the real world then it can be said to be non-ideological. If, on the other hand, it *misrepresents* the world then it can accurately be described as presenting an incomplete or ideological account of the world.

In the second place, since both workers and capitalists develop ideological understandings (or misunderstandings) of the world, and since there is an assumption that working-class ideology is in some way 'better' or more *positive* than bourgeois ideology, it is necessary to describe the criteria by which an ideology can be regarded as positive and therefore beneficial to society, or negative and therefore socially divisive. Again following Marx's argument, the most important difference between a positive ideology and a negative one, is that 'negative' ideologies tend to support the *specific interests* of one group in society, while 'positive' ideologies are intended to support *universal interests*. Moreover, these tendencies are not accidental, but actively provide an essential reason for developing ideologies in the first place. Ideologies, in other words, are put forward by competing groups for *specific purposes*; they do not represent the interests of a particular group by chance. For Marx, therefore, the essential difference between negative bourgeois ideology and positive working-class ideology is that the former represents the interests of a minority, while the latter represents the interests of a majority. Further, even if working-class ideas are ideological in the sense of partly misunderstanding the world, they can still be regarded as positive if this misunderstanding is well-intentioned. In sum, therefore, it can be said that while all distorted beliefs are ideological, some ideologies are more negative than others.[3] It should be emphasised again that this does not mean that all these 'ideas' are necessarily ideological, nor that ideas which are not generated by the ruling class are non-ideological. What it does suggest, however, is that, within capitalism at least, distorted ideas or ideologies tend to serve the interests of the advantaged minority *only*.

With regard to the *effects* of ideology, it is important to remember that although ideologies have an impact upon the way in which individuals perceive the world *intellectually*, for example by providing a frame of reference within which to understand the relations between different facets of society, it is their *material effect* which is much more important. This is not to say that ideologies have a physical form in themselves (since by definition ideologies are metaphysical), but rather that to the extent that they influence the development and character of particular institutions and practices, at least some aspects of ideologies become manifest in the material world. The working class, in other words, is not controlled or dominated by ideology as such, but by the institutions and practices which derive from it. If, within capitalism, the majority of the population participates in the institutional practices of bourgeois society, this participation does not in itself signify that these individuals necessarily agree with or share the particular interpretation of reality which lies behind them. It is for this reason that Marx emphasises that *in themselves* ideologies cannot change the world; only practical action can do this. As noted above, Marx assigns the proletariat the task of challenging the inherent distortions of capitalist reproductive practice through revolutionary practice. Since the contradictions of capitalism can be overcome only by radical changes in the means by which individuals produce their livelihood, changes in consciousness alone can only ever represent *partial* solutions to the problem. In Larrain's words: 'Ideology is therefore, a solution in the mind to contradictions which cannot be solved in practice; it is the necessary projection in consciousness of man's practical inabilities' (Larrain, 1979: 46).

This emphasis upon the material origins of consciousness, ideas and ideologies, and upon the superiority of action over thought, is further elaborated in the third stage where Marx develops a detailed analysis of capitalist social reality itself. A central part of his argument turns on the distinction between the 'essence' of reality and its outward 'appearance'. Lukács summarised the significance of this distinction in the following way:

> If the facts are to be understood, this distinction between their *real existence* and their *inner core* must be grasped clearly and precisely. This distinction is the first premise of a truly scientific study which in Marx's words, 'would be superfluous if the outward appearance of things coincided with their essence'. Thus we must detach the phenomena from the form in which they are immediately given and discover the intervening links which connect them to their core, their essence ... the simultaneous recognition and transcendence of immediate appearances is precisely the *dialectical* nexus. (Lukács, 1968: 8; cf. Marx, 1959: 209; emphasis added)

The relationship between inverted reality and distorted ideas is thus 'mediated and complexified by a level of appearances constitutive of reality itself'. The process of reaching a true understanding of society, in other words, is made doubly difficult because the basis of this interpretation is itself partly made up of appearances only. From this perspective, it can be suggested that although many aspects of capitalist relations of production *appear to be* coherent, natural and legitimate, they are *in essence* profoundly incoherent, synthetic and illegitimate. In Marx's words:

> The final pattern of economic relations as seen on the surface in their real existence and consequently in the conceptions by which the bearers and agents of these relations seek to understand them, is very much different from, and indeed quite the reverse of, their inner but concealed essential pattern and the conception corresponding to it. (Marx, 1959: 209)

In summary, then, and as Larrain suggests, Marx's definition of ideology is essentially *negative* or *pejorative* since ideological forms of consciousness are always the result of a distorted perception and misunderstanding of reality. Within capitalist society, these misunderstandings and misrepresentations derive from the fact that this form of social organisation is based upon an incomplete and contradictory mode of practice. In producing his own analysis of capitalist society, particularly in *Capital*, Marx sought to provide an *undistorted* account of the essence of capitalism which could be used as a basis for deciding between what is essential and real and what is temporary and illusory. He criticises the analyses of bourgeois political economists precisely on the grounds that their theoretical understanding is based upon observations and conclusions at the level of appearances only. As these distorted representations originate in real material practices (albeit incomplete practices), their dissolution can be achieved only through the practical re-appropriation of economic and thus social relations by the propertyless industrial proletariat. For Marx, the forward development of productive technique and thus the ability for society to provide for the needs of all, would be accompanied by a growing realisation of the contradictory nature of capitalism, and in turn with the collapse of bourgeois ideology. The proletariat would then develop its own 'true' understanding of society and seek to implement necessary changes through revolutionary practice. Marx's *Capital* can be seen as an attempt to help create this new understanding by exposing the inversions and distortions of bourgeois ideology.

As noted above, however, in placing so much emphasis in his own analysis upon the influence of 'structural' economic phenomena on our understanding of reality, Marx underestimated the degree to which consciousness in general and 'class consciousness' (the awareness of shared interests and goals) in particular is also formed as a consequence of participating in a complex range of 'superstructural' practices, many of which may not be specifically concerned with economic production. Despite the fact, in other words, that individuals' perceptions of reality fundamentally derive from the practical experience of entering into a particular set of working relationships, *it is also formed* in response to the experience of living within other superstructural institutions such as the political system, the law and the Church. In order to change society through revolutionary practice it is therefore not sufficient to analyse economic practices in isolation, but to analyse and understand *every* source of consciousness *including those aspects* which are an intellectual reflex to the experience of living in a society where the institutions of the superstructure are an unavoidable part of daily life.

As suggested at the start of this chapter, Gramsci's concept of hegemony can be seen as a later and more adequate development of the concept of ideology in Marx. It will therefore be useful to look briefly at the intermediate stages of this development as they emerge through the work of Lenin and Lukács.

Lenin and Lukács: an extension of the concept ideology

The contributions of Lenin and Lukács to the development of the concept of ideology can usefully be seen as an attempt to overcome the shortfalls in Marx's analysis of the barriers to the development of class consciousness and revolutionary practice discussed above. Writing at a time when the potential for revolution seemed to have reached its peak, Lenin and Lukács were necessarily deeply concerned with the ways in which adverse ideological influences upon class consciousness might interrupt the revolutionary process. Lenin believed that the full development of class consciousness (and therefore of revolutionary practice) could be achieved only if the proletariat developed a distinctive ideology and political consciousness of its own. He also recognised, however, that, in the West, bourgeois ideology represented a powerful force which acted directly against this possibility. The extent of this influence was in proportion to the fact that, because of their dominant position, the bourgeoisie not only had access to far greater resources with which to propagate their world-view, but that they were also much better organised: 'Bourgeois ideology is far older in origin than socialist ideology, it is more fully developed and has at its disposal *immeasurably* more means of dissemination.' (Lenin, 1947: 42). He was therefore very doubtful whether the proletariat would be able to develop an alternative ideology 'spontaneously' as Marx had suggested and, even if it was able to, whether this ideology would be contaminated and thus weakened by aspects of bourgeois ideology, albeit in residual form:

> There is much talk of spontaneity. But the *spontaneous* development of the working-class movement leads to its subordination to bourgeois ideology . . . for the spontaneous working-class movement is trade-unionism, is *Nur-Gewerkschaftlerei*, and trade-unionism means the ideological enslavement of the workers by the bourgeoisie. Hence our task, the task of Social-Democracy, is to *combat spontaneity, to divert* the working-class movement from this spontaneous, trade-unionist striving to come under the wing of the bourgeoisie, and to bring it under the wing of revolutionary Social-Democracy. (Lenin, 1947: 41; original emphasis)

Having pointed to the limitations of 'spontaneous consciousness', arising from 'the spontaneous practice of the class as expressed in trade unionism', Lenin goes on to develop the idea of a 'political and theoretical form of consciousness' which is 'developed by intellectuals outside the spontaneous movement of the class' (Larrain, 1983: 65). Because, in other words, the proletariat could not be relied upon to move from 'spontaneous' to 'political and theoretical' consciousness of its own accord, this 'higher' consciousness would have to be brought to the proletariat from outside by an intellectual 'revolutionary vanguard' who would, as it were, 'enlighten' the working classes and so nurture a truly alternative 'proletarian ideology' amongst them.[4] Although this raising of consciousness would take place in organisations such as the trade unions within the economic structure, it would also have to operate within the realm of the political superstructure. As Larrain points out: 'the accentuation of the struggle necessarily leads to intense confrontation on all fronts, especially in the field of ideas', and so: 'the political ideas of the classes in conflict acquire a new importance and need to be theoretically accounted for' (Larrain, 1983: 64). The intellectual vanguard thus emerges as the catalyst through which the working class can pursue the ideological and political struggle. In emphasising the necessity of developing an *alternative ideology* which accurately expresses the world-view of the working class, Lenin moves away from Marx's understanding of ideology as necessarily negative, towards a more *neutral* definition of ideology as 'class political ideas' (Larrain, 1983: 64). It should be emphasised that this extension of the revolutionary struggle to include the conflict of ideas within the political institutions of the superstructure does not mean that practical changes in the structure are no longer necessary since, by definition, proletarian revolution is based upon such changes; rather, that the process of changing the latter may partly depend upon winning control over the former. As Marx says: 'theory also becomes a material force once it has gripped the masses' (Marx, 1975: 251). In a different context, Barry Smart has pointed out that: 'It is not so much the case that men take on only those problems that they can resolve as that they can only take on those problems which they can *identify*' (Smart, 1976: 61; emphasis added). For Lenin, it was the intellectual élite who would, as it were, take on this task of 'identification'.

In his analysis of class consciousness, Lukács follows Lenin in placing great stress upon the necessity for ideological maturity if revolutionary practice is to be achieved:

> When the final economic crisis of capitalism develops the fate of the revolution (and with it the fate of mankind) will depend upon the ideological maturity of the proletariat i.e. on its class consciousness.
> It is an ideological crisis which must be solved before a practical solution to the world's economic crisis can be found. (Lukács 1968: 70, 79; emphasis removed)[5]

Following Lenin's concern that the new ideology might be contaminated as a result of the bourgeois milieu within which it develops, Lukács turns his attention to some of the ways in which working-class consciousness tends to be affected by bourgeois ideology. In order to do this, he elaborates upon the dichotomy described above between essence and appearance. Lukács suggests that one of the means by which bourgeois ideology both propagates itself and is also propagated *within* the consciousness of the proletariat is through the device of substituting fragmented or partial aspects of 'reality' (formed at the level of appearances), some of which may or may not be 'true', for unified or 'total' aspects of true reality at the level of the contradictory essence. Bourgeois ideology, in other words, takes a number of superficial ideas and then constructs around these an overall interpretation which it passes off as being 'the whole story':

When bourgeois thought 'transforms the different limbs of society into so many separate societies' it certainly commits a grave theoretical error. But the immediate practical consequences are nevertheless in harmony with the interests of capitalism. The bourgeoisie is unable in theory to understand more than the details and the symptoms of economic progress. (Lukács 1968: 74; cf. Marx, 'The Poverty of Philosophy'; McLellan, 1977: 203)

In order to break this cycle of deception, Lukács suggests that individual proletarians and their intellectual guides should try to reconstruct the whole of which bourgeois ideology presents only a part. He therefore advocates a 'holistic' or all-inclusive description and critique of social reality in order to neutralise and ultimately reverse the development of what he labels 'false consciousness'.

Lenin's critique of spontaneous trade-union consciousness and of 'economism' re-emerges at this point, as the reformist tendencies of spontaneous trade-union consciousness tend to become fixated with 'particular' and relatively minor complaints about capitalism and so end up ignoring or obscuring 'universal' and more fundamental issues about how to bring about a much more fundamental restructuring of society. So, for example, by entering into negotiations with their capitalist employers over such things as rates of pay and working conditions, trade unionists and their organisations become part of the fabric of society and so contribute to the apparent legitimacy of capitalist society. Once they have become absorbed in this way, the survival of these organisations and their own career structures becomes dependent upon the survival of capitalism itself. In his analysis of capitalist society, Ralph Miliband makes the point that 'reforming intellectuals' have always offered the Labour movement 'a certain kind of political guidance – away from "wild" strivings, unreasonable militancy, doctrinaire Marxism, and towards gradual, piecemeal and moderate reform *within* the framework of the political system and in accordance with its political, parliamentary and electoral procedures' (Miliband, 1982: 90; emphasis added). A further important consequence of particularistic reformism is that it tends to cause divisions not only *between* different groups *within* the urban proletariat, but also between the urban proletariat and other sections of the working class as a whole. Lukács therefore argues that holistic or 'true' consciousness must be developed by a *united class*; a class acting *for* itself as a class rather than as an assembly of associated groups or craft-based unions. In discussing the role of anarchism and the peasantry, for example, Lukács comments:

We cannot really speak of class consciousness in the case of these classes (if indeed we can even speak of them as classes in the strict Marxist sense of the term): for a full consciousness of their situation would reveal to them the hopelessness of their particularist strivings in the face of the inevitable course of events. (Lukács, 1968: 61).

Having argued that a holistic conception is essential at the level of critical theory and consciousness, Lukács goes on that in terms of practical strategy it is not possible to dissolve bourgeois ideology, achieve true consciousness and engage in revolutionary practice in a single spontaneous outburst:

> There can be no single act that will eliminate reification in all its forms at one blow; it means that there will be a whole host of objects that at least in appearance remain more or less unaffected by the process. (Lukács, 1968: p.206)

Consequently, it is likely that the development of revolutionary consciousness will be a *gradual process*:

> The self-education of the proletariat is a lengthy and difficult process by which it becomes 'ripe' for revolution, and the more highly developed capitalism and bourgeois culture are in the country, the more arduous this process becomes because the proletariat becomes infected by the life-forms of capitalism. (Lukács, 1968: 264)

Further still, it is unrealistic to hope that every potentially revolutionary member of the proletariat will achieve the necessary level of enlightened consciousness either at the same time as everyone else or even *before* the point of crisis has been reached:

> It is certainly true that even those groups and masses whose class situation gives them a direct interest, only free themselves inwardly from the old order *during* (and very often only *after*) a revolution. They need the evidence of their own eyes to tell them which society really conforms to their interests before they can free themselves inwardly from the old order. (Lukács, 1968: 258)[6]

Even after people have become involved in revolutionary practice it is necessary to guard against the revival of 'false' consciousness since clearly the ideas of the bourgeoisie are likely to survive at least during the early stages of social transformation. The danger of retrospective contamination affects members of both the revolutionary class who may be forced 'to take power at a time and in a state of mind in which it inwardly still acknowledges the bourgeois social order as the only authentic and legal one', and, more significantly, members of the displaced dominant class who will still see the world in terms of their own ideology:

> [The bourgeoisie] must first be broken ideologically before it will voluntarily enter the service of the new society and before it will begin to regard the statutes of that society as legal and as existing of right instead of as the brutal facts of a temporary shift in the balance of power which can be removed tomorrow. (Lukács, 1968: 266)[7]

In summary, then, for Lukács the development of revolutionary practice necessarily involves dealing with the problem of false consciousness which emerges as a consequence of the actual experiences of living within the capitalist relations of production. Because, in the first instance at least, the workingclass' understanding of the world is deeply embedded in bourgeois ideology, the formation of true consciousness must to some extent depend upon the *prior* development of an alternative conception of the world, a proletarian *weltanschaung*, which can overcome the deceptions of appearance-based bourgeois ideology by revealing the real and fundamental contradictions of working and living within capitalist society. As long as this new world-view is based upon *universal concerns*, and as long these concerns are expressed by a *united class*, the limitations and self-defeating tendencies of false trade-union consciousness can also be overcome. Once the revolutionary process is under way, the practical experience of an alternative socialist structure will lead to a greater understanding and appreciation of the new world-view, the legitimacy of which will be correspondingly enhanced.

Discussion and summary

From Marx via Lenin and Lukács, the concept of ideology partially loses its exclusively *pejorative* and *negative* meaning and becomes instead a *positive* concept. Broadly speaking, with Lenin the significance of the struggle within the political sphere between alternative ideologies becomes a crucial determinant of successful revolutionary practice. With Lukács, false consciousness which arises when the proletariat absorbs elements of bourgeois ideology is recognised as one of the forces which is most likely to jeopardise the revolution. As a solution to the difficulties thus perceived, Lenin advocates the need for an intellectual vanguard élite who will bring the working classes a suitable ideological and political framework within which to develop the ideas they need in preparing for the critical moment of revolution. Lukács advocates the need for a more thorough understanding of the origins and mechanisms through which false consciousness is produced. His emphasis is therefore very much one of ideological critique conceived *negatively* with regard to the bourgeoisie and *positively* with regard to the proletariat.

Despite the fact that these developments made up for some of the shortcomings in Marx's original approach, a number of criticisms can be made of the theoretical and practical developments associated with Lenin and Lukács. In the case of the former, for example, questions remain as to who should become a member of the intellectual vanguard and how this group relate to the initially 'unenlightened' proletariat. If, as Lenin seems to suggest, not all these individuals originate within the working class, and since alienation arises directly out of the experience of living and working within the capitalist relations of production, the question remains as to how the vanguard can become experts in the problems and experiences of that class. Aside from the fact that the whole process of enlightenment 'from above' seems rather patronising, there is the possibility that the vanguard might end up using the masses for their own particular rather than universal ends.[8] Similarly, Lukács can be criticised for shifting the emphasis of revolutionary practice away from organisational problems towards the 'academic' or theoretical intricacies of false consciousness. As Larrain points out: 'Lukács consistently overrates the role of ideology and ideological struggle to the point that they seem to substitute for real political practice and real class struggle' (Larrain, 1983: 77). What concerns us here, however, is that through the work of Lenin and Lukács a new emphasis has emerged in the analysis and understanding of the mechanisms of social change which acknowledges that superstructural institutions and practices require analysis *in their own right*, and that revolutionary consciousness is a highly complex phenomenon which is unlikely to develop of its own accord.

This new paradigm in the analysis of social change centres round a set of closely related issues: the significance of 'ideas' and their combination in the form of ideologies; the origins, development and propagation of ideas and the ways in which they become materialised through practice within both the economic and non-economic institutions of society; the role of intellectuals as the practitioners of a new universal and positive ideology and the means by which they can or cannot convey their perceptions of reality to other members of society; and finally the probability that radical social change can be achieved only with the *prior* formation of an alternative world-view.

As the discussion in the following chapters will show, Gramsci's concept of hegemony can be seen as an attempt to engage with these new considerations and to develop a revised strategy for revolution which takes them fully into account. In anticipation of this discussion, a number of comparisons with the foregoing discussion can be made. First, with regard to the concept of ideology, Gramsci continues the trend noted above and further displaces the negative connotations which Marx associated with ideology. Used as a concept of ideology, the term hegemony emerges as a way of describing the world-view which *any social group must have* if it is to gain power and hold on to it. The development of a coherent and legitimate world-view, in other words, becomes a prerequisite for successful revolution. It is for this reason that Gramsci emphasises that, although proletarian hegemony is quite different in *content* to bourgeois hegemony, the two are very similar in *form*. This is why Gramsci directs much of his analysis towards analysing the processes by which bourgeois hegemony is constructed and maintained.

Gramsci recognises that ideology has acquired a pejorative meaning, but suggests that this is due to a confusion between (positive) ideology as 'the necessary superstructure of a particular structure' (which is to say as the commonplace and necessary intellectual understanding of something and how it should be organised), and (negative) ideology as 'the arbitrary elucubrations of particular individuals' (*SPN*, p.376) which, as noted above, are constructed in the interests of a particular group only. He goes on to define the former as 'historically organic ideologies . . . which are necessary to a given structure' and therefore have 'a validity which is "psychological"; they "organise" human masses and create the terrain on which men move, acquire consciousness of their position, struggle, etc.', and ideologies that are 'arbitrary, rationalistic or "willed"' and therefore 'only create individual "movements", polemics and so on' (*SPN*, p.377). For Gramsci, therefore, *positive organic ideologies are legitimate*, 'they organise human masses' and are thus effective through practice, giving 'a sense of unity of faith between a conception of the world and a corresponding norm of conduct' (*SPN*, p.326).

The second similarity, the perceived necessity for the *prior formation* of an alternative world-view, is common to both Lukács and Gramsci. For the former, holistic perception is seen as a necessary defence against the misrepresentations of reality which arise through the distorting, fragmenting lens of bourgeois theory. This new perception amounts to the re-assembly of these fragments in order to allow a true perception of the 'totality' of structural contradictions. For Gramsci, achieving a *total conception* of the social structure depends not only upon recognising and overcoming the inequalities of capitalist society in its material economic manifestations, but also of understanding other aspects of social practice *including* political and necessary ideological practices. He seeks, in other words, to transcend the assumption that social change is affected only by purely structural considerations.

Thirdly, for both Gramsci and Lenin *the political dimension* of the struggle is of paramount importance. There are strong parallels between the Bolshevik 'soviets' and Gramsci's development of the 'factory councils', both of which are seen as a means of organisation, 'leadership' and discipline. Similarly, the intellectuals are seen as playing an important role in stimulating political consciousness and class solidarity, and in developing the appropriate strategy in preparation for revolution. Gramsci goes beyond Lenin in this respect, however, by developing a much more sophisticated analysis of the intellectuals and the necessity that they should originate *from within* the working class rather than being imposed from outside or 'above' it. (These issues are discussed in Chapters 7 and 8.)

Finally, for Gramsci and Lukács the need for a thorough re-examination of revolutionary *strategy* forms a central aspect of their thought. The transition proposed by Gramsci from outright frontal assault towards a more gradual (though not necessarily reformist) tactical strategy can be seen as an extension of Lukács' belief in the need to undermine bourgeois ideology *before* the decisive seizure of power can be achieved. Gramsci also emphasises that once they have gained control over the productive processes, the working class must *continue* to exercise 'direction' and leadership.

Having outlined how hegemony can be seen as a concept of ideology, it is now necessary to discuss the other major elements which Gramsci also includes within this multifaceted concept. Of particular importance are the concepts of 'historical bloc', civil society / political society and the State, and 'war of position / war of manoeuvre'.

Notes

1. Larrain (1979), (1983).
2. Larrain takes this chronology from the work of R. Echeverria (1978), 'Marx's concept of Science'. Doctoral thesis, Birkbeck College, London.
3. Deciding where a particular ideology lies along this positive–negative continuum is of course very difficult. It would be ridiculous to claim, for example, as Marx tends to do, that all working-class ideologies are necessarily 'good'. Male-centred and paternalistic attitudes towards women at work, for example, are a clear example of a particularistic and therefore negative working-class ideology. Sim-ilarly, some sets of ideas which may or may not be ideological are clearly not class-based. Environmental 'ideology', for example, is universal and therefore positive, but may none the less be seen as negative by multi-national organisations for whom 'cleaning up the environment' may be seen as unwelcome interference.
4. For a discussion of this issue see Karabel (1976), Colletti (1971), and Magri (1970).
5. For a more detailed discussion see also Lukács (1970).
6. It was this view which led Lukács to develop the idea of the *Teilaktionen* offensive or 'partial actions' against the State, which would, in Anderson's words, have a 'subjective impact on the consciousness of the working class' and thus '"awaken" the proletariat from its reformist torpor' (Anderson, 1976: 56). It was this kind of strategy which underlay the KPD offensives in Germany in March 1921. For more details see note 10 in Chapter 3 above and Chapter 5 below. Gramsci's view of this form of revolutionary strategy in discussed in Chapter 5.
7. The survival of pre-revolutionary perceptions is associated with the kind of material effect which ideologies acquire once they have become operationalised through practice. During and immediately after the revolution, many of the institutions which are already well established, such as power supply and adequate means of communication, will have to be maintained. To the extent that the organisation of these institutions originate in bourgeois society, their continued use implies an at least partial acknowledgement of the bourgeois world-view. It is practical difficulties of this nature which may hinder the process of conceiving alternatives as the dominant class is likely

to present 'alternatives' and the individuals who put them forward as impractical and naive. Early attitudes towards environmentalists as being rather eccentric is a clear example of this tactic.
8. For example, see Larrain (1983): 67.

5

The concept hegemony: a variable definition

As noted in the Introduction, the fragmented nature of Gramsci's writings and, in the case of the *Prison Notebooks*, the extremely difficult circumstances in which they were written, presents the reader with a number of problems. One problem is that Gramsci's writings represent *a process* of intellectual and theoretical development and not a *finished project*. We are offered a series of combinations and theoretical analogies rather than a single coherent 'grand theory'. A second problem is that, since Gramsci applies his terms and concepts in a variety of different combinations and historical contexts, the precise definition of *the terms themselves* tends to vary according to the particular issue he is addressing. As such Gramsci's ideas form a kind of crustacean; a whole which adheres in a general way, but whose individual elements may not always be entirely consistent with one another.[1]

With this in mind, the concept hegemony is itself used by Gramsci in a number of different ways depending upon which relationship of social forces is being addressed. A number of general observations can, however, be made at the outset. First, as a description of process and evolution it is useful to consider the concept of hegemony as essentially *organic*: 'Hegemony is actually a process of struggle, a permanent striving, a ceaseless endeavour to maintain control over the "hearts and minds" of subordinate classes. The work of hegemony, so to speak, is never done' (Miliband, 1982; 76).

Second, the agents of hegemony are conscious and reflective human agents; hegemony is not therefore a mysterious metaphysical force or 'spirit' lying beyond the control of social agents, it is actively created, maintained and reproduced by real individuals:

We have to emphasise that hegemony is not singular; indeed that its own internal structures are highly complex, and have continually to be renewed, recreated and defended; and by the same token that they can be continually challenged and in certain aspects modified. (R. Williams, 1973: 8)

Thirdly, hegemony describes a process of conscious intellectual reflection and synthesis, which leads (1) to a greater understanding of material reality, and (2) to the development of a new form of political strategy and action. In this sense hegemony is a form of *praxis*, a realisation through action of conscious, critical self-reflection.

Hegemony and 'historical bloc'

In an article entitled 'The antinomies of Antonio Gramsci', Perry Anderson traces the origin of the concept hegemony and argues that: 'The term *gegemoniya* (hegemony) was one of the most central political slogans in the Russian Social-Democratic movement, from the late 1890s to 1917' (Anderson, 1976: 15). Its usage was established in the writings of Plekhanov and Axelrod, the latter writing in 1901: 'By virtue of the historical position of our proletariat (its all-national revolutionary significance), Russian Social Democracy can acquire hegemony (*gegemoniya*) in the struggle against absolutism.'[2] Subsequently, in one of his many polemics against the Mensheviks, Lenin wrote: 'Renunciation of the idea of hegemony is the crudest form of reformism in the Russian Social-Democratic movement:

> From the stand-point of Marxism the class, so long as it renounces the idea of hegemony or fails to appreciate it, is not a class, or yet a class, but a *guild* or the sum total of various guilds . . . . It is the consciousness of the idea of hegemony and its implementation through their own activities that converts the guilds (*tsekhi*) as a whole into a class. (Lenin, 1963: 57–8; Anderson, 1976: 17)

In this usage, hegemony refers to the need to amalgamate at a political level all sections and aspirations of the working class into a greater whole with a single unified aim, which, as noted in the previous chapter, transcends the inherent divisiveness of economistic trade-union consciousness.

As already noted in Chapter 1, considerable debate has arisen over the extent to which Gramsci adopts an orthodox Leninist perspective. Although it seems clear that Gramsci inherited the term hegemony from the various documents of the Comintern (Anderson points out, for example, that Gramsci 'naturally had an intimate knowledge of the Comintern resolutions of the period'; Anderson, 1976: 18), and although in the *Prison Notebooks* Gramsci attributes the concept directly to Lenin,[3] it is also clear that he went on to extend the concept well beyond its original use.[4] Indeed, it is Gramsci's extension of the concept hegemony which provides the innovative substance of his theory of political organisation and action.

This extension contains three essential elements. First, Gramsci places much greater emphasis on the synthesis of what he calls 'intellectual and moral unity', which is to say of concerns which go beyond immediate and practical economic problems:

> Previously germinated ideologies become "party", come into confrontation and conflict, until only one of them, or at least a single combination of them tends to prevail, to gain the upper hand, to propagate itself throughout society – bringing about not only a unison of economic and political aims but also intellectual and moral unity, posing all the questions around which the struggle rages not on a corporate but on a "universal" plane, and thus creating the hegemony of a fundamental social group [the proletariat] over a series of subordinate groups. (*SPN*, pp.181–2).

The second extension involves a much more explicit indication of the need to develop productive communication with, and assimilation of, other social groups which are, in the first instance at least, and in a predominantly economic sense, 'friendly' towards the proletarian class:

> An appropriate political initiative is always necessary to liberate the economic thrust from the dead weight of traditional policies – i.e. to change the political direction of certain forces which have to be absorbed if a new, homogeneous politico-economic historical bloc, without internal contradictions is to be successfully formed. Force . . . can be employed against enemies but not against a part of one's own side which one wishes rapidly to assimilate and whose 'good will' and enthusiasm one needs. (*SPN*, p.168)

The third extension relates to the fact that Gramsci applies his analysis to *all forms* of class association and homogenisation *including* that of the dominant social group. As Anderson explains:

Gramsci extended the notion of hegemony from its original application to the perspectives of the working class in a bourgeois revolution against a feudal order, to the mechanisms of bourgeois rule over the working class in a stabilised capitalist society. (Anderson, 1976: 209)

Through these extensions the concept hegemony can be used to develop a more general analysis of the form and content of social structures as a necessary precursor to the development of an appropriate revolutionary strategy. For Gramsci, in other words, the successful overthrow of the bourgeoisie depends upon a satisfactory analysis *of how this class itself holds power*. In this respect, Gramsci goes beyond the more limited idea of hegemony used previously by Lenin and others as a way of describing only working-class solidarity. (This aspect of hegemony as a strategic necessity will be discussed in relation to the notion of 'war of position' below.)

As noted above, Gramsci employs the concept hegemony in a variety of forms and contexts. The most frequent use of the term, and the one which is most commonly used in recent Marxist discourse, is to denote a form of social and political 'control' which combines physical force or *coercion* with intellectual, moral and cultural persuasion or *consent*. In the context of complex western societies, Gramsci views the consensual aspect of this dual strategy as particularly important:

> The methodological criterion on which our own study must be based is the following: that the supremacy of a social group manifests itself in two ways, as 'domination' and as 'intellectual and moral leadership'. A social group dominates antagonistic groups, which it tends to 'liquidate' or to subjugate perhaps even by armed force; it leads kindred and allied groups. A social group can and indeed must already exercise 'leadership' before winning governmental power (this indeed is one of the principal conditions for the winning of such power); it subsequently becomes dominant when it exercises power, but even if it holds it firmly in its grasp it must continue to 'lead' as well. (*SPN*, pp.57–8)

There is therefore a *dialectical strategy* available to the dominant group in society. Either it can use direct physical force by such means as the army and the penal system to overcome its opponents, or it can gain their support as it were 'voluntarily' by persuading them to accept and assimilate the norms and values of its own prevailing world-view. Elsewhere Gramsci refers to this 'unity of the moments of force and consent' through the notion of the 'dual perspective' and by means of the analogy of Machiavelli's Centaur:

> The dual perspective can present itself on various levels from the most elementary to the most complex; but these can all theoretically be reduced to two fundamental levels, corresponding to the dual nature of Machiavelli's Centaur – half-animal and half-human. They are the levels of force and of consent, authority and hegemony, violence and civilisation, of the individual moment and of the universal moment. (*SPN*, pp.169–70)

Provisionally, therefore, hegemony can be defined in terms of the latter 'positive' aspects of social control.

Two further aspects of hegemony are described here. First, hegemony entails and requires '*direzione*' or *leadership*, which means that hegemonic social control (social control which is predominantly consensual) does not emerge spontaneously but has to be *actively created*.[5] Second, if a social group is to be successful in its aims, it must exercise leadership *before* the critical moment of social upheaval. The extent to which it can 'lead' depends upon the extent to which it is genuinely representative of a cohesive and purposeful alliance or 'historical bloc' of social groups and their aspirations. Furthermore, an emergent historical bloc will be able to take power only once it has developed a universal perspective which transcends the particular self-interests of its component parts. Although the interests of the various groups which make up the new alliance are principally concerned with structural or 'economic-corporate' issues, these concerns will inevitably be reflected in the political and moral spheres. The successful emergence of an alternative hegemony must therefore develop a new economic, political and moral 'leadership', which recognises and is prepared to engage with practical and ideational issues, within both the economic structure and the political superstructure.

Having recognised that structural economic contradictions can be resolved only in combination with changes in the institutions of the superstructure, Gramsci frequently refers to the structure–superstructure relationship specifically in terms of these properties of the historical bloc:

> But can one really speak of a dialectic of distincts, and how is the concept of a circle joining the levels of the superstructure to be understood? Concept of 'historical bloc' i.e. unity between nature and spirit (structure and superstructure), unity of opposites and distincts. (*SPN*, p.137)

And elsewhere: 'Structures and superstructures form an "historical bloc". That is to say the complex, contradictory and discordant ensemble of the superstructures is the reflection of the ensemble of the social relations of production' (*SPN*, p.366). (A detailed analysis of the structure–superstructure relationship is given in the following chapter.)

The relationship between hegemony and historical bloc should not, however, be seen as entirely direct. As Adamson has argued; 'hegemonies always grow out of historical blocs, but not all historical blocs are hegemonic' (Adamson, 1980: 177–8). This is an important point because societies inevitably produce a whole series of alliances or blocs based upon mutual interest, only very few of which will actually become dominant for any length of time. In combination with the notion of historical bloc, however, the concept hegemony can be very useful in analysing eventualities of this kind. For example, in analysing what Williams has called 'historical questions' rather than concentrating upon 'epochal questions',[6] the concept hegemony can help in analysing the likely displacement of one historical alliance by another. The non-inevitable correspondence between historical bloc and hegemony also emphasises the possibility of internal deficiencies *within* social groupings. As Adamson says: 'A social group or class which establishes an "intellectual and moral bloc" will by definition be hegemonic vis-a-vis itself, but its political alliances with other such groups may or may not develop into a hegemonic relationship' (Adamson, 1980: 179).[7] It is for this reason that leadership must be established *before* significant change is likely to occur. It is extremely unlikely, in other words, that a social alliance will be able to achieve a hegemonic dominant position *retrospectively*. Where a non-hegemonic alliance does achieve power through perhaps a violent *coup d'état*, the social order it establishes is likely to be fragile and unstable *precisely because* it lacks sufficient hegemonic social legitimation. In all likelihood it will have to rely much more heavily upon the coercive dimension of the force/consent strategy.[8]

Having gained power, the new historical bloc must *continue* to build hegemony both within itself and with other classes or social groups: 'when a class is in power it becomes dominant, but continues to "lead" as well', (*SPN*, p.57, note 5). During this post-revolutionary phase, in other words, the function of hegemonic leadership does not disappear but changes its character. This emphasis upon the continuing need for hegemonic control can be seen as an acknowledgement of the reactionary potential of the defeated bloc discussed by Lukács. Gramsci's use of hegemony is particularly useful in this respect as it recognises this danger while at the same time suggesting how it can be neutralised. Establishing hegemony, in other words, is at one and the same time the *precondition* for social change and the only defence against *subsequent* challenges to it.

Having outlined Gramsci's use of hegemony as a way of describing the emergence and essential characteristics of an ascendant social group or alliance, it is now necessary to consider the various social realms or contexts within which the dual strategy of coercion and consent operates.

Civil society, political society and the State

It has been shown above that Gramsci's concept of hegemony made three significant advances over the earlier use of the concept: first in emphasising its cultural and 'moral' aspects; second by describing the process of necessary assimilation of sympathetic groups; and third, as a means of analysing bourgeois domination over subordinate, predominantly proletarian groups. This latter shift of emphasis emerges most graphically in Gramsci's analysis of the relationship of civil society with political society/the State.[9]

It will be recalled that hegemony has provisionally been defined as consensual control in contrast to coercive control. Gramsci goes on to elaborate the particular institutional domains where the dialectical strategy is employed:

> What we can do for the moment is to fix two major superstructural 'levels': the one that can be called 'civil society', that is the ensemble of organisms commonly called 'private', and that of 'political society' or 'the State'. These two levels correspond on the one hand to the function of 'hegemony' which the dominant group exercises throughout society and on the other hand that of 'direct domination' or command exercised through the State and 'juridical' government. (*SPN*, p.12)

In a letter written from prison in 1931, Gramsci reiterates this point: 'Political society (or dictatorship, or coercive apparatus, for the purpose of assimilating the popular masses to the type of production and economy of a given period)', and 'civil society (or hegemony of a social group over the entire national society exercised through so-called private organisations such as the Church, the trade unions, the school etc.)' (Gramsci, 1947: 137; Femia, 1981, 25–6; Anderson, 1976: 22).

It should be emphasised that Gramsci locates civil society within the superstructure. This is a departure from the orthodox Hegelian and Marxist topography of social analysis, where the 'civil' institutions of economic relations and commercial life and 'the public services needed to maintain order within them e.g. civil courts, police etc.' (Femia, 1981: 26), are usually located within the economic structure. This issue and the problems it causes in understanding Gramsci's analysis of the relationship between the structure and superstructure will be discussed in the following chapter. For now it is important to note that although on the basis of these two quotations we can say that for Gramsci 'public' political society/the State is the primary source of coercive domination, while 'private' civil society is the primary source of consensual hegemony, what he actually means by political society/the State and civil society tends to vary. In his analysis of Gramsci's political theory, Anderson has paid particular attention to the various definitions and relationships which Gramsci associates with these terms, and consequently with the coercive or consensual forms of social control which they represent. He suggests that 'in effect three distinct versions of the relations between Gramsci's key concepts are simultaneously discernible in his Prison Notebooks' (Anderson, 1976: 25). In order to understand the subtleties of hegemony as a mode of social control, it will be useful to discuss the first two of these here.

In the first configuration, and as a result of his analysis of the relative complexity of western society compared with the more rudimentary society with which the Russian Bolsheviks had to contend, Gramsci concludes that:

> In the East [Russia] the State was everything, civil society was primordial and gelatinous; in the West there was a proper relation between State and civil society and when the State trembled a sturdy structure of civil society was at once revealed. The State was only an outer ditch behind which there stood a powerful system of fortresses and earthworks: more or less numerous from one State to the next, it goes without saying – but this precisely necessitated an accurate reconnaissance of each individual country. (*SPN*, p.238)

As Anderson notes, there is some inconsistency here with regard to the precise nature and importance of the State. If in the West the State is in a 'proper relationship' with civil society, it cannot at the same time be only an 'outer ditch', as this implies that the State, and consequently the institutions of coercive control which it operates, is in some way superficial and apparently unimportant. In a different passage, and as part of his discussion of 'permanent revolution',[10] Gramsci seems to contradict this analysis by suggesting that as part of the 'massive structure' of western society, the institutions of the State constitute a major barrier to revolution:

> The massive structures of the modern democracies, both as State organisations and as complexes of associations in civil society, constitute for the art of politics as it were the 'trenches' and the permanent fortifications of the front in the war of position: they render merely 'partial' the element of movement which before used to be 'the whole' of war. (*SPN*, p.243)

Further still, as Anderson points out: 'These oscillations moreover, concern only the relationship *between* the terms. The *terms themselves*, however are subject to the same sudden shifts of boundary and position.' He goes on to suggest that elsewhere 'Gramsci speaks of the State itself as inclusive of civil society . . . and in other passages he goes further and directly rejects any opposition between political and civil society as a confusion of liberal ideology' (Anderson, 1976: 12–13).[11] Of the first configuration Anderson concludes:

> The preponderance of civil society over the State in the West can be equated with the predominance of 'hegemony' over 'coercion' as the fundamental mode of bourgeois power in advanced capitalism. Since hegemony pertains to civil society, and civil society prevails over the State it is the cultural ascendancy of the ruling class that essentially ensures the stability of the capitalist order. For in Gramsci's usage here, hegemony means the ideological subordination of the working class by the bourgeoisie, which enables it to rule by consent. (Anderson, 1976: 26)

Anderson is not at all happy with this position, however, as it implies that the bourgeoisie exercises control not only primarily through the institutions and practices of *civil society* rather than through the repressive institutions *of the State*, but that it is *ideational persuasion* rather than the threat of *physical force* which ensures the 'consent' of the proletariat. Hegemonic consent, in other words, eclipses coercion as the primary means of social control: 'It is the strategic nexus of civil society which is believed to maintain capitalist hegemony within a political democracy, whose State institutions do not directly debar or repress the masses' (Anderson, 1976: 27).

Against this view and the implication that the working class can be liberated through a purely counter-ideological offensive within civil society, Anderson first stresses the importance of ideological pressures which stem from the institutional practices of the State. In particular, he points to the way in which the practices of the parliamentary system constitute 'the formal framework of all other ideological mechanisms of the ruling class'. For Anderson, Gramsci is therefore wrong to 'partition the ideological functions of bourgeois class power between civil society and the State', since 'the fundamental form of the Western parliamentary State – the juridical sum of its citizenry – *is itself the hub of the ideological apparatus of capitalism*' (Anderson, 1976: 28–9; emphasis added). For Anderson, therefore, it is active and apparently willing participation in the parliamentary process of the State which is the primary source of ideational consent in modern democratic societies. Ideational consent which originates in civil society through what Anderson calls 'the ramified complexes of the cultural control-systems within civil society – radio, television, cinema, churches, newspapers, political parties', on the other hand, is also important but its impact should not be 'counterposed to the cultural-ideological role of the State itself' (Anderson 1976: 29).

This analysis relates to the discussion of the appearance/essence dialectic discussed in the previous chapter. At a superficial level, the citizenry of parliamentary states elect their own representatives without any apparent need for overt coercion. In doing this, individuals express a belief in the 'democratic equality of all citizens' and a corresponding '"disbelief" in the existence of any ruling class' (Anderson, 1976: 30). In essence, however, this belief in the 'equality' of individuals and their ability to affect government policy is nothing but a façade. In reality, widely differing levels of access to the necessities of life render people profoundly *unequal*: 'The bourgeois State thus by definition "represents" the totality of the population abstracted from its distribution into social classes' (Anderson, 1976: 28). It should be emphasised once again that this subjugation is not simply 'ideological' *but is manifest in actual material practices*; people actually vote, discuss election issues and so on, they are not simply 'indoctrinated' in some abstract way but are *active participants* in the process itself.

With these criticisms in mind, Anderson outlines a second configuration presented by Gramsci. Picking up the idea of a 'proper relationship between State and civil society', Gramsci suggests that since there is 'an equilibrium of political society (the State) and civil society', it follows that social control must be expressed by both force and consent; hegemony, in other words, is constituted by *a combination of force and consent*: 'The normal exercise of hegemony on the now classical terrain of the parliamentary regime is characterised by the combination of force and consent, which balance each other reciprocally, without force predominating excessively over consent' (*SPN*, p.80, note. 49). Gramsci goes further than this, however, and suggests ways in which the State can exercise, or at least make use of, a number of *ideological* functions. Not only, in other words, is social control exercised by both the State and civil institutions and by force and consent, but the State itself uses ideological control rather than force alone. In the first place, Gramsci discusses the idea of the 'ethical State' and the 'cultural State', suggesting that some institutions of the State such as the judiciary and the education system perform important hegemonic functions:

> Every State is ethical in as much as one of its most important functions is to raise the great mass of the population to a particular cultural and moral level. . . . The school as a positive educative function and the courts as a repressive and negative educative function are the most important State activities in this sense. (*SPN*, p.258)

In the second place, and as Femia has pointed out, Gramsci suggests that, when necessary, the State can make use of the communicative facilities of the 'private' institutions of civil society: 'The State, when it wants to initiate an unpopular action or policy creates in advance a suitable, or appropriate public opinion; that is it organises and centralises certain elements of civil society.' (Gramsci, 1951: 158; Femia, 1981: 27).

Third, and having explained that the State does not operate exclusively by coercion, Gramsci argues that, conversely, the institutions of civil society can also exercise coercive force. As Femia puts it: 'certain hegemonic institutions of civil society, such as political parties and organised religion, are transmuted, in specific historical situations and periods, into constituent components of the state apparatus' (Femia, 1981: 28).

In summary, then, through the concept hegemony, Gramsci emphasises that social control is maintained by a combination of force and consent, and that although these forms of control are usually associated with the State and civil society respectively, either means of social control is available within both institutional realms.

Once again Anderson is not happy with this analysis which he feels makes the error of associating coercion with the institutions of civil society. Rather, following Engels and Weber he holds that: 'coercion is precisely a legal monopoly of the capitalist State. . . . The exercise of repression is juridically absent from civil society' (Anderson, 1976: 32). While Anderson is certainly correct to stress the powerful coercive resources available to the State (police, judiciary, army and intelligence agencies and so on), it is also important to acknowledge, as Gramsci does, that the institutions of civil society are able to exercise repression, albeit in a different way. In religious practice, for example, coercive authority operates along a spiritual dimension and is not therefore 'physically' violent. To a dissenting individual, however, the threat of excommunication or social exclusion may *in effect* be just as debilitating as physical punishment. Similarly, the practice of racial and gender discrimination in educational and other 'civil' institutions may inflict considerable anguish, again without the exercise of actual physical force. Further still, within the 'private' institution of the family it can be suggested that the socialisation process is in itself a highly coercive but none the less 'private' practice. As Althusser points out in his analysis of 'Ideological State Apparatuses', which in this context can be equated with the institutions of civil society:

> It is essential to say that for their part the Ideological State Apparatuses function massively and predominantly by ideology, but they also function secondarily by repression, even if ultimately, but only ultimately, this is very attenuated and concealed, even symbolic. (There is no such thing as a purely ideological apparatus.) (Althusser, 1971: 138)[12]

To sum up, then, although Gramsci uses the terms political society/ the State and civil society in a variety of different ways, it is clear enough that the coercive aspect of social control is predominantly associated with the institutions of the State, while ideological or consensual control derives from the institutions of civil society. At the same time, however, and partly because of the methodological difficulty of trying to analyse these 'public' and 'private' institutions separately when in reality they are so closely interwoven, Gramsci shows that, whatever their position in Marxist topography, all institutions have both an ideological and practical effect upon individuals; the State does not have a monopoly on coercive control, and neither do the institutions of civil society have a monopoly on ideological control. Even if ultimately the dominant group maintains the consent of other groups by the threat of force, and even if this force is operated through the State rather than through civil society, its legitimacy still depends upon a minimal degree of conscious and 'voluntary' consent on the part of the population at large.

Having outlined Gramsci's use of hegemony as a way of describing the various institutional contexts within which coercive and consensual social control operate, it is now necessary to see how Gramsci uses this analysis to determine what kind of revolutionary strategy is appropriate in a particular historical context.

'War of position' and 'war of manoeuvre'

As the above references to the *Prison Notebooks* show, Gramsci often illustrates his analysis through an analogy with military strategy. So, for example, he writes that the 'massive structures of the modern democracies constitute for the art of politics the "trenches" and the permanent fortifications of the front in the war of position'; that in the East 'the State was only an outer ditch behind which there stood a powerful system of fortresses and earthworks'. This language shows that Gramsci is constantly concerned with the *practical problems* of revolutionary strategy and organisation. This is the language of revolution not of abstract academic debate. As discussed in Chapter 3, by the time Gramsci became concerned with the differences between a potential revolution in the West and the successful revolution in Russia, the excitement and optimism of the immediate post-war period had waned. In view of the fact that the 1917 Revolution had not had the kind of domino effect throughout central and western Europe which Lenin and others had expected, the problem of revolutionary strategy had risen to the top of the agenda. In particular, it was recognised that it was no good simply to organise a carbon copy of the Russian Revolution since conditions in the West were entirely different. In a letter written to Togliatti and others from Vienna in February 1924, for example, Gramsci reflects that:

The determination, which in Russia was direct and drove the masses onto the streets for a revolutionary uprising, in central and western Europe is complicated by all these political super-structures, created by the greater development of capitalism. This makes the action of the masses slower and more prudent, and therefore requires of the revolutionary party a strategy and tactics altogether more complex and long-term than those which were necessary for the Bolsheviks in the period between March and November 1917. (*SPWII*, pp.199–200)

The failure of the German and Hungarian communists to mount a revolution of this kind in 1919 and 1921 confirmed the truth of this observation. Gramsci became one of the main advocates of the need for a new strategy, and much of his writing is devoted to this problem.

The need for a new strategy which Gramsci calls a tactical 'war of position',[13] was further confirmed following the abortive attempt during March 1921 of the KPD to overthrow the German State by mounting a series of 'partial actions' or violent 'armed attacks'. (Anderson, 1976: 56). This tactic of *Teilaktionen* was developed by Lukács, Thalheimer and Fohlich in the belief that immediately following the events in Russia: 'The actuality of the revolution is no longer only a world historical horizon arching over the self-liberating working class, but that revolution is already on the agenda . . . . The actuality of the revolution provides the key-note of the whole epoch' (Lukács, 1977: 12; Anderson, 1976: 56). In the event, the KPD offensive was a complete failure and succeeded only in demoralising the German working class whose membership of the KPD fell by 50 per cent. In the light of this failure, Lenin and Trotsky soundly criticised the strategy of sporadic frontal attack represented by the *Teilaktionen* offensive: 'It is absolutely self-evident that tactical theories of this sort have nothing in common with Marxism. To apply them in practice is to play directly into the hands of the bourgeoisie's military–political leaders and their strategy' (Trotsky, 1945: 295–6; Anderson, 1976: 58).

In describing the futility of this form of 'frontal attack' against the resourceful institutions of a well-developed western bourgeois State, Gramsci again uses a military analogy:

> In war it would sometimes happen that a fierce artillery attack seemed to have destroyed the enemy's entire defensive system, whereas in fact it had only destroyed the outer perimeter; and at the moment of their advance and

attack the assailants would find themselves confronted by a line of defence which was still effective. (*SPN*, p.235)[14]

For Gramsci, in other words, the tactics of the KPD had focused on the 'outer perimeter' and had not appreciated the importance of the much larger and more robust institutions and forces which lay behind. Gramsci therefore distinguishes between two distinct strategies or phases of revolutionary action. First, an all-out frontal attack or 'war of manoeuvre' designed to take control of society in one move by overthrowing the coercive agencies of the State and its military forces in particular. Coercive force is needed to counter coercive force. Second, a more gradual and subversive strategy or 'war of position' whose object is the progressive undermining of the 'trench systems', 'earthworks' and 'permanent fortifications' of civil society. Since the control exercised by these civil institutions is primarily consensual, they must be tackled in and on their own terms through ideological and political 'attack'. The choice between these two tactics is determined by the institutional complexity of the society over which control is being sought. If, as in tsarist Russia, the institutions of civil society are 'primordial and gelatinous', war of manoeuvre is appropriate. Alternatively, in societies where 'civil' institutions and the democratic structure in particular are well-established, war of position is appropriate *at least in the first instance*, since the defences of the State merely constitute an 'outer ditch'. Having made this distinction between two types of revolutionary practice, Gramsci warns that waging of a war of position, the process of 'passive revolution' will be particularly arduous: 'The war of position demands enormous sacrifices by infinite masses of people, so an unprecedented concentration of hegemony is necessary' (*SPN*, p.238).[15] This phase of revolutionary practice 'is concentrated, difficult and requires exceptional qualities of patience and inventiveness' (*SPN*, p.239). And again emphasising the importance of *leadership*: 'Only a very skilful political leadership, capable of taking into account the deepest aspirations and feelings of those human masses, can prevent disintegration and defeat' (*SPN*, p.88).

Gramsci's understanding of the new and more protracted nature of revolutionary practice can be seen as essentially parallel to the views developed by Trotsky and Lenin during the early 1920s. (This is despite the fact, as Anderson has pointed out, that in his prison writings Gramsci mistakenly associates Trotsky's concept of 'Permanent Revolution' with the now outmoded strategy of war of manoeuvre.)[16] Gramsci firmly believed that: 'Lenin understood that a change was necessary from the war of manoeuvre applied victoriously in the East in 1917, to a war of position which was the only form possible in the West.' For Gramsci, 'this is what the formula of the "United Front" seems to me to mean . . . it corresponds to the conception of a single front' (*SPN*, pp.237–8). As Anderson and Hoare and Nowell Smith have pointed out, however, at the time that the 'united front' policy was launched by the Comintern in 1921, Gramsci firmly rejected it. As noted in Chapter 3, the main reason for this was his fear that uniting with the PSI maximalists might add to the tensions within the PCI between Bordiga's 'left' and Tasca's 'right'. It does seem, however, that after he had assumed the leadership of the PCI during the summer of 1924, and subsequently in the *Prison Notebooks*, Gramsci did give his support to the idea of establishing a united front, particularly with the peasantry, as long as this was formed from below rather than from above.[17] Indeed, this attitude is self-evidently expressed in his emphasis on the need to assimilate sympathetic groups in forming a new hegemonic historical bloc. Gramsci's distinctions between the strategies of war of manoeuvre and war of position, tend to leave two crucial issues unresolved. First, to what extent has the war of position *displaced* or superseded the war of manoeuvre in revolutionary practice, and, second, if it is accepted that the war of position is a necessary precursor to revolution, does it not imply that the decisive revolutionary moment of confronting the defensive forces of the State is likely to be postponed almost indefinitely? Is the war of position, in other words, merely a further if somewhat more sophisticated form of reformism or the 'parliamentary road to socialism'?

In the case of the first of these issues, Anderson has suggested that: 'Gramsci expressly relegated "war of movement" to a merely preliminary role in the West and promoted "war of position" to the concluding and decisive role in the struggle between labour and capital' (Anderson, 1976: 71). Since for Anderson the coercive strength of the bourgeoisie ultimately lies within the repressive agencies and institutions of the State, including its armed forces, and since the emergent social group must overcome these forces if it is to win power, this recommendation of a more 'passive' strategy is somewhat problematic. It can be argued, however, that although Gramsci writes that: 'In politics the "war of position" once won is decisive definitively. . . . the war of manoeuvre subsists so long as it is a question of winning positions that are non decisive' (*SPN*, p.239), what he actually means is that *even when* all the institutions of the State including its military forces have been overcome by frontal attack, the newly emerged historical bloc must follow up this victory by leading the alliance of social groups of which it is composed into a position of control over the institutions and practices of civil society. War of position is necessary, in other words, to ensure the *definitive* decisiveness of revolutionary practice *in addition to* the essential but *relatively partial victories* achieved through frontal attack: 'A war of position is not, in reality, constituted simply by the actual trenches, but by the whole organisational and industrial system of the territory which lies to the rear of the army in the field' (*SPN*, p.234). On this understanding, it can be argued that Gramsci does not mean, as Anderson suggests, that war of manoeuvre has been completely superseded by the war of position, but rather that 'the war of manoeuvre must be considered as reduced to a more *tactical* than *strategic* function'. Frontal attack is still essential, but in and of itself cannot be decisive; it has become, in other words, *an aspect* of the overall tactical possibilities contained *within* the larger 'positional' strategy.

Because the ideological and political sources of bourgeois hegemony are concentrated in civil society, and since the business of gaining control over them takes time, this phase of revolutionary practice must come before the final and relatively short phase of 'military' assault. In his notes on the strategy of Mazzini and the Action Party during the *Risorgimento* for example, Gramsci elaborates on this point and argues that the frontal attack *cannot itself occur* without a considerable amount of previous 'ideological and political preparation'. This is to say that the tactics of manoeuvre *are themselves formed upon the basis of a prior and over-arching positional strategy*:

> The concentrated or instantaneous form [i.e. frontal attack] was rendered impossible by the military technique of the time – but only partially so; in other words the impossibility existed [for direct frontal attack] in so far as that concentrated and instantaneous form was not preceded by long ideological and political preparation, organically devised in advance to re-awaken popular passions and enable them to be concentrated and brought simultaneously to detonation point. (*SPN* p.110).

In the same way, therefore, that hegemony should be seen as operating through a *combination* of force and consent, the war of position should also be seen as a new form of revolutionary practice which *combines* the tactics of position and frontal attack within a single overall strategy. Femia makes this point: 'The graduations of social integration, Gramsci seems to believe, can be arranged like consent, along a continuum, an infinite range of strategies [tactics] is therefore possible' (Femia 1981: 55). Because the circumstances in each country are likely to vary, the precise moment of application of each tactic will be determined by a number of different factors including: the ideological and 'military' preparedness of the emergent group; the nature and complexity of the particular reproductive practice which the emergent group is trying to overthrow, and an accurate and realistic assessment of the likely bourgeois response and possible counter-attack. It is for this reason, already noted above, that 'a precise reconnaissance of each individual country' is needed. It would seem, therefore, that Gramsci's formulation of revolutionary practice accords with Trotsky's view (of which Anderson approves) that: 'Defense and offense enter as variable moments into combat. . . . Without the offensive, victory cannot be gained. But victory is gained by him who attacks when it is necessary to attack and not by him who attacks *first*' (Trotsky, 1969: 47; Anderson, 1976: 74).

In respect of the first ambiguity noted above – that war of position has completely displaced frontal attack – we can therefore say that Gramsci sees these tactics as two phases of a single strategy, each of which has an important part to play in successful revolution. This goes a long way towards resolving the second issue of the 'reformist' implications of war of position. In the first place, and as the above reference to the possibility of an internal division within the PCI during and after 1922 has emphasised, both Gramsci and Bordiga were very hostile to the prospect of any amalgamation with the PSI *precisely because* of the PSI's tendency towards reformism. Similarly, the whole history of the PSI and Gramsci's role in its eventual split with the formation of the PCI in 1921, provide ample evidence of his unrelenting belief in the self-defeating tendencies of the reformist strategy. Indeed, the defeats of the council movement in April and September 1920 certainly gave Gramsci no reason to change his opinion of the divisiveness of 'economic-corporatism'. In the second place, and in terms of the strategy itself, it is clear that Gramsci relates the actual timing of frontal attack to prevailing historical circumstances. In the Italian situation, the militancy of the working class during and immediately after the war, the concentration of the urban proletariat in the north and its growing organisation during 1919–20, and the assassination of Matteotti by the Fascists in 1924, are all examples of particular situations where Gramsci felt that frontal attack was appropriate. Further still, Gramsci often refers explicitly to the military aspects of the Party and the working-class struggle and to what he calls the 'third' or military 'moment' of 'the relations of forces'.[18] Clearly, however, decisions about the preparedness of the working class and assessments of the moment of attack are functions of the political and 'intellectual' leadership. If this leadership decides, as arguably Stalin did when he put forward the concept of 'socialism in one country', that circumstances are not right for revolution, then frontal attack will indeed be postponed. The point is that the positional strategy, at least as put forward by Gramsci, is not *in itself* meant to justify postponement. If circumstances remain unfavourable for any length of time, then this would imply either that the agents of revolution no longer want a revolution, or that circumstances have changed to such an extent that an alternative new strategy will have to be developed.[19]

Summary

This chapter has discussed three ways in which Gramsci uses the concept hegemony. First, in relation to the concept of historical bloc, Gramsci emphasises that the successful overthrow of one social group or class by another (in this context of the bourgeoisie by the proletariat), depends upon the prior formation of solidarity both *within* that social group itself, and *between* it and other sympathetic groups. Most importantly, the new historical bloc must transcend the *particular* interests of its component parts and establish a new and universal world-view. In order to win the support of the population at large, that is to say of other groups which are not initially part of the alliance, the emergent social group must give 'leadership' and 'direction' both before, during and after the crucial moment of revolution. When these conditions are fulfilled, the new social group can be said to be hegemonic. The extent to which the revolution is likely to succeed and, more importantly, *to last* is the extent to which hegemony has been achieved.

Second, Gramsci uses the concept hegemony to describe the various modes of social control available to the dominant social group. He distinguishes between *coercive control* which is manifest through direct force or the threat of force, and *consensual control* which arises when individuals 'willingly' or 'voluntarily' assimilate the world-view or hegemony of the dominant group; an assimilation which allows that group to be hegemonic. He then goes on to discuss the institutions and practices through which these two basic forms of control operate. In their purest form, coercion is exercised 'physically' through the repressive institutions of the State, most notably the army, police and penal system, while consent is exercised 'intellectually' through the institutions of civil society such as the Church, the education system and the family. Most importantly, however, Gramsci recognises that *all institutions* have both a material and ideational impact upon individuals, and that therefore, in reality, coercion and consent tend to combine. The association of coercion with the State and of consent with civil institutions, in other words, is ideal rather than absolute.

Third, and having emphasised that the bourgeoisie in 'modern' democratic western societies maintain power primarily through consensual or hegemonic control, Gramsci argues that a challenge to its power must, at least in the first instance, take place on the political and intellectual terrain of both the structure and the superstructure. He therefore proposes that the emergent group should wage a war of position aimed both at freeing individuals' minds from the distortions of bourgeois ideology through a process of hegemonic critique, and at freeing their bodies from the contradictory practices of bourgeois society through the gradual subversion of these practices. Once these 'positions' have been won, and once the new hegemony has been established, the earlier tactic of frontal attack can be used to achieve the final, and if necessary violent, overthrow of the bourgeoisie's military defences. For Gramsci, the formation of an emergent historical bloc based upon an effective and realistic counter-hegemony constitutes, in the context of the evident relapse in the proletarian struggle after 1917, the only feasible strategy for revolutionary practice.

One important theme which has emerged in this chapter is the nature of the relationship between different types of institutions and their relative importance in the process of social change. Having emphasised the need for mounting an ideological and political challenge to the ruling hegemony, questions remain as to the practical means by which the emergent historical bloc can take control over the economic institutions of society. As has already been noted, Marx focuses his attention almost exclusively upon the need to change these latter institutions as a prerequisite for genuine social change. Political and ideational change, in other words, does not in itself constitute revolution. As Gramsci analyses the apparently non-economic or superstructural institutions in so much detail, much debate has arisen as to whether he agrees or disagrees with Marx on this point. The following chapter examines this debate.

Notes

1. It is of course partly because of this variability that Gramsci's ideas have provoked such a large amount of analysis and reapplication, since it is possible to take a single fragment, or combination of fragments, and re-apply them in a number of alternative ways and historical contexts. In this respect, a certain amount of confusion has proved to be very stimulating.
2. *Perepiska G.V.Plekhanova i P.B.Axelrod*, Moscow (1925), 11, p.142; Anderson (1976): 15–16.
3. He writes, for example, that: 'the theorisation and realisation of hegemony carried out by Ilich [Lenin] was a great "metaphysical event" ' (*SPN*, p.357), and later that: 'The theoretical-practical principle of hegemony has also epistemological significance, and it is here that Ilich's greatest theoretical contribution to the philosophy of praxis should be sought' (*SPN*, p.365).
4. In addition to Anderson (1976), see the discussions in Femia (1981): 25 and Adamson (1980): 172. The implications of Gramsci's relationship to Lenin with regard to the organisation and conduct of the Communist Party are discussed in Chapter 8.
5. The precise meaning of the Italian word '*direzione*' as used by Gramsci is a clear example of the problems of translation noted in the Introduction. For a discussion of the range of meanings which this notion of 'leadership' contains see Hoare and Smith's comments in *SPN*, p.55, note 5.
6. It is worth noting in full the distinction that Williams makes between 'epochal' and 'historical' questions:

> One thing that is evident in some of the best Marxist cultural analysis is that it is very much more at home in what one might call epochal questions than in what one has to call historical questions. That is to say, it is usually very much better at distinguishing the large features of different epochs of society, as between feudal and bourgeois, or what might be, than at distinguishing between different phases of bourgeois society, and different moments within the phases: that true historical process which demands a much greater precision and delicacy of analysis than the always striking epochal analysis which is concerned with main lineaments and features. (R. Williams, 1973: 8)

7. During the 1980s, for example, the failure of the newly reunited Liberal and Social Democrat Parties in Britain to emerge as a realistic alternative to the Conservative and Labour Parties, and the long-standing inability of the Democrats in the United States to displace the Republicans, can be seen as

examples of potential historical blocs which have not attracted sufficient public support to establish a new hegemony.

8. It is worth noting that this kind of reliance sometimes makes it possible for foreign dominant groups to co-opt the ruling élites of fragile governments through the provision of materials, expertise and personnel which are necessary for the maintenance of coercive control. This form of imperialism, which arises as a direct consequence of non-hegemonic rule, was very characteristic of North American interventionist foreign policy in Central and South America during the 1970s and 1980s. Similarly, the British government's reliance upon the use of military force in Northern Ireland suggests a lack of hegemonic leadership over this part of the 'British' population.

9. As Femia points out, Gramsci uses at least two definitions of the State: 'a broad [or integral] definition of the state, comprehending all institutions which whether formally public or private, enable the dominant group to exercise power: "State in the integral sense: dictatorship + hegemony" (Gramsci, 1951: 72)', and 'a more conventional narrow [or limited] conception of the state as political society'. (Femia, 1981: 28). Generally speaking, it is the integral definition of the State which is used most often in the *Prison Notebooks*.

10. For a discussion of what Gramsci means by this term see *SPN*, p.80, note 49.

11. See, for example:

> For it should be remarked that the general notion of State includes elements which need to be referred back to the notion of civil society (in the sense that one might say that State = political society + civil society, in other words, hegemony protected by the armour of coercion). (*SPN*, p.263)

And:

> The ideas of the Free Trade movement are based on a theoretical error whose practical origin is not hard to identify; they are based on a distinction between political society and civil society which is made into and presented as an organic one, whereas in fact it is merely methodological. Thus it is asserted that economic activity belongs to civil society, and that the State must not intervene to regulate it. But since in actual reality civil society and State are one and the same, it must be made clear that *laissez-faire* too is a form of State 'regulation' introduced and maintained by legislative and coercive means. (*SPN*, pp.159–60)

12. For a comparative discussion of Althusser and Gramsci on this point see Mouffe, 1981: 167–87. It can also be added that many forms of authority

and control within the labour-process of civil society are based upon coercive practices. For an introduction to this topic see P. Thompson (1983): esp. ch. 5 and 6.

13. Anderson notes that the distinction between two types of strategy had received attention prior to Gramsci's work on the subject. He points out that Karl Kautsky had counterposed 'a strategy of attrition' to a 'strategy of overthrow', and that this had been the substance of a 'famous debate' between Kautsky and Rosa Luxemburg in 1910. Anderson further suggests that Kautsky had himself 'borrowed' the terms from Hans Delbruck 'the most original military historian of his day'. For a full account of this chain of development see Anderson (1976): 61–6.

14. Gramsci uses a similar analogy in his analysis of 'colonial wars or to old wars of conquest' when, following a successful frontal attack, 'the defeated army is disarmed and dispersed but the struggle continues on the terrain of politics and of military "preparation"' (*SPN*, p.229).

15. For the genealogy of the term 'passive revolution' see *SPN*, p.106. For a discussion see Buci-Glucksmann (1979): 207–36.

16. For a discussion of this error see Anderson (1976): 73; and *SPN*, p.236, note 35.

17. Compare, for example, the view expressed by *L'Ordine Nuovo* in April 1922 that:

> The reporter [Gramsci] then went on to explain another argument which makes the implementation of the political united front impossible in Italy, which is the relation of forces existing in Italy between workers and peasants. . . . When one speaks of a political united front, and hence of a workers' government, one must understand a 'united front' between parties whose social base is furnished only by industrial and agricultural workers, and not by peasants (small-holders, share-croppers, husbandmen, etc.). In Italy there do not exist, as in Germany, exclusively workers' parties between which a political united front too can be conceived. In Italy, the only party which has such a character is the Communist Party. (*SPWII*, 123–4)

In the Lyons Theses of 1926, however, Gramsci and Togliatti suggest that:

> The task of uniting the forces of the proletariat and all the working class on a terrain of struggle is the 'positive' part of the united front tactic; in Italy, in the present circumstances, this is the party's fundamental task. . . . [Communists] must be capable of working in every way to achieve this end. Above all, they must become capable of drawing close to the workers of other parties and those without a party, overcoming unwarranted hostility and incomprehension, and

in all cases presenting themselves as the advocates of unity of the class in the struggle for its defence of liberation. (*SPWII*, p.372)

18. For example, in reply to the suggestion by the CGL that 'the workers, since they did not fight in the war, cannot combat and defeat fascism on the terrain of armed violence', Gramsci writes that:

    The Turin workers have the following 'war' experiences: general strike of May 1915, armed insurrection lasting five days in August 1917, manoeuvres involving broad masses on 2–3 December 1919, general strike with episodic use of Irish tactics and development of a unitary strategic plan in April 1920, occupation of the factories last September [1920] with the accumulation of a wealth of experience in the military sphere. (*L'Ordine Nuovo*, January 1921; *SPWII*, pp.5–60)

    The 'third moment' of military confrontation is discussed in Chapter 6 below.

19. The development of Eurocommunism could of course be seen as a direct example of this kind of strategic development.

6

□

Structure and Superstructure

As noted in Chapter 1, much debate has arisen within Marxism concerning the relative importance of structural and superstructural practices and institutions in maintaining a particular form of society. For Marx, the economic structure provides a foundation upon which all other institutions and practices are built. Consequently, if the economic structure changes then so too will the institutions of the superstructure. Revolutionary practice must therefore concentrate on changing the methods and working relationships by which goods and services are produced. Since Marx's time, and partly in response to the fact that the proletarian revolution has not occurred, much more attention has been focused on the need to challenge bourgeois hegemony as manifest through other practices which are less obviously 'economic'. As the previous chapter has shown, in emphasising the need for establishing a legitimate alternative world-view which includes not only economic but also ideational, cultural and intellectual practices, Gramsci's analysis represents one of the most forthright attempts to achieve this form of critique. In placing so much emphasis upon these latter practices, however, the Gramscian analysis is open to the interpretation that economic practices should not be regarded as the basis of all other practices, as Marx suggested but that, in the context of modern societies, superstructural practices exert pressures upon individuals (of both a coercive and consensual nature) *in their own right*. They should not, in other words, be dismissed as an unmediated reflection of the economic structure.

Further evidence of this apparent deviation from Marx stems from Gramsci's unorthodox categorisation of the institutions of civil society, including the economic institutions, as lying within the superstructure rather than structure. Two authors who have analysed this feature of Gramsci's work are Norberto Bobbio and Jacques Texier,[1] and a brief discussion of their alternative points of view provides a useful means of understanding Gramsci's perspective on this point. Before proceeding, it is necessary to consider a number of preliminary issues which form the broader context of the discussion, and to give an outline of Gramsci's own analysis of the 'moments' and 'levels' of the development of political consciousness through which he suggests that the structure is transcended by superstructural political practice as the 'mature' arena for hegemonic activity.

Preliminary issues

The first issue concerns what Marx means when he says that economic institutions 'determine' all other institutions. In *The German Ideology* Marx and Engels explain that:

> A certain mode of production or industrial stage, is always combined with a certain mode of co-operation or social stage, and this mode of co-operation is itself a 'productive force'. Further, that the multitude of productive forces accessible to men determines the nature of society, hence, that the 'history of humanity' must always be studied and treated in relation to the history of industry and exchange. . . . This conception of history depends upon our ability to expound the real process of production starting out from the material production of life itself, and to comprehend the form of intercourse connected with this and created by this mode of production (i.e. civil society in its various stages) as the basis of all history; and to show it in its action as State, to explain all the different theoretical products and forms of consciousness, religion, philosophy, ethics etc., and trace their origins and growth from that basis; by which means of course, the whole thing can be depicted in its totality (and therefore too, the reciprocal action of these various sides on one another). (Marx, and Engels, 1977b: 166, 172)

From this quotation, and following Hall's analysis of it,[2] a number of points can be made. First, 'the nature of society' is 'combined with' (or determined by) the 'multitude of productive forces accessible to men'. 'Productive forces' are taken to be inclusive of a 'mode of co-operation' or 'social stage' since without co-operation between individuals no form of material production would be possible. To this extent, co-operative social practices can be understood as *including* practices which are not *exclusively involved* in direct economic production ('the material production of life itself'),³ although ultimately all social practices do tend to reflect aspects of economic activity. Second, the relationship between economic production in civil society and its various manifestations or reflections in the superstructural State, is variously described as 'connected with', 'created by', 'in its action as'. The relationship between economic and non-economic activities need not therefore be seen as *direct* and *linear*, but rather as *interactive* and *circular*. Marx suggests, in other words, that the method of Historical Materialism recognises the holistic nature of society while at the same time helping to explain the 'reciprocal action of these various sides on one another'.

This interpretation of 'determination' as circular and interactive has also been put forward by Raymond Williams. He points out that there are two 'quite different possible meanings and implications of the word "determine"':

> There is on the one hand, from its theological inheritance the notion of an external cause which totally predicts or prefigures, indeed totally controls a subsequent activity. But there is also, from the experience of social practice, a notion of determination as setting limits, exerting pressures. (Williams, 1973: 4)

Williams goes on to suggest that it is the former sense of the word which has predominated and that it would be much more instructive to follow Marx's original meaning and emphasise the latter:

> We have to revalue 'determination' towards the setting of limits and the exertion of pressures and away from a predicted, prefigured and controlled context. We have to revalue 'superstructure' towards a related range of cultural practices, and away from a reflected, reproduced or specifically dependent context. (Williams, 1973: 8)⁴

The second issue relates to what Marx means by 'economic production'. It is important to stress that, in Hall's words: 'Mode of production is already conceptualised as consisting, neither of economic relations per se nor of anything so vulgarly material as "level of technology", but as a combination of relations – productive forces, social relations of production' (Hall, 1977: 51). This implies that the Marxian notion of human productive activity goes well beyond the relatively mundane experience of earning a living, and also includes participation in many other forms of co-operative behaviour and creativity, the 'productivity' of which should not be assessed exclusively in terms of economic criteria. From a Marxist point of view, in other words, 'human activity' can be seen in terms of a set of interacting realms of activity; economic activity is therefore only *part of* a much larger realm of productive activity.[5] Williams also stresses this point in emphasising that 'the received notion of the base' has led, 'as a matter of verbal habit' to a very superficial and increasingly unconsidered set of assumptions as to what exactly constitutes the economic basis of society. As a consequence: 'The base has come to be considered virtually as an object or in less crude cases it has been considered in essentially uniform and usually static ways.' In reality, however, the practices of economic production (let alone productive activity more generally), are dynamic phenomena which change according to developments in human inventiveness; 'there is therefore the continual possibility of the dynamic variation of these forces' (Williams, 1973: 5).

Indeed, it is the manifestation of this variation which allows Marx to trace the transcendence not only of one form of society by another, but of alternative manifestations of the same society: 'The same economic basis . . . due to innumerable different empirical circumstances, natural environment, racial relations, external historical influences etc., [is not prevented] from showing infinite variations and gradations in appearance' (Marx, 1959: 791–2). For Williams, therefore: 'We have to revalue "the base" away from the notion of a fixed economic or technological abstraction and towards the specific activities of men in real social and economic relationships containing contradictions and variations and therefore always in a state of dynamic process' (Williams, 1973: 6). By adopting a more comprehensive definition of productive activity: 'We are less tempted to dismiss as superstructural, and in that sense as merely secondary, certain vital productive social processes, which are in the broad sense, from the beginning basic' (Williams, 1973: 6).

The third issue relates to the conceptual difficulties which arise from the topographical metaphor of base and superstructure itself. It is important to remember that this simple spatial image is a convenient way of discussing society from a methodological and analytical point of view; it is not meant to represent the actual complexity of the 'real world'. It is therefore important not to confuse analytical distinctions with actual social phenomena and the relationships between them.

Having said this, it is not difficult to see how this type of confusion may arise since Marx often uses the base/superstructure metaphor in his own analysis. In the *Preface* of 1859, for example, Marx observes that:

> In the social production of their life, men enter into definite relations that are indispensable and independent of their will, relations of production which correspond to a definite stage of development of their material productive forces. The sum total of these relations of production constitutes the economic structure of society, the real foundation on which rises a political superstructure and to which correspond definite forms of social consciousness. (Marx, 1977: 389)

As Jakubowski explains, however, although in Marx 'the economy is assigned a special place in the totality of social relations':

> This does not mean that economic relations are to be strictly separated from the rest, nor that they can be, even in a purely conceptual sense. The unity of social life is so strong that the only possible distinction is a methodological one for the purpose of throwing light on any particular relationship. It is a complete mistake to think that Marx's differentiation between base and superstructure was an absolute distinction between two different, unoverlapping spheres. (Jakubowski, 1976: 37)

Jakubowski goes on to make a second important distinction between economic *relations* (understood as co-operative relationships between people) and *economic interests* (understood as the desire for economic gain or profit). What he means by this is that, although Marx and Engels place a firm emphasis upon economic relations, they do not intend to suggest that other non-economically motivated (but none the less productive) forms of social motivation – political, cultural, ideational and so on – cannot or do not, under particular historical circumstances, have considerable influence over the social structure. In a letter to Bloch in September 1890 Engels makes this point:

> The economic situation is the basis, but the various components of the super-structure – political forms of the class struggle and its consequences ... juridical forms, and even the reflections of all these actual struggles in the minds of the participants, political, juristic, philosophical theories, religious views and their further development into systems of dogmas – also exercise their influence upon the course of historical struggles and in many cases determine their *form* in particular. (Marx and Engels 1977a, 75–8; Jakubowski, 1976: 38)

It is Marx's realisation of the tendency for political, legal and ideational forces to intervene through the practices which they generate which leads him to develop an analysis of them elsewhere in his writings, despite the fact, as Engels explains, that he and Marx 'had to emphasise the main principle over and against our adversaries who denied it. We had not always the time, the place or opportunity to let the other factors involved in the interaction to be duly considered' (Marx and Engels, 1977: 78). Hall points out, for example, that in *The 18th Brumaire of Louis Bonaparte* (1851), *The Class Struggles in France* (1850) and in the *Notes on Britain* (1850):

> Marx is not only dealing with concrete social formations at a specific historical moment, but his intention is focused on one level of the superstructure – the *political* instance ... they contain essential insights into how, in detail, Marx thought of the 'effectivity of the superstructures'. (Hall, 1977: 54)

Gramsci makes a very similar reference to Marx's political analysis:

> The claim presented as an essential postulate of historical materialism, that every fluctuation of politics and ideology can be presented and expounded as an immediate expression of structure, must be contested in theory as primitive infantilism and combated in practice with the authentic testimony of Marx, the author of concrete political and historical works. Particularly important from this point of view are *The 18th Brumaire* and the writing on the Eastern Question, but also other writings (*Revolution and Counter-Revolution in Germany, The Civil War in France* and lesser works). (*SPN*, p.407)

To some extent, Gramsci's own work has also suffered from the same kind of crude reapplication of abstracted methodological distinction to actual material reality sometimes attributed to Marx. As shown in the previous chapter, for example, the distinctions Gramsci draws between coercion and consent (which is itself presented through the metaphor of Machiavelli's Centaur), and between war of position and war of manoeuvre, are convenient ways of expressing his analysis. In reality, these phenomena have to be understood as continua; there is no such thing as 'pure' consent or exclusively 'positional' warfare. Indeed, in the case of the latter Gramsci reminds us that: 'In saying all this, the general criterion should be kept in mind that comparisons between military art and politics, if made, should always be taken *cum grano salis* (with a pinch of salt) – in other words, as stimuli to thought or as terms in a *reductio ad absurdum*' (*SPN*, p.231).

The formation of political consciousness

One of the most important features of the historical bloc is that the hegemony it develops is at least as much political and ideational as it is economic. In order to be successful, the new alliance must move beyond the particular economic (self-) interests upon which it is initially based, towards universal concerns. With regard to the institutional realms wherein the new hegemony develops, Gramsci implies that economic structural institutions give way to superstructural political or ideational ones. To use the Marxist metaphor discussed above, the development of 'mature' political consciousness transcends or 'moves up' from the base to the superstructure.

Gramsci paraphrases as his starting point the proposition made by Marx in the Preface to *A Critique of Political Economy* that 'no society sets itself tasks for whose accomplishment the necessary and sufficient conditions do not already exist or are at least beginning to emerge and develop' (meaning that industrial technique and work organisation have advanced to the point where further productive capacity can be achieved) and, further, that 'no society breaks down and can be replaced until it has first developed all the forms of life which are implicit in its internal relations' (meaning that the demise of a dominant social order occurs only after it has exhausted its own productive potential) (*SPN*, p.177).[6] Having recognised these *general* principles of social decay and crisis, it is important to distinguish between two different types of critical expression which develop during a *particular* historical period. Gramsci calls the first of these 'organic moments' which are 'relatively permanent' and 'give rise to sociohistorical criticism, whose subject is wider social groupings beyond the public figures and beyond the top leaders'. This constitutes general criticism of the overall world-view of the dominant group. These are contrasted with 'conjunctural phenomena' which appear as 'occasional, immediate almost accidental' and 'do not have any very far-reaching historical significance' (*SPN*, pp.177–8).[7] These constitute specific criticisms such as pay and working conditions. When 'incurable structural contradictions have revealed themselves', a crisis develops and the dominant group engages in heightened political activity and tries to resolve the crisis and to preserve the structure in its present form. Significantly, 'these incessant and persistent efforts . . . form the terrain of the "conjunctural", and it is upon this terrain that the forces of opposition organise' (*SPN*, p.178). These immediate short-term criticisms are 'developed in a series of ideological, religious, philosophical, political and juridical polemics, whose concreteness can be estimated by the extent to which they are convincing, and shift the previously existing disposition of social forces' (*SPN*, p.178). In the long term (organic moment), the emergent group establishes the 'truth' or legitimacy of its claim that the present mode of production has exhausted its own potential by showing that the possibility (in terms of both technique and organisation) now exists for establishing a new organisation of the productive process. The point at which this truth 'becomes a new reality', is the point at which radical social change actually occurs.[8]

For Gramsci, therefore, participation in political practices – practices which take the form of 'ideological, religious, philosophical, political and juridical polemics', and which are embedded in short-term and 'immediate' criticisms of a 'minor day to day character' (*SPN*, p.177 – is a necessary part of the business of overcoming the long-term contradictions of capitalism. The successful emergence of an alternative historical bloc therefore depends upon a correct assessment of the interdependence *of all levels of social practice*, and of 'the correct relation between what is organic and what is conjunctural'. He warns for example, that 'presenting causes as immediately operative which in fact only operate indirectly' or that 'asserting that the immediate causes are the only effective ones', leads, in the case of the former, 'to an excess of "economism" and in the case of the latter 'to an excess of "ideologism"' (*SPN*, p.178). Showstack Sassoon summarises this position:

> Realising that there is a dialectical if uneven relationship between organic contradictions at the base, and the playing out of the political and ideological struggle in the superstructure is crucial to a correct understanding of the relationship between base and superstructure. Only in this way can the status of the political be delineated correctly. (Showstack Sassoon, 1987: 183)

In describing this relationship and its implications for revolutionary practice, Gramsci suggests that there are three basic *moments* in the 'relation of forces'. At the *first moment* there is 'a relation of social forces which is closely linked to the structure, objective, independent of human will, and which can be measured with the systems of the exact or physical sciences'. An assessement of the relations of forces at this level, the level of the structure, will show whether the two preconditions proposed by Marx have been met.[9] The second or *'subsequent moment'* is 'the relation of political forces' which allows for 'an evaluation of the degree of homogeneity, self awareness and organisation attained by the various social classes' (*SPN*, p.180). Since, however, the development of political consciousness is extremely variable, even to the extent, as Showstack Sassoon argues, 'that a social force does not necessarily have a political existence at all' (Showstack Sassoon, 1987: 185), Gramsci subdivides this second 'moment' into three further '*levels*':

> The first and most elementary of these is the economic-corporate level: a tradesman feels *obliged* to stand by another tradesman, a manufacturer by another manufacturer etc., but the tradesman does not yet feel solidarity with the manufacturer; in other words, the members of the professional group are conscious of its unity and homogeneity, and of the need to organise it, but in the case of the wider social group this is not yet so. (*SPN* p.181)

At the *second level* 'consciousness is reached of the solidarity of interests among all the members of the social class – but still in the purely economic field.' At this stage the class seeks to pursue its interests with the State: 'The right is claimed to participate in legislation and administration, even to reform these – but within the existing fundamental structures' (*SPN* ,p.181). At the *third* and most decisive level, individuals come to realise that their own corporate interests

> in their present and future development, transcend the corporate limits of the purely economic class, and can and must become the interests of other subordinate groups too. This is the most purely political phase and marks the decisive passage from the structure to the sphere of the complex superstructures. (*SPN*, p.181)

Once the development of political consciousness has reached the third level, the struggle can be conducted in terms of *universalistic* rather than *particularistic* goals, and a new hegemonic historical bloc can develop.

Gramsci emphasises, however, that *the form* that this development takes and *the type of society* which subsequently emerges will necessarily be influenced by both 'external' influences such as the international context, and by the way that political and ideational practices actually develop. Since significant aspects of the new society are bound to be primarily structural (in the sense, for example, that the 'political' introduction of proportional representation is not going to displace the 'economic' need for electricity production), the range of political possibilities *is ultimately limited by the availability of particular economic forces and practices*. This dynamic and reciprocal view of social interaction closely resembles the full Marxist notion of determination discussed above. As Femia suggests:

> Gramsci it would appear, believes only that *the basic trajectory of human history* is explained by the development of productive forces. *The specific course of any given society*, however, may vary in accordance with the dynamics of its own individual situation . . . . The economic base sets, in a strict manner, the range of possible outcomes, but free political and ideological activity is ultimately decisive in determining which alternative prevails. (Femia, 1981: 116, 121; original emphasis)

Although it may not be possible to specify in advance the precise composition of an alternative historical bloc, under certain circumstances and depending upon how clear an analysis has been made of the nature of the 'crisis' which has developed, it may be possible to predict with some accuracy both the likely *content* of the universalistic concerns being expressed and which groups are likely to express it. What *is* clear, however, as Showstack Sassoon emphasises, is that the nature of this level of consciousness is inherently political since, by definition, hegemony must encompass all realms of activity. The struggle for hegemony

> is thus conducted on the intellectual and moral fronts as well as the economic and strictly political. Consequently in the context of this struggle for hegemony, all areas of society acquire a *political* significance. It is not the site of the struggle which makes it political . . . *it is the way in which questions are posed in a 'universal' rather than a corporative manner which makes the struggle political or not*. (Showstack Sassoon, 1987: 118; emphasis added)

The *third moment* is characterised by 'the relation of military forces, which from time to time is directly decisive'. This moment has a dual character as it encompasses the military 'in the strict or technical military sense', meaning actual armaments, and 'the level which may be termed politico-military' (*SPN*, p.183). This latter aspect encompasses the question of the morale, political motivation and solidarity of both the dominant and dominated alliances, since, as Gramsci tirelessly emphasises, an emergent group is unlikely to achieve its aims if it does not *already* lead with the consent of its individual members. The question of military strategy has been discussed in the previous chapter.

To summarise, for Gramsci the economic development of society establishes the momentum of and for social change. Awareness of the need for change passes through a number of stages, culminating in the emergence of 'mature' or truly hegemonic universalistic consciousness. This consciousness takes on a political character and is expressed through a wide range of practices including: industrial action; provision of new information about the contradictions of present society; cultural and ideological critique; and attempts to nurture solidaristic alignments with other individuals and groups. Since this advanced consciousness is particularly associated with superstructural practices, and since Gramsci seems to locate important aspects of what Marx regarded as structural civil society within the superstructure, it is important to examine the implications of this apparent topographical relocation both for Gramsci's own perspective and for our own understanding of contemporary society.

Norberto Bobbio: Gramsci and the conception of civil society

Bobbio begins his analysis by emphasising that 'Gramsci's theory introduces a profound innovation with respect to the whole Marxist tradition: *Civil society in Gramsci does not belong to the structural moment, but to the superstructural one*' (Bobbio, 1979: 30; original emphasis).[10] It has already been noted that Gramsci's terminology is somewhat variable, particularly with regard to the relationship between civil society and political society/the State. Despite this, and despite Bobbio's suggestion that Gramsci interprets Hegel's civil society as including trade unions and other organisations which express structural contradictions 'politically', it is fairly clear, as Femia points out, that Gramsci's interpretation of Hegel was 'at least in this respect, rather idiosyncratic; for Hegel clearly understood by civil society the complex of commercial and industrial life, the totality of economic instruments and relations, together with the public services needed to maintain order within them' (Femia, 1981: 26). Bobbio goes on to say that, for Gramsci, civil society is seen as existing within the superstructure and that it is the superstructure which 'although still considered in reciprocal relations' to the structure, is seen as 'primary and subordinating'. Quoting Gramsci: 'It is not the economic structure which directly determines the political action, but it is the interpretation of it and of the so-called laws which rule its development' (Bobbio, 1979: 33). As noted above, the development of political consciousness signifies the transition from the economic-corporate to the universalistic, a process which Gramsci describes as 'catharsis':

> The term 'catharsis' can be employed to indicate the passage from the purely economic (or egoistic-passional) to the ethical-political moment, that is the superior elaboration of the structure into superstructure in the minds of men. This also means the passage from 'objective to subjective' and from 'necessity to freedom'. (*SPN*, p.366; Bobbio, 1979: 33–4)

Having reached this highest form of consciousness, in other words, individuals no longer conceive of society within the limitations of economic and ideological discourse but they come to see it in its totality. Further still, they come to realise that since 'freedom' rather than 'necessity' is the ultimate aim of society, material production *is subordinate* to the needs of individuals, rather than being a force which subjugates or oppresses them. With this new knowledge and consciousness of necessity, individuals reassert themselves as the true 'subjects' of history, and structural practice comes to be seen as an essentially *subordinate* means by which individuals can achieve their ends:

> It is the active subject of history who recognises and pursues the end, and who operates within the superstructural phase using the structure itself as an instrument. Therefore, *the structure is no longer the subordinating moment of history, but it becomes the subordinate one.* (Bobbio, 1979: 34; emphasis added)

For Bobbio, Gramsci's attribution of primacy to the superstructure and of ideational-political practice over structural economic practice is the first of 'two fundamental differences between Marx's and

Gramsci's conception of the relations between structure and superstructure' (Bobbio, 1979: p.33). The second difference 'develops within the sphere of the superstructure between the moment of civil society and the moment of the state . . . and consists in *the prevalence within the superstructure itself, of the ideological moment over the institutional moment*' (Bobbio, 1979: pp.35, 36; emphasis added). This is taken to be a reversal of Marx's order of determination, where 'ideologies *always* come *after* institutions as a secondary moment within the same secondary moment [i.e. a subdivision within the superstructure] because they are considered as posthumous and mystified-mystifying justifications of class domination' (Bobbio, 1979: 35: original emphasis).[11]

Combining this inversion with the first, Bobbio concludes 'the ideologies become the primary moment of history and the institutions the secondary one'. Once individuals have achieved the highest form of political consciousness in the manner described above, their actual universalistic needs, desires and aims expressed as 'positive' ideologies enable them to reassert their control over structural practices and to develop whatever institutions may be necessary to achieve their desired ends. When, in other words, the 'cathartic' transition to true consciousness takes place, 'ideologies are seen as forces capable of creating a new history and of collaborating in the formation of a new power, rather than to justify a power which has already been established' (Bobbio, 1979: 36). In this and in the first inversion, superstructural civil society – in the sense that Gramsci understands it as 'the whole of ideological-cultural relations' and 'the whole of spiritual and intellectual life' (Bobbio, 1979: 30–1) – is seen as positive, primary, subordinating and determinant; first as it is the sphere within which 'true' consciousness develops, and secondly as this consciousness, instigated through ideational practice, subjugates or brings under its control structural economic practice.

Having outlined these two differences between Gramsci and Marx, Bobbio goes on to suggest that in combination with the concept of historical bloc (understood as the 'totality of a historical situation' including both structural and superstructural elements), Gramsci's 'more complex scheme' has two important practical advantages. First, in the analysis of historical development, the first dichotomy (of superstructure over base and of freedom over necessity) 'serves to define and to delimit a determinate historical bloc'; for example, that the Moderate Party emerged over the Action Party during the

Risorgimento because its political consciousness, and therefore its hegemonic position, was more advanced. The second dichotomy (of ideologies over institutions) 'serves to distinguish a progressive historical bloc from a regressive one' (Bobbio, 1979: 37); for example, the situation in Italy during the 1920s where the system of coalition governments under Giolitti finally lost the ideational support it needed, leaving the way open to fascism. The second practical advantage relates to the analysis of the appropriateness of particular types of 'political action': 'The first dichotomy constitutes the grounds for [Gramsci's] continued polemic against economism', i.e. against a simplistic emphasis on purely structural economic issues, while 'the second dichotomy is one of the greater if not the greatest source of reflection from the *Prison Notebooks*, where the stable conquest of power by the subordinate class is always considered as a function of the transformation which must first be operated in civil society' (Bobbio, 1979: 37).

In sum, Bobbio's reading of Gramsci attributes great importance to the role of the political and ideational practices of superstructural civil society in bringing about the replacement of one historical bloc by another. The development of true political consciousness signifies, first, that the emergent group has become aware of the need to reassert its authority over the means of material production, and, second, that it is the realm of ideas which leads the way in transcending the contradictions of the present society. The economic structure therefore becomes subordinate and secondary to the battle of ideas in the political superstructure.

A number of criticisms can, however, be made both of Bobbio's assessment of Gramsci's understanding of civil society as being located exclusively within the superstructure, and of the determining influence he apparently attributes to ideational and political practices. It may be the case, for example, that Gramsci does not so much relocate the economic institutions and practices of 'civil society' *en masse* to the superstructure, but that in wanting to emphasise *the ideational and political aspects of these practices* he tries to separate them as it were 'methodologically' from their material manifestations, and thus gives the unintended impression of topological relocation. Similarly, even though political and ideational practices play an important part in revolutionary practice, the new society still has to solve the *practical problems* of how to produce goods and services. Since these solutions are evidently structural, and since new superstructural institutions will necessarily have to take any new arrangement of the productive forces fully into account as part of its own development, then clearly the extent to which superstructural practices can develop *autonomously* is strictly limited. It will be useful to illustrate some of these points by reference to Texier's alternative interpretation of Gramsci.

Jacques Texier: Gramsci, theoretician of the superstructure

With regard to the first inversion of the superstructure over the economic base, four points should be made. First, Bobbio's reading of Gramsci tends to suggest that Gramsci adopts a somewhat limited understanding of the economic structure as constituting little more than the most mundane, laborious and essentially unfulfilling activities necessary for sustaining material life. These activities are then represented as being incompatible with any 'higher' and more 'philosophical' engagement with reality. Acting within the structure, individuals are therefore regarded as somehow unable to consider anything which lies beyond or outside economic production; their motivation is seen as exclusively related to and derived from immediate economic interests only. Bobbio then attributes to Gramsci the belief that the possibility of salvation, or 'freedom' from mere 'economic' existence, can be found only within practices which, superficially at least, are not tied up with production; practices which in conceptual terms are superstructural rather than structural. The transcendence of economic practice ('the decisive passage from the structure to the sphere of the complex superstructures', 'the superior elaboration of the structure into superstructure in the minds of men') is thus equated not only with a down-grading of some practices in relation to others, but also with an elevation in consciousness so that 'higher' forms of consciousness are associated with 'superior' aspects of the social structure. It has already been pointed out, however, that the economic base and the practices which constitute it are more complex and potentially much more fulfilling than Bobbio's 'mechanicist' reading of Marx suggests. He adopts, in other words, a shallow conception of what constitutes 'the base', which both Hall and Williams reject as inadequate.

Second, Bobbio tends to attribute to Marx a very rigid and direct understanding of the effect that economic practices have over other social practices. As such he uses the pejorative and 'totalistic' sense of the process of determination and thus makes the error of confusing economic *relations* with economic *interests*. As the above references to Jakubowski have shown, this may represent a superficial interpretation of Marx, for whom economic relations are merely *one aspect* of 'the totality of social relations'; the aspect which provides a necessary point of departure for other more diverse types of co-operative activities and social relations. It is precisely because true freedom can be achieved only *once physical needs have been met* that Marx places so much emphasis upon the need to overcome the structural contradictions of capitalism. Having achieved this freedom, individuals will then be able to spend time in non-work activities of a more personal or autonomous kind. There is no particular reason to think, however, that these activities are any more superstructural than basic. On this understanding, the means–end relation to which Bobbio refers (superstructural freedom is the end to which economic production is the means) would seem to be somewhat superfluous since, once productive activity is seen in its broadest sense, the means and the ends become one and the same thing. As Texier points out:

> Man's creativity furthermore, should not be understood merely on the 'political' or superstructural level. It occurs – and should first of all be thought – in the development of the productive forces of social work. This is the point of departure for Gramsci and marxism. (Texier, 1979: 60)

Third, the division which Bobbio pursues between different realms of social practice tends to result in a fictitious separation not only of one moment of activity from another, but more significantly of the various aspects of *the same* moment. He suggests that Gramsci separates the two fundamental moments of human creativity, the moments of conception and execution (this is to say of conceiving what needs to be done and of actually bringing it about), allocating the former to the superstructure and the latter to the structure. However, this interpretation would not seem to accord with Gramsci's view. With regard to the separation of structure from superstructure Gramsci is quite clear that:

> Structures and superstructures form an 'historical bloc'. That is to say the complex, contradictory and discordant *ensemble* of the superstructures is the reflection of the *ensemble* of the social relations of production . . . this reasoning is based on the necessary reciprocity between structure and

superstructure, a reciprocity which is nothing other than the real dialectical process. (*SPN*, p.366)

In his notes on 'quality and quantity', Gramsci is equally forthright with regard to the separation of the intellectual and practical aspects of activity. He concludes that: 'There cannot exist quantity without quality or quality without quantity (economy without culture, practical activity without the intelligence and vice versa) any opposition of the two terms is rationally a nonsense' (*SPN*, p.363).

Finally, although Gramsci emphasises the importance of the political and ideational aspects of the new historical bloc and its alternative hegemony, he continues to acknowledge the significance of economic practice. He does not, as Bobbio suggests, relegate these to a secondary or subordinate position in relation to superstructural practices. In the first place, Gramsci clearly relates political consciousness to the development of crises within the economic structure. This is why he begins with the two fundamental principles from Marx's *Preface* of 1859, which relate specifically to the present and future development of the productive process. Economic crises, in other words, provide both *the point of departure* and *the driving force* of new forms of society. Although the need for change and the appropriate strategy has to be expressed politically, *actual change* can be achieved only through a transformation of the productive process. Ideational reform finds expression only by and through structural reform: 'Intellectual and moral reform has to be linked with a programme of economic reform – indeed the programme of economic reform is precisely the concrete form in which every intellectual and moral reform presents itself' (*SPN*, p.133).

In the second place, 'though hegemony is ethical-political, it must also be economic, must necessarily be based on the decisive function exercised by the leading group in the decisive nucleus of economic activity' (*SPN*, p.161). Texier reinforces this point:

> The new social group must be revolutionary in economic terms, that is it must be capable of transforming the economic base and establishing such production relations as will permit the new development of productive forces. Its political hegemony will therefore have an economic base and content. (Texier, 1979: 64)[12]

Turning to the second inversion proposed by Bobbio, the inversion within the superstructure characterised by the 'prevalence' of the ideological moment over the institutional moment, a number of further points should be made. It will be recalled that methodological distinctions should not be taken as 'real'. Texier agrees with Bobbio that it is 'useful and necessary to establish this distinction between the [ideological and institutional] moments, aspects or phases of superstructural activity', but stresses with Gramsci that 'a methodological distinction' should not be confused with an 'organic distinction' since: 'a distinction between political society and civil society [is] in fact merely methodological . . . in actual reality civil society and the state are one and the same' (*SPN*, p.160; Texier, 1979: 51).[13] Having established that, for Gramsci, the State in its integral sense is inclusive of both political and ideationally-based civil practices, we can now establish the direction of influence between ideational and institutional moments. It has already been noted that Marx recognised that ideological, political and cultural practices constitute forces which not only modify the conscious awareness of material production but that, under particular historical circumstances, these forces may play a leading role. In the *Prison Notebooks* Gramsci makes reference to Marx's *Preface* of 1859 (in which he refers to 'political, religious, aesthetic or philosophical – in short, ideological forms in which men become conscious of conflict and fight it out'), and to Engels's letter to Bloch (see above), concluding that: 'It is on the level of ideologies that men become conscious of conflicts in the world of the economy' (*SPN*, p.162; Texier, 1979: 56). Similarly, in the notes on 'the concept of "ideology" ' Gramsci writes:

> To the extent that ideologies are historically necessary they have a validity which is 'psychological'; they 'organise' human masses, and create the terrain on which men move, acquire consciousness of their position, struggle etc. . . . The analysis of these propositions [that popular conviction often has the same energy as a material force] tends I think, to reinforce the conception of *historical bloc* in which precisely material forces are the content and ideologies are the form. (*SPN*, p.377)

It would seem, therefore, that, following Marx, Gramsci recognises the reciprocity of 'ideological forms' and material forces and suggests that individuals become aware of and arrive at *intellectual* resolutions of *material* contradictions. It is also consistent to suggest that once a correct and undistorted intellectual solution has been formed, this solution becomes a 'material force' through revolutionary practice. This does not mean, however, either that intellectual hypotheses have an automatic *priority* over their material manifestations, nor that intellectual solutions are in any way a *substitute* for practical-material solutions: 'This distinction between form and content [ideologies and material forces] has purely didactic value since the material forces would be inconceivable historically without form and the ideologies would be individual fancies without the material force' (*SPN*, p.377).

It would therefore be a mistake to suggest that Gramsci reverses the direction of influence between one form of social practice and another. In reality, all forms of social practice are necessarily bound up with the continued existence, through reproductive practice, of contradictory productive practices and the relations between individuals which they generate. The extent to which practices *appear to be* either independent or autonomous of economic practices is a cypher of the degree to which the dominant group has succeeded in masking these essential contradictions. It is for this reason that, under some circumstances, political or ideational practices play a leading role in the maintenance of social control. Texier gives a number of examples of how these 'superstructural activities' may operate:

> The ruling class *maintains* the economic system (juridical consecration of a regime of property, and protection of this regime by coercion), *impels* and *controls* the development of the productive apparatus (creation of a type of *homo oeconomicus* consistent with the type of production and relations of production at a given moment by means of juridical coercion and education), guarantees its power by developing a system of political and social alliances and an ethico-political system which permits it to exercise its hegemony and rule over society as a whole. (Texier, 1979: 71) [14]

Summary

This chapter has discussed a number of issues relating to Gramsci's understanding of the relationship between economic and non-economic institutions, and of how revolutionary consciousness develops within and between them. Taking Marx as his starting point, Gramsci suggests that once the existing social order enters into crisis, a crisis which in the first instance is economic, the emerging social group passes through three stages or 'moments' of struggle with the dominant group. The first stage involves criticism of the immediate contradictions of the productive system. These criticisms are primarily expressed *economically*, perhaps through strike action and claims for reform in the organisation of work. The second stage, which subdivides into three 'levels', signifies the evolution of political consciousness from economic-corporate through economic-solidaristic to universal-solidaristic. During this evolution, the expression of criticism becomes increasingly political, and addresses itself specifically to the fundamental contradictions of the present system. Finally, in the third stage, the new historical bloc displaces the old by taking control of the institutions of the State, including its coercive military forces. Depending on particular historical circumstances and upon the strength or legitimacy of the new hegemony, this final stage may or may not involve direct physical confrontation.

This transition *in consciousness* from particular-economic to universal-political is associated with a transition from structural to superstructural forms of practice. It is, however, important not to confuse transitions between methodological or analytical categories with actual transitions in the real world, nor to confuse these with distinctions between the ideational and material aspects *of the same* practice. For Gramsci, in the same way that the distinction between force and consent is primarily methodological, so too are the distinctions between the structural and the superstructural (civil society and political society), and between conception and execution. In reality, individuals are immersed in a whole host of different material practices and ideational interpretations through which the dominant group exercises varying degrees of social control. The purpose of revolutionary consciousness, therefore, is to separate out those practices which are the fundamental source of this control, and those which are secondary. In order to do this it is necessary to distinguish between different types of practice and to confront them in the most appropriate way. Since the institutions of the superstructure, including the political and democratic institutions of the State, exercise considerable control, revolutionary practice must include a critique of them *on their own terms*. Once this critique is under way, and once the prevailing hegemony has been sufficiently displaced, it will then be possible to bring about fundamental changes in the economic structure itself.

It was noted in Chapter 4 that one of the most difficult aspects of conducting a successful revolution is precisely the problem of how and when a sufficient proportion of the population not only becomes aware or conscious of the need for change, but becomes actively involved in bringing this change about. This and the previous chapter have outlined Gramsci's detailed analyses of these problems in terms of the need for a new historical bloc, the development of an appropriate strategy, the importance of the political aspect of the struggle, and the development of a universalistic political consciousness. A number of issues remain to be resolved, however. First, to what extent do individuals and groups develop political consciousness as it were spontaneously, and to what extent do they need expert guidance? Second, having acknowledged that political consciousness is a prerequisite of revolution, how exactly is the new historical bloc to be organised and led? Gramsci's discussion of education, the intellectuals and appropriate forms of political organisation addresses these problems, and it is to these issues that the following chapters now turn.

Notes

1. See Bobbio (1979), and Texier (1979).
2. See Hall (1977).
3. For example, individuals co-operate as part of the family, while at school and while involved in a whole range of recreational activities. This co-operation, the experience and necessity of doing things with other people, both extends and reflects the kind of behaviour and intellectual habits which are essential in order to gain access to the means of livelihood.
4. See also Williams (1977), for a more extended discussion of this topic.
5. It is worth noting that the commonplace association of 'productivity' with economic production, where the *worth* of a particular activity is almost always calculated in terms of economic criteria and 'profitability', is a key feature of bourgeois ideology. Conversely, the *usefulness* of an activity, either in terms of individual fulfilment and gratification or in terms of the community more generally, is often ignored. For a discussion of the relationship between different realms of activity and a critique of capitalistic economic rationality see Gorz (1989).
6. The full version of this passage is as follows:

   No social order ever perishes before all the productive forces for which there is room in it have developed; and new, higher relations of production never appear before the material conditions of their existence have matured in the womb of the old society itself. Therefore mankind always sets itself only such tasks as it can solve; since, looking at the matter more closely, it will always be found that the task itself arises only when the material conditions for its solution already exist or are at least in the process of formation. (Marx, 1977: 390)

7. Gramsci defines the conjuncture as: 'The set of circumstances which determine the market in a given phase, provided that these are conceived of

as being in movement, i.e. as constituting a process of ever-changing combinations, a process which is the economic cycle' (*SPN*, p.177, note 79).

8. In contemporary society, for example, economic recession or increases in unemployment may stimulate this kind of defensive political activity on the part of the dominant group. Statements are made about a whole range of international trends and statistical factors which are presented as the actual causes of immediate problems. Spokespeople of opposition parties and trade unions will then enter the debate in the hope of gaining a political advantage. Unless opposition groups succeed in exposing the fundamental and long-term deficiencies of the economic system, however, it is likely that the immediate crisis will subside leaving the status quo intact.

9. For Marx, for example, advances in productive technologies during the mid-nineteenth century together with the emergence of a very large industrial workforce, had rendered the capitalist system of production obsolete and therefore liable to collapse. In contemporary society, the perceived incompatibility of capitalism with environmental conservation has cast similar doubts upon our present methods of production and organisation of work.

10. It will be recalled that Gramsci suggests: 'What we can do for the moment is to fix two major superstructural "levels": the one that can be called "civil society", that is the ensemble of organisms commonly called "private", and that of "political society" or "the State"' (*SPN*, p.12). For Marx, however:

> Civil Society embraces the whole material intercourse of individuals within a definite stage of the development of productive forces. It embraces the whole commercial and industrial life of a given stage and, in so far, transcends the State and the nation, though, on the other hand again, it must assert itself in its foreign relations as nationality and inwardly must organise itself as State. (Marx and Engels, 1935: 76; Bobbio, 1979: 29–30)

11. This relates back to the discussion in Chapter 4 of the pejorative definition of ideology used by Marx. On this understanding, bourgeois theory or ideology is based upon a distorted and incomplete analysis of society, and is developed as a means of justifying or explaining structural contradictions *retrospectively*.

12. Texier notes Gramsci's more explicit examination of this point:

> If it is true that no type of State can avoid passing through a phase of economic-corporate primitivism, it may be deduced that the content of the political hegemony of the new social group which has founded the new type of State must predominantly be of an economic order: what is involved is the reorganisation of the structure and the real relations between men on the one hand and the world of the economy of production on the other. (*SPN*, p.263; Texier, 1979: 64 note 47)

13. Texier expresses this in the following way:

> It would seem quite impossible . . . to separate the concepts of civil and political society on the one hand and the concept of infrastructure on the other. The form of the superstructural activities may well be ideological, but their content is economic and social and the struggle to win hegemony is a struggle for power. This is why civil and political society are identical in actual reality. (Texier, 1979: 65)

14. It will be recalled that Anderson makes a similar point with regard to the effects of mass participation in the electoral processes of modern States:

> The existence of the parliamentary State thus constitutes the formal framework of all other ideological mechanisms of the ruling class. It provides the general code in which every specific message elsewhere is transmitted. The code is all the more powerful because the juridical rights of citizenship are not a mere mirage: on the contrary, the civic freedoms and suffrages of bourgeois democracy are a tangible reality, whose completion was historically in part the work of the labour movement itself and whose loss would be a momentous defeat for the working class. (Anderson, 1976: 28)

7

☐

Political consciousness: education and the intellectuals

From the discussion presented in the previous chapters, it is clear that the process of hegemony is dependent upon a suitably educated and politically conscious population; there can be no formation of an alternative hegemony or legitimate emergent historical bloc without political education. The discussion has also shown, however, that the processes of hegemonic development at both the individual and social levels are by no means direct and unproblematic. Gramsci was therefore keenly interested in the problem of how individuals reach an understanding of their circumstances and of how this awareness subsequently develops into the kind of advanced political consciousness discussed in the previous chapter. Although this interest is reflected throughout his writings, perhaps the clearest exposition of this topic is set out in his suggestions for school education, and in his analysis of the origins and roles of 'the intellectuals'.

The common school

Gramsci sees the development of advanced political consciousness culminating in the formation of an alternative hegemony, in terms of the passage of the individual from pre-school kindergarten, through the 'common school' and university or specialised technical training, to active and fully democratic participation in the organisation and 'control' of society as a whole. The institutions of education and of the 'educating intellectuals' within them, are fundamental to this process: 'The problem of education is the most important class-problem'; 'the first step in emancipating oneself from political and social slavery is that of freeing the mind' (Davidson, 1974: 126).[1]

As noted in the previous chapter, Gramsci emphasises the importance of developments in productive technologies as one of the driving forces of society. These developments inevitably generate a need for new skills or 'specialisations', and the modern school system therefore plays an important part in providing individuals with appropriate skills. This is an ongoing process, since these skilled individuals will also stimulate the continued development of new technologies and industrial processes. Speaking of his own time, Gramsci felt that: 'The educational crisis raging today is precisely linked to the fact that this process of differentiation and particularisation is taking place chaotically, without clear and precise principles, without a well-studied and consciously established plan' (*SPN*, p.26).[2] Gramsci's response was to propose 'a rational solution' composing two basic elements. First: 'a common basic education, imparting general, humanistic, formative culture.' This would be a form of basic education aimed at the development of general 'intellectual capacities' (the ability to read and write, to express thoughts and arguments) which are not directed towards any particular occupation. Second, 'from this type of common schooling, via repeated experiments in vocational orientation, pupils should pass on to one of the specialised schools or to productive work'(*SPN*, p.27). This would be a form of vocational schooling specifically designed to develop manual and 'technical' skills appropriate for modern industry. The common school, 'the school of humanistic formation', would therefore 'aim to insert young men and women into social activity after bringing them to a certain level of maturity, of capacity for intellectual and practical creativity, and of autonomy of orientation an initiative' (*SPN*, p.29). In order to ensure that the common school should provide education to all people 'without division of group or caste', which is to say irrespective of their class origins, a number of structural changes would have to be made in the education system itself. The school should be publicly funded; 'the teaching body would have to be increased'; the construction and layout of the school would have to be changed since 'this type of school should be a college, with dormitories, refectories, specialised libraries, rooms designed for seminar work etc.'. Finally, and most importantly, the school should facilitate 'a collective life by day and by night' (*SPN*, pp.30–1).

Partly as a result of the rather fragmented nature of his own education in Sardinia, Gramsci felt that the education system should provide pupils with a strong sense of continuity from kindergarten to the world of work. Entry to the common school should therefore be preceded by 'a network of kindergartens and other institutions [in which] children should be habituated to a certain collective discipline and acquire pre-scholastic notions and attitudes' (*SPN*, p.31). During primary school, pupils should not only be introduced to 'the first "instrumental" notions of schooling – reading, writing, sums, geography, history,' they should also be made aware of 'rights and duties' in order to establish 'the first notion of the State and society, as primordial elements of a new conception of the world' (*SPN*, p.30). This latter aspect is most important because it challenges what Gramsci calls 'magical' or 'folkloristic' conceptions of how the world has come to be as it is. This relates back to the discussion of ideology in Chapter 4 where it was emphasised that 'true' consciousness must penetrate the inversions and misrepresentations of bourgeois ideology. For Gramsci, folkloristic conceptions are an example of 'false' consciousness, since individuals may attribute their circumstances to mystical forces beyond their control. Elsewhere, Gramsci refers to these conceptions as constituting part of what he calls 'common sense' or 'good sense' through which individuals arrive at an understanding of the world without being 'distracted by fancy quibbles and pseudo-profound, pseudo-scientific metaphysical mumbo-jumbo' (*SPN*, p.348).[3] Following the common school and in order to avoid the 'brusque and mechanical', 'real break in continuity' between school and university or work:

> the last phase of the common school must be conceived and structured as the decisive phase, whose aim is to create the fundamental values of 'humanism', the intellectual self-discipline and the moral independence which are necessary for subsequent specialisation – whether it be of a scientific character (university studies) or of an immediately practical-productive character (industry, civil service, organisation of commerce etc.). (*SPN*, p.32)

From the particularly detailed outline of the common school developed by Gramsci, it is possible to locate a number of central themes which re-emerge throughout his discussion of the development of political consciousness and democratic participation. First, the full development of the individual originates from an interplay of communal and individual experiences. On this understanding, the extent to which an adult will be able to play a full and unselfish role in society is dependent upon childhood experiences of individuality and communality. Through the experience of the common school, each individual will discover that his or her well-being and creativity are bound up with the creativity and well-being of others and that a harmonious and progressive society is dependent upon autonomously developed but heteronomously expressed productive activities. This synthesis of the personal and the communal is closely related to achieving a sense of *continuity* between the development of intellectual abilities and the subsequent preparedness to participate in the democratic institutions of society. Gramsci suggests that:

> Democracy, by definition, cannot mean merely that an unskilled worker can become skilled. It must mean that every 'citizen' can 'govern' and that society places him, even if only abstractly, in a general condition to achieve this. Political democracy tends towards a coincidence of the rulers and the ruled (in the sense of government with the consent of the governed), ensuring for each non-ruler a free training in the skills and general technical preparation necessary to that end. (*SPN*, p.40)

Second, and closely related to this intellectual-democratic or intellectual-political continuity, Gramsci points to a second type of continuity, that between school and the world of work: 'The advent of the common school means the beginning of new relations between intellectual and industrial work, not only in the school but in the whole of social life' (*SPN*, p.33). This synthesis between both the appropriateness of school activities to working activities, and between the conceptual and practical aspects of activity of whatever kind, is essential to Gramsci's whole philosophical understanding of human nature and society. Individuals must perceive that society and the complex variety of practices through which it is constituted are essentially the consequence of past, present and future productive activity:

> The discovery that the relations between the social and natural orders are mediated by work, by man's theoretical and practical activity, creates the first elements of an intuition of the world free from all magic and superstition. It provides a basis for the subsequent development of an historical, dialectical conception of the world, which understands movement and change, which appreciates the sum of effort and sacrifice which the present has cost the past and which the future is costing the present,

and which conceives the contemporary world as a synthesis of the past, of all past generations, which projects itself into the future. (*SPN*, p.34–5)

In combination, these continuities of intellectual and practical abilities should stimulate a sense of 'totality' in the understanding of society. Once established, this may also create the potential for making a positive assessment of what forms a particular society may take in the future. Gramsci believed, however, that if people don't get into the habit of seeing things in this way at an early age, their future attitudes towards society may become fragmentary and selfish. As a result, the business of developing an alternative hegemony and of seeking common cause with other groups would be much more difficult.

Third, and again reflecting his own childhood experiences, Gramsci emphasised that personal and therefore social development demands considerable efforts of self-discipline, concentration and perseverance:

> The child who sweats at *Barbara, Baralipton* is certainly performing a tiring task . . . but it is also true that it will always be an effort to learn physical self-discipline and self-control; the pupil has, in effect, to undergo a psycho-physical training. Many people have to be persuaded that studying too is a job, and a very tiring one, with its own particular apprenticeship – involving muscles and nerves as well as intellect. It is a process of adaption, a habit acquired with effort, tedium and even suffering. (*SPN*, p.42)

Fourth, and related to the above, an element of 'authority' or 'leadership' is required to the extent that it is necessary to create the correct environment within which learning can take place. For Gramsci, this authority, expressed through the agency of teachers and senior students, should be based upon mutual recognition of communal needs and not upon the arbitrary exercise of coercive force. It should, in other words, be *enabling* rather than *disabling* authority. Similarly, the aims of the 'educator' should be determined by the demands of those being educated rather than by an arbitrary doctrine. The educator should therefore see her or himself as a facilitator of knowledge and learning rather than as a 'superior' individual.

Taking these points together, it can be seen that Gramsci's educational programme has considerable points of overlap, first with Marx's analysis of the educating intellectuals, and second with Paulo Freire's concept of an 'activist pedagogy'. With regard to Marx and as Adamson has argued, Gramsci's scheme may partly solve the dilemma inherent in Marx's writing with regard to 'who shall educate the educator'. This problem stems from the fact that although it may be legitimate for some 'enlightened' individuals (including Marx himself, of course) to show the proletariat the way towards revolution, who is to say that the educators themselves are right and what guarantee is there that their own ideas will change as new circumstances arise? In his analysis of this dilemma, Adamson suggests that, in addition to the 'self-educative' potential of the 'school of labour' where individuals learn about society through their own first-hand experiences of work, 'Marx worked with at least two images of worker education' coming from *outside* the proletariat. The first of these is a 'therapeutic image' wherein the role of the educator 'is to act as a kind of non-directive therapist who . . . only facilitates but does not impose a new and more correct praxis'. The second is a more 'directive image' wherein 'bourgeois intellectuals would play an active, educative role in bringing the proletariat to critical consciousness' (Adamson, 1978: 435).

The inherent problem of the directive image is that it implies a division between the proletariat proper and a stratum of educators who might, as it were, 'tower above them'. Adamson continues that inheritors of this dilemma, particularly during the Second International, were divided between the alternatives of 'orthodox' spontaneism advocated by Kautsky, Plekhanov and later by Luxemburg, and by Lenin's 'voluntarism'. The former felt that direct experience of 'the harsh but hardening school of labour' would be sufficient to bring the proletariat to the point of 'critical consciousness' and thus revolution. The latter argued that 'the school of labour' could in and of itself produce only elementary and possibly reformist trade-union consciousness, and therefore that 'education' would have to be brought to the revolutionary class from outside.[4]

Adamson suggests that Gramsci's perspective displaces the third 'directive' image while producing a 'fusion' of the 'self-educative' and 'therapeutic' images developed by Marx. In the first place, through personal experience of the world of work individuals are able to build upon and expand their self-education. In the second place, through the new institutions of the common school, technical education and university, the educators are able to share their knowledge with other individuals, and so provide them with a source of legitimate *comparative experience* on the basis of which they can continue to develop their own understanding of the world. Because the experiences of the educators are so close to those being educated, they will be able to filter out the distortions of bourgeois ideology. Even if, therefore, the knowledge of the educated is *quantitatively* different to that of the educators, if, that is, they have less experience of the world and the process of interpreting it, their knowledge will none the less be *qualitatively* the same. As Femia notes: 'Ways must be found of reaching the masses in terms of their ideas, their aspirations, their reality. The desired result is "a reciprocal relationship" in which "every teacher is always a pupil and every pupil a teacher" ' (Femia, 1981: 161; Gramsci, 1949: 26).

With regard to the work of the radical Brazilian educationalist Paulo Freire, two clear similarities should be noted. In the first place, and as noted above, Gramsci suggests that the displacement of 'traditional' or 'direct' teaching methods by the more 'active' and self-directive methods of the common school ensures that the educators do not 'tower above'. In his analysis, Freire makes a very similar distinction between the advantages of the 'problem-solving concept' of education as opposed to the 'banking concept' where 'knowledge is a gift bestowed by those who consider themselves knowledgeable upon those whom they consider to know nothing'. Through the former, however:

> breaking the vertical patterns characteristic of banking education, can fulfil its function of being the practice of freedom only if it can overcome the above contradiction. Through dialogue, the teacher-of-the-students and the students-of-the-teacher ceases to exist and a new term emerges: teacher-student with student-teacher. The teacher is no longer merely the-one-who-teaches, but one who is himself taught in a dialogue with the students, who in their turn while being taught also teach. They become jointly responsible for a process in which all grow. (Freire, 1972a: 46, 52)

In the second place, Gramsci's belief that political consciousness develops out of the personal experience of the need for change is very similar to what Freire calls 'conscientization' (the acquisiton of critical consciousness) which enables individuals 'to take action against the oppressive elements of reality'. Freire writes, for example:

> The starting point for organizing the programme content of education or political action must be the present, existential, concrete situation, reflecting the aspirations of the people. Utilizing certain basic contradictions, we must pose this existential, concrete, present situation to the people as a problem which challenges them and requires a response – not just at the intellectual level, but at the level of action. . . . It is not our role to speak to the people about our own view of the world, nor to attempt to impose that view on them, but rather to dialogue with the people about their view and

ours. We must realise that their view of the world, manifested variously in their action, reflects their situation in the world. (Freire, 1972a: 68)[5]

Up to this point, this chapter has concentrated on how the principles of individuality and communality, of continuity between intellectual and democratic, and between school and work skills, and of the need for self-discipline, can be developed through the early and intermediate stages of education. It is now necessary to discuss how these skills provide a foundation for the development of full political consciousness and for participation in the democratic institutions of political practice. Although Gramsci emphasises that every individual has the *potential* to engage in these latter types of activity, he none the less recognises that some individuals will take on *the particular task* of organising and leading the new historical bloc. We have already seen for example, that some individuals take on the particular role of educators in the common school and the training colleges or universities. Similarly, and in the same way that industrial development creates a need for new skills, so too does the development of political society. The development of an alternative hegemony, in other words, poses new problems which, in the first place at least, require a concentration of political and ideational effort. For Gramsci, the individuals who play a leading role in this process are the intellectuals.

The intellectuals

Generally speaking, the notion of the intellectual is of a person who develops and communicates ideas and theoretical constructs based upon the careful study of a particular aspect of the social universe. In Miliband's words: 'Intellectuals is here used in a fairly loose sense to denote the people who are mainly concerned with the formation, articulation and dissemination of ideas – theorists, publicists, academics and the like' (Miliband, 1982: 87). Because this type of occupation entails a relatively high proportion of cognitive, mental or 'intellectual' activity, as opposed to instinctual, manual or emotional activity, the notion of the intellectual tends to imply a sense of superiority, a more highly developed sense of rationality and deeper knowledge of the world, and possibly of more 'advanced' cultural tastes. This definition therefore derives from generalisations made on the basis of the *specific attributes* of the occupation itself; the relatively high proportion of thought-based over action-based activity. If an individual is engaged in these kinds of activity, then, by definition, he or she must be an intellectual since non-intellectuals are largely unable to perform these activities. For Gramsci, however, in trying to answer the question 'Are intellectuals an autonomous and independent social group, or does every social group have its own particular specialised category of intellectuals?', and, further, 'What are the "maximum" limits of acceptance of the term "intellectual"?' (*SPN*, pp.5, 8), this simplistic definition is based upon a fundamental misconception of the criterion upon which such a definition should be based:

> The most widespread error of method seems to me that of having looked for this criterion of distinction in the intrinsic nature of intellectual activities, rather than in the ensemble of the system of relations in which these activities (and therefore the intellectual groups who personify them) have their place within the general complex of social relations. (*SPN*, p.8)

For Gramsci, in other words, the categorisation of a particular task or individual as 'intellectual' should not be based on the fact that some activities are intrinsically more cognitive than others, but rather on the basis of the *relative function* they perform within social practice. Since in every activity 'even the most degraded and mechanical, there exists a minimum of technical qualification, that is, a minimum of creative intellectual activity . . . *All men are intellectuals*, but not all men have in society *the function* of intellectuals' (*SPN*, pp.8, 9, emphasis added).

Having made the point that all activities require a certain amount of creative intellectual effort, Gramsci goes on to give a number of examples of the different functions which particular individuals may perform 'within the general context of social relations'. He discusses 'the industrial technician' who keeps the production process going, 'the specialist in political economy' who plans the broader context and priorities of production, and 'the organisers of a new culture, of a new legal system etc.,' who create the structural and superstructural institutions of society (*SPN*, p.5). If these occupations are placed along a continuum, we can say that, *in terms of their social function*, the individuals who perform the latter occupations have a *more intellectual* function or role than the former, although each of these occupations necessarily involves intellectual capacity.

Having settled the question of definition, Gramsci extends this analysis to look at how and why different occupational groups and their intellectual 'strata' come into being. As his examples show, Gramsci argues that, initially, it is developments within the economic structure which generate the need for intellectuals:

> Every social group, coming into existence on the original terrain of an essential function in the world of economic production, creates together with itself, organically, one or more strata of intellectuals which give it homogeneity and an awareness of its own function not only in the economic but also in the social and political fields. (*SPN*, p.5)

In capitalist society, for example, the entrepreneur can be categorised as an intellectual since he or she 'must have a certain creative and technical (i.e. intellectual) capacity'. Most importantly, however, and having become qualified in the technical sense to take part in the productive process, these individuals also play a role at 'a higher level of social elaboration'. The entrepreneur, in other words, must also be 'an organiser of masses of men; he must be an organiser of the "confidence" of investors in his business, of the customers for his product etc.' (*SPN*, p.5). Although this wider organisational function relates particularly to spheres of activity 'which are closest to economic production', Gramsci implies that they may also take a leading role in the political and cultural spheres. In contemporary society, for example, 'the captains of industry' very often become involved in professional organisations which, to use Showstack Sassoon's phrase, express economic questions 'politically'. Similarly, workers may become trade-union representatives and elected members of the legislature. A key feature of these types of intellectuals is that they go hand in hand with the forward development of productive practices. They do not come into being of their own accord (since they would be function*less*) but are *organically* created by these practices. So, for example, capitalism creates a need for entrepreneurs and other 'experts in political economy' to establish and maintain the complex system of economic exchange upon which it is based. In turn, it also creates a demand for many other individuals to maintain institutions which are necessary for its wider organisation and control of society, and to perform more diverse intellectual-political and intellectual-cultural functions:

> If not all entrepreneurs, at least an *élite* amongst them must have the capacity to be an organiser of society in general, including all its complex

organism of services, right up to the state organism, because of the need to create the conditions most favourable to the expansion of their own class. (*SPN*, p.5)[6]

Having argued that social development stimulates the need for intellectuals, the question then arises of what happens to these individuals as further development takes place. Similarly, because social development is a dynamic process, each emergent social group and its own intellectual strata have found 'categories of intellectuals already in existence which seemed indeed to represent an historical continuity uninterrupted even by the most complicated and radical changes in political and social forms' (*SPN* pp.6–7). Following the definition of intellectuals in terms of their functions, Gramsci suggests that organic intellectuals do not disappear but take on new functions. He calls this category the 'traditional intellectuals' who, although originating in response to previous economic and social developments, see themselves in the context of 'their uninterrupted historical continuity and their special qualification [as] autonomous and independent of the dominant social group ... endowed with a character of their own' (*SPN*, pp.7–8). Traditional intellectuals, in other words, see themselves, and are seen by others, as largely 'independent' of the contemporary dominant group. The activities or functions they perform are judged to be of *mutual* benefit to all social groups, and are in principle carried out with a high degree of *impartiality* and neutrality.

As an example of the process by which organic intellectuals are displaced and subsequently take on the functions of traditional intellectuals, Gramsci discusses the ecclesiastics 'who for a long time held a monopoly of a number of important services: religious ideology, that is the philosophy and science of the age, together with schools, education, morality, justice, charity, good works etc.'. As society became more and more developed, this group was displaced as the central power of the absolutist monarchs generated a new stratum of organic intellectuals: 'Thus we find the formation of the *noblesse de robe*, with its own privileges, a stratum of administrators, etc., scholars and scientists, theorists, non-ecclesiastical philosophers, etc.' (*SPN*, p.7). In broad terms, the residue of the organic intellectuals of one historical period (or, more precisely, of an earlier form of the organisation of economic practices) form the basis of the traditional intellectuals of the subsequent society. So, for example, teachers and academics, judges and lawyers, and some practitioners of 'high culture' and 'the arts' can be seen as fulfilling the role of the traditional intellectuals. In contemporary society, this group can be contrasted to organic intellectuals involved, for example, in research into artificial intelligence, genetic engineering and bio-technology.

To summarise, Gramsci believes that every social activity requires a balance of conception and execution: '*homo faber* cannot be separated from *homo sapiens*' (*SPN*, p.9). It is not therefore legitimate to distinguish between different activities solely on the basis of 'the relationship between efforts of intellectual-cerebral elaboration and muscular-nervous effort'. For this reason, Gramsci therefore emphasises that:

> Each man, outside his professional activity, carries on some form of intellectual activity, that is, he is a 'philosopher', an artist, a man of taste, he participates in a particular conception of the world, has a conscious line of moral conduct and therefore contributes to sustain a conception of the world or to modify it, that is, to bring into being new modes of thought. (*SPN*, p.9)

Since all activities take place in the context of social practices more generally (only very few activities are entirely arbitrary), it is the precise nature or 'function' of a particular activity which allows us to describe a particular activity or individual as being intellectual. The continuous development or 'elaboration' of new organic intellectuals is brought about by the development of economic practices which constantly generates new 'specialisations'. In the first instance, these new tasks are concerned with the direct maintenance of the current economic system, and a stratum of economic-corporate intellectuals is established in accordance with these needs. Subsequently, and once the immediate 'technical functions' have been met, a second stratum of intellectuals emerges which is concerned with the intellectual-political dimensions of social control. That is to say, with maintaining a particular political and cultural milieu which is conducive to the means of production itself.[7] As productive technologies continue to develop, and as the political and cultural environment changes its character, a process of what can be called 'intellectual regeneration' takes place as these strata of organic intellectuals are displaced in terms of authority, power and leadership from central to increasingly peripheral positions. These former organic intellectuals are then assimilated into the stratum of traditional intellectuals, where they continue to perform useful functions in an apparently impartial or neutral way.

Gramsci's analysis of the origins and functions of the intellectuals is very useful as a means of making distinctions between the broad categories of the organic and the traditional. Clearly, however, the ever-changing nature of society means that broad distinctions are not entirely appropriate. Since Gramsci sees the intellectuals as playing an important part in constructing an alternative hegemony and in leading and organising revolutionary practice, it is necessary to consider some of the more ambiguous characteristics of the intellectuals.

Discussion

First then, in referring to 'one or more strata of intellectuals', Gramsci recognises that other categories can be distinguished both within and between the organic and traditional categories defined above. Some intellectuals, in other words, *perform more than one function*. It has already been noted, for example, that in addition to their instrumental role in industry, the entrepreneurs provide an élite who 'must have the capacity to be an organiser of society in general'. Although, therefore, the elaboration of intellectuals in response to the demands of production creates *an initial sense of parity* between intellectuals, some intellectuals *are more influential than others*. Further, this élite group will take responsibility for delegating its authority: 'They must possess the capacity to choose the deputies (specialised employees) to whom to entrust this activity of organising the general system of relationships external to the business itself' (*SPN*, p.6). This suggests the formation of an *intermediate* category of intellectual functionaries who will be responsible for this process of delegation. Significantly, individuals who carry out these tasks acquire their authority from the élite group. Gramsci compares the function of these 'intellectuals of the urban type' to that of 'subaltern officers' in the army:

> They have no autonomous initiative in elaborating plans for construction. Their job is to articulate the relationship between the entrepreneur and the instrumental mass and to carry out the immediate execution of the production plan decided by the industrial general staff, controlling the elementary stages of work. (*SPN*, p.14)

In analysing the origins and functions of the *organic* intellectuals, we can therefore say that a distinction should be made between those categories which arise *directly* as a result of the specific or 'technical' requirements of the economic structure, and those which arise in response to its *secondary* requirements. The hierarchy of intellectuals therefore extends beyond production itself (economic-corporate functions), through a series of intermediate groups (distributional and administrative intellectuals), and into the realm of more diffuse political-cultural and intellectual-moral functions. In Gramsci's words: 'The democratic-bureaucratic system has given rise to a great mass of functions which are not all justified by the social necessities of production, though they are justified by the political necessities of the dominant fundamental group' (*SPN*, p.13). This distinction is important as it emphasises that the authority of the political and cultural intellectuals (both organic and traditional), and the apparent legitimacy of what they say, derives from their association with the controllers of the economic system; their authority is therefore *derivative* rather than *autonomous*. To this extent, both the ways in which particular issues are constructed and discussed, and their actual content and substance are likely to be framed within the agenda of the dominant group. The political, intellectual and cultural character of a particular society should not therefore be seen as 'above' or 'outside' the less glamorous world of production, but as a necessary extension of it.

Another important group of intellectuals is made up of occupations which *anticipate* future developments. The dominant group might, for example, decide to employ a number of intellectuals to counter potential threats to the existing hegemony, even if these threats have not yet materialised. Once in place, the dominant group can then protect itself by mobilising 'the apparatus of state coercive power which "legally" enforces discipline on those groups who do not "consent" either actively or passively' (*SPN*, p.12). This category of intellectuals would, for example, include the leaders of the armed forces, the police and the intelligence-gathering agencies of the State. Since this category is at least partly formed *in advance* of the circumstances in which it might become active, these intellectuals could be considered to be both organic and traditional at one and the same time. As organic intellectuals, they function on the basis of perceived present and future threats to the hegemony and social control of the dominant group. As traditional intellectuals, they constitute a residue of past experiences of opposition and conflict. Although, therefore, these intellectuals are organically produced by actual historical circumstances, the activities they are engaged in may become a *permanent feature* of social control. Furthermore, in discussing the loyalties of the army in times of political crisis, for example, Gramsci suggests that since 'the army's duty is to defend the Constitution – in other words the legal form of the State together with its related institutions [their] so-called neutrality only means support for the reactionary side' (*SPN*, p.212).

Turning to the origins and functions of traditional intellectuals a number of further points should be made regarding their apparent 'neutrality'. First, it should be emphasised that traditional intellectuals are not accepted as being economically and politically neutral as it were automatically, but that they have *actively to create* this appearance. As noted above, these intellectuals justify their image as 'autonomous and independent of the dominant group' on the basis that both they and the institutions and practices through which they express themselves 'represent an historical continuity uninterrupted even by the most complicated and radical changes'. This 'historical continuity' has both a material and an ideational form. In the case of the former, it should be emphasised that the considerable influence exercised by the political and cultural institutions including the democratic, legal and education systems in particular, often directly support the interests of the dominant group. To the extent that the traditional intellectuals help maintain these institutions, their neutrality may be more apparent than real. Similarly, in the ideational field, the dominant group will try to present these institutions as being in some way part of the inevitable fabric of society. In order to do this, it will enlist the support of a number of traditional intellectuals to create the impression that its own world-view is similarly 'natural' or inevitable. Among other things, this process of hegemonic maintenance will be articulated through general appeals to social norms, values and ideals. In contemporary society, for example, intellectual élites in the USA have presented the virtues of 'the freedom of the individual', of 'the right to individual development' and of the importance of 'national identity' as inalienable features of the 'American Way'. In Britain, similar 'universal' concerns relating to individual self-determination, 'freedom of choice' and 'self-reliance' have been presented in terms of 'national sovereignty'. By co-opting these universal values into their own world-view and in presenting themselves as the protectors or guardians of these 'rights', the dominant group is able to present alternative views as largely heretical, and the individuals who put them forward as the 'enemies of freedom'. In a slightly different context, Richard Hyman has argued that claims regarding 'the national interest' may also fall into this category:

> 'The national interest' is the type of abstract idea which orients people's thinking in a particular direction. In this case, people are led to view the interests of a particular social group as common to the whole society – even though a fundamental conflict of interests may exist. Such powerful abstractions are a modern parallel to the fetish-objects worshipped by 'primitive' peoples. (Hyman, 1984: 155)

Although there may be nothing intrinsically wrong with the ideals themselves, and although they may be presented as constituting an accumulation of non-partisan values and beliefs about the nature of society, *the particular historical manifestation of them* will invariably be subsumed by the dominant group as one way of protecting its hegemonic control over society. Since these discourses are often conducted through the agency of traditional intellectuals, at least some categories of traditional intellectuals, and therefore of the institutions which their activities support, should more properly be described as reactionary rather than neutral.

The second point which should be made with regard to the traditional intellectuals, is that some categories *may reproduce themselves* without passing through an organic stage at all. Many traditional intellectuals for example, perform intellectual functions within the various bureaucracies of the State. Since their personal careers, status and income are dependent upon the continued existence of the bureaucracy which employs them, these individuals have a vested interest in the preservation of the State in its current form. Similarly, it is likely that they will see other similar institutional practices and their intellectual personnel as equally legitimate and subsequently develop the kind of reactionary *'esprit de corps'* to which Gramsci refers. Since new recruits are likely to adopt a similar attitude to that of their senior colleagues, it can be suggested that some occupations may generate *new* 'traditional' intellectuals without the need to wait for the temporal absorption of organic intellectuals. Gramsci suggests, for example, that:

One of the characteristics of the [traditional] intellectuals as a crystallised social group (one that is, which sees itself as continuing uninterruptedly through history and thus independent of [the class struggle] . . . is precisely that of connecting itself, in the ideological sphere, with a preceding intellectual category by means of a common conceptual nomenclature. . . . If the 'new' intellectuals put themselves forward as the direct continuation of the previous 'intelligentsia', they are not new at all (that is, not tied to the new social group which organically represents the new historical situation) but are a conservative and fossilised left-over of the social group which has been superseded. (*SPN*, pp.452–3)

In the legal profession, for example, great reliance is placed upon continuity of practice based upon case law and legal precedent. Changing economic and political circumstances may bring about the organic development of new specialisations to take account of such changes but, on the whole, retrospective continuity aimed at the preservation of both the status quo and of personal status and prosperity is their main priority.

Third, Gramsci notes that the development of intellectual strata is by no means a free and universal characteristic of all social groups: 'The elaboration of intellectual strata in concrete reality does not take place on the terrain of abstract democracy but in accordance with very concrete traditional historical processes' (*SPN*, p.11). This does not mean that some social groups are inherently *unable* to develop their own intellectual 'leadership', but that some groups or classes develop intellectual strata *more easily than others*. Thus, Gramsci suggests that: 'Strata have grown up which traditionally "produce" intellectuals and these strata coincide with those which have specialised in "saving" i.e. the petty and the middle landed bourgeoisie and certain strata of the petty and middle urban bourgeoisie' (*SPN*, p.11). This implies that, partly as a result of the kinds of self-reproduction and preservation of material advantage discussed above, the most underprivileged groups in society tend to be at a disadvantage in terms of intellectual representation. Two factors might contribute to this relative disadvantage. In the first place, if an individual or group of individuals is largely preoccupied with the business of earning a living, then the time available for intellectual development and subsequently for participation in democratic practices will be more limited. In the second place, although these individuals may see society as divisive and inequitable, they may lack the necessary material resources to gain access to the means of expressing their criticisms. Paradoxically, it is precisely the personal experience of relative deprivation and injustice which constitutes the bedrock of oppositional consciousness. As Sartre suggests: 'If the intellectual wishes to understand the society in which he lives, he has only one course open to him and that is to adopt the point of view of its most underprivileged members' (Sartre, 1974: 255).

Having discussed a number of characteristics of the various strata of intellectuals, and having emphasised their relations with, and support for, the dominant group, it should be clear that one of the tasks of the organic intellectuals of the emergent group is to challenge the authority and legitimacy of the current strata of intellectuals. Indeed, in the intellectual and cultural spheres in particular, this process of challenge and critique is part and parcel of the business of building an alternative hegemony. It will be useful to list briefly a number of different tasks involved in this process.

First, Gramsci's analysis provides a useful means of establishing the *reliability* of working-class intellectuals (to ensure in other words that they don't impose their own views or 'tower above'), and to distinguish the *relative importance* of various intellectual functions:

> It should be possible both to measure the 'organic quality' (*organicita*) of the various intellectual strata and their degree of connection with a fundamental social group, and to establish a gradation of their functions and of the superstructures from the bottom to the top (from the structural base upwards). (*SPN*, p.12)

Further, after the revolution, this type of scrutiny can be applied to decide whether a particular occupation is still required. If, for example, large segments of the intermediate managerial and bureaucratic strata can be shown to be a *particular* requirement of *capitalistic* relations of production, serving purely second-order administrative functions, then the future reorganisation of work may render them functionless and thus dispensable.[8]

Second, with regard to the problem of penetrating the inversions of bourgeois hegemony, the intellectuals should help individuals both to *demystify* this hegemony and to construct new forms of discourse through which effective opposition and critical expression can be achieved. It may be necessary, in other words, to create new agendas for political discussion and to raise issues which the intellectuals of the dominant group choose to avoid.[9]

Third, with regard to the problems of achieving the *prior formation* of a new historical bloc, the intellectuals will be required to act as negotiators and arbitrators to convey from one group to another a clear understanding of their common interests. They will also be instrumental in anticipating the kinds of divisionary tactics which the displaced group may try to use in its defence.

Fourth, in terms of developing *appropriate forms of revolutionary practice*, the intellectuals will have to provide organisation and leadership to ensure that the chosen strategy remains relevant to changing circumstances. This may include striking the correct balance between reformism and adventurism, that is, to help individuals to distinguish actively between 'conjunctural' (i.e. temporary and partial) and 'organic' (i.e. permanent and fundamental) forms of critical expression.

Finally, the intellectuals will play a central role in articulating the particular form and characteristics of the new hegemony. This will require a great deal of objective analysis and creativity to understand which aspects of present social practices should be sustained and developed, and which should be allowed to 'wither away'. This is perhaps the most crucial sphere of intellectual activity since the emergence of a sustainable future society will be directly dependent upon the practicality of its programme.

Summary

This chapter has discussed the problem of how individuals reach an understanding of their circumstances, and of how the ability to develop this understanding coincides with the development of skills which are necessary for active participation in both the economic and political institutions of society. Through the common school and other educative institutions, in other words, individuals will not only develop instrumental skills appropriate for modern industry, but also more general intellectual skills which will enable them to play a full and 'humanitarian' part in the democratic institutions of society. Because of the way society develops, different groups of individuals will be required to take on particular tasks. Gramsci suggests that although all tasks require a degree of intellectual and creative ability, some individuals will be required to perform tasks or functions which are overtly intellectual. In the first instance, these occupations are associated with the particular technical requirements of the economic system. Subsequently, they may be associated with the more general administrative and organisational institutions which synchronise the activities of the economy with those of society as a whole. In the political sphere, each social group or class (which is itself brought into being by the particular way in which economic practices are organised) generates a need for intellectuals who both represent the interests of that class and develop its ideational understanding of the world.

In order to differentiate between different types of intellectuals, Gramsci distinguishes between organic intellectuals who emerge in response to particular historical developments, and traditional intellectuals whose 'organic' role is transcended as society enters a new stage of development. Although they have been displaced from their original functions, traditional intellectuals are tolerated since, superficially at least, they are seen as playing an independent and impartial role in maintaining the institutions of society. Since, however, social development is an ongoing process, and since some intellectuals play an ambiguous role, there are subdivisions within these broad categories. In particular, not all groups of intellectuals are equally powerful; some take on the function of delegating tasks to others while a further group may be regarded as both 'organic' and 'traditional' at one and the same time. Similarly, because the traditional intellectuals often play an important role in maintaining the hegemony of the dominant group, there is some doubt as to their actual neutrality or impartiality.

Having considered how individuals acquire the basic skills necessary for social participation, and having looked at why some individuals take on particularly intellectual functions, the question now arises as to how these rudimentary or latent forms of consciousness can develop into the kind of mature intellectual-political consciousness discussed in the previous chapter. This process is inevitably bound up with the development of organisations through which members of the emergent social group can express their hegemonic aspirations. Gramsci's suggestions for political participation are discussed in the following chapter.

Notes

1. Elsewhere Gramsci refers to hegemony specifically in terms of education. He writes:

Every relationship of 'hegemony' is necessarily an educational relationship and occurs not only within a nation, between the various forces of which the nation is composed, but in the international and world-wide field, between complexes of national and continental civilisations. (*SPN*, p.350)

2. As Hoare and Nowell Smith point out, Gramsci is directing some of his comments towards Mussolini's education reforms of 1923 (see *SPN*, p.24). It is clear, however, that Gramsci had already developed his own ideas about the appropriate form of working-class education. In an article for *Avanti!* in December 1916, under the heading 'Socialists and Education' he writes:

> What the proletariat needs is an educational system that is open to all. A system in which the child is allowed to develop and mature and acquire those general features that serve to develop character. In a word, a humanistic school, as conceived by the ancients, and more recently by men of the Renaissance. A school which does not mortgage the child's future, a school that does not force the child's will, his intelligence and growing awareness to run along tracks to a predetermined station. A school of freedom and free initiative, not a school of slavery and mechanical precision. (*SPWI*, pp.26–7)

3. More specifically:

> Every social stratum has its own 'common sense' and its own 'good sense', which are basically the most widespread conception of life and of man ... Common sense is not something rigid and immobile, but is continually transforming itself, enriching itself with scientific ideas and with philosophical opinions which have entered ordinary life. 'Common sense' is the folklore of philosophy, and is always half-way between folklore properly speaking and the philosophy, science, and economics of the specialists. (*SPN*, p.326, note 5)

4. For further discussion on this topic see Karabel, 1976, and Hoffman, 1984, esp. ch.4. A more detailed account of Lenin's view is given in Chapter 4 above.

5. In addition to Freire (1972a), see also Freire (1974) and Freire (1972b). A useful commentary on Freire is given in Mackie (1980).

6. This 'organism of services' can be taken to include not only infrastructural services such as communications and transport, but also a legal system which acknowledges the legitimacy of private property, and a number of State bureaucracies for organising such things as taxation, welfare and health care.

7. This state of convivial equilibrium between the productive process and the society to which it gives rise is well described in Gwyn Williams' definition of hegemony:

By 'hegemony' Gramsci seems to mean a socio-political situation . . . in which the philosophy and practice of a society fuse or are in equilibrium; an order in which a certain way of life and thought is dominant, in which one concept of reality is diffused throughout society in all its institutional and private ramifications, informing with its spirit all taste, morality, customs, religious and political principles, and all social relations, particularly in the intellectual and moral connotation. (G. Williams, 1960: 587)

8. In a more radical vein, analysis might show that many of the criteria against which we measure our present concept of 'work' have become outdated and therefore inappropriate to future requirements. Persistently high levels of unemployment during the 1980s, for example, may indicate that 'formal paid employment' is no longer a reliable mechanism for the distribution of income.

9. Discussions of racial and gender discrimination, and of the true nature of the relationships between work and community, for instance, can be taken as examples of this process of agenda-change. More recently, environmentalists have created a new framework within which the 'local' consequences of industrial production can be seen in terms of their often highly destructive 'distant' effects.

8

Political participation: the council movement and the political party

As noted in Chapter 6, Gramsci suggests that emergent groups or classes can form an hegemonic historical bloc only if they transcend their particular economic-corporate concerns through the development of mature and universal intellectual-political consciousness. The previous chapter has discussed how the common school and other educational institutions can prepare individuals in general 'abstract' terms for this later 'cathartic' development. Clearly, however, actual social change will come about only if this potential for revolutionary consciousness is realised *in practice*. Throughout his life, both as a practising revolutionary and subsequently while in prison, Gramsci was centrally concerned with this problem. His writings on hegemony and historical blocs, on the relationship between structural and superstructural institutions, and on the different phases of revolutionary consciousness and strategy are all aimed at its solution. Unfortunately, however, Gramsci's analysis of the actual *organisations* through which political consciousness can be expressed is not entirely straightforward. Broadly speaking, it seems that up until 1921 Gramsci believed that the proletarian revolution should be primarily organised through the factory councils. With the collapse of the council movement following the September strike in 1920, however, he became convinced that a successful revolution could be conducted only with the help and leadership of a centralised *communist* party based on the Russian Bolshevik model. As Femia and others have pointed out,[1] Gramsci's successors, not least in Italy itself, have hotly debated the implications of this apparent change of mind. In the first place, much argument surrounds the question of the extent to which Gramsci's 'conversion' to Leninism did or did not signify an abandonment of the role of the factory councils. In the second place, while recognising that Gramsci certainly acknowledged the role of the Party, did he see this as being hierarchical, centralised and essentially authoritarian, or as being more diffusely democratic? For present purposes it is not necessary to go into these debates any further; it is, however, worth noting Davidson's suggestion that to some extent these problems are a result of a particular 'historical method' whereby both Gramsci's and Lenin's theory are viewed 'from the point of view of Marxist theory as a whole':

> In this enquiry the meaning of both theories is theoretically, but perhaps not practically, *outside them* and what is significant in their work is established not by *what they thought was significant*, nor by *what they directed most of their attention to*, but *by what our present revolutionary/practical understanding renders significant* in their work. This reading is an implicit reading in which our perspective renders visible what was latent. (Davidson, 1974: 142; original emphasis)

Whatever the final outcome of these debates, it is clear that Gramsci's analysis of appropriate forms of working-class organisation did pass through a number of stages, and that these developments corresponded to changes in the actual situation of the Italian working class. It is also reasonable to suggest that many of the themes of participatory education discussed in the previous chapter are evident throughout Gramsci's writings on political participation. In particular, the organic intellectuals of the working class are seen as playing a key role in the revolutionary process, however it is organised.

The factory councils

Prior to the foundation of *L'Ordine Nuovo* in 1919, Gramsci had pursued the idea that political education should be imparted through the traditional media of the press, lectures and seminars. To this end, in December 1917, Gramsci had formed the *Club di Vita Morale* through which he proposed:

To accustom young people in the socialist movement to dispassionate discussion about social and ethical problems. We want them to become used to research, to read in a methodological and disciplined fashion, to expound their convictions simply and with equanimity. (Gramsci to Giuseppe Lombardo-Radice, March 1919; Davidson 1974: 127)

During this period, and despite Bordiga's view that 'the need for study should be proclaimed in a congress of school-teachers, not socialists. You don't become a socialist through instruction but through experiencing the real needs of the class to which you belong' (Bordiga in *Avanguardia*, 20 October 1912; Davidson, 1974: 128), Gramsci clearly believed that the self-education of the working class was the necessary starting point for political consciousness. Gradually, however, and partly as a result of his increasing personal involvement with the Turinese proletariat, Gramsci began to turn away from 'cultural messianism' as the exclusive means to the revolutionary end, in favour of a more explicit analysis of the role that active participation in working-class organisations could play in providing individuals with the skills and outlook necessary for achieving a radical transformation of society. Significantly, however, and with regard to workplace organisation, Gramsci felt that the 'traditional' trade unions of the CGL no longer constituted a sufficiently revolutionary forum within which individuals could develop these skills and consciousness. As more information became available about the role of the soviets or workers' councils in the Bolshevik Revolution, Gramsci adopted the idea that the Italian working classes should organise soviets or factory councils of their own. In October 1919 he writes that:

> The Council is the most effective organ for mutual education and for developing the new social spirit that the proletariat has successfully engendered from the rich and living experience of the community of labour. Whereas in the union, workers' solidarity was developed in struggle against capitalism, in suffering and sacrifice, in the Council this solidarity is a positive, permanent entity that is embodied in even the most trivial moments of industrial production. It is a joyous awareness of being an organic whole, a homogeneous and compact system which, through useful work and the disinterested production of social wealth, asserts its sovereignty, and realises its power and its freedom to create history. (*SPWI*, pp.100–1)

As this quotation implies, Gramsci's view of the factory councils reflects a number of the themes outlined in the previous chapter. In the first place, participation in the factory councils stimulates a sense of continuity between organising a particular aspect of production and organising society more generally:

> Everyone is indispensable, everyone is at his post, and everyone has a function and a post. Even the most ignorant and backward workers, even the most vain and 'civil' of engineers, will eventually convince himself of this truth in the experience of factory organization.

In the second place, experience of the factory council should generate a new consciousness or way of looking at the world based on experiences which are familiar to them. It should, in other words,

> effect a radical transformation of the worker's mentality, should make the masses better equipped to exercise power, and finally should diffuse a consciousness of the rights and obligations of comrade and worker that is both concrete and effective, because spontaneously generated from living historical experience. (*SPWI* p.68)

Third, since the councils nurture a universal rather than economic-corporate view of society, the councils themselves provide a practical example of how the future society will operate. The councils are, in other words, not only necessary in order to instigate the revolution, but *subsequently* their organisation will provide a model for the future State:

> The Factory Council is the model of the proletarian State. All the problems inherent in the organisation of the proletarian State are inherent in the organisation of the Council . . . . Factory organization will bind the class (the whole class) into a homogeneous and cohesive unit corresponding perfectly to the industrial process of production and controlling it by taking it over once and for all. In other words, organization based on the factory embodies the proletarian dictatorship, the communist State, that destroys class domination in the political superstructures and throughout its entire fabric. (*SPWI*, pp.100, 102)

Finally, a key feature of the factory councils and consequently of the kind of society to which they will give rise, is the fact that they are both highly organised and fundamentally democratic:

> The socialist State already exists potentially in the institutions of social life characteristic of the exploited working class. To link these institutions, co-ordinating and ordering them into a highly centralized hierarchy of

competences and powers, while respecting the necessary autonomy and articulation of each, is to create a genuine workers' democracy here and now. (*SPWI*, p.65)

As noted above, Gramsci's proposals for the factory councils developed out of his critique of the trade unions as currently constituted. The councils, in other words, were not simply meant to modify the traditional unions, but rather to supplement and later replace them altogether.[2] As indicated in Chapter 3, this critique formed part of Gramsci's wider attack on the reformism of the other principal organisation of the working class, the Socialist Party. Before discussing Gramsci's views on the role of the political party in the second part of this chapter, it will be useful to consider the principal deficiencies he associated with what were effectively the pre-Leninist organisations of the Italian working class.

The discussion in previous chapters has shown that Gramsci assesses the current state of society on the basis of a detailed analysis of the configuration of economic practices by and through which it produces and re-produces itself. So, for example, in Chapter 7 it was noted that the foundation upon which an alternative hegemonic historical bloc can be formed must, in the first instance at least, be economic in character. It must take as its starting point the satisfactory transcendence of economic-corporate interests through the formation of a new and universal hegemony. Similarly, in the previous chapter it was shown that, for Gramsci, the necessary elaboration of organic intellectuals and the subsequent (partial) displacement of traditional intellectuals comes about as a direct consequence of the productive system for ever more diverse specialisations. Their development is therefore an unavoidable consequence of developments in productive technique. Following the same pattern of analysis, Gramsci's critique of the trade unions arises out of his assessment of how Italian capitalism had developed since the end of the First World War.

First, then, Gramsci argues that imperialism and the development of large monopolies have brought about profound changes in the character of capitalism: 'In the present period capitalism is characterised by the predominance of finance over industrial capital, of the bank over the factory, of stock exchange over the production of commodities, of monopoly over the traditional captain of industry' (*SPWI*, p.257). These monopolies have had the effect of stifling the competitive freedom which capitalism needs in order to survive. Once this has happened: 'The capitalist regime has reached deadlock. It loses all reason for its existence and progress; its institutions become rigid, parasitical encrustations, without useful role or prestige' (*SPWI*, p.69). Second, and as noted in Chapter 3, improvements in technology and changes in the organisation of work have created new groups of skilled and semi-skilled workers and new struggles within the economic structure:

> Four years of war have rapidly changed the economic and intellectual climate. Vast work-forces have come into being, and a deeply-rooted violence in the relations between wage-earners and entrepreneurs has now appeared in such an overt form that it is obvious to even the dullest onlooker. (*SPWI* p.57)

Because of the increasingly specialised nature of industrial production, the potential power and influence of the proletariat have therefore increased: 'Capitalist concentration has reached its maximum possible level, with the achievement of a global monopoly of production and exchange. The corresponding concentration of the working masses has given the revolutionary proletarian class an unprecedented power' (*SPWI*, p.77). Since capitalism is a world system, Italian capitalism is necessarily affected by this process of change and crisis: 'This dependence of national affairs on external laws, that came into play suddenly and in an unpredictable and uncontrollable fashion, places Italian society in the same position as a collection of animals cowering before an earthquake' (*SPWI* p.71). Most significantly, Gramsci believed that the crisis of capitalism could be resolved only by the working class:

> Only the working class can save society from plunging into the abyss of barbarism and economic ruin towards which the enraged and maddened forces of the propertied class are driving it. It can do this by organizing itself as the ruling class, to impose its own dictatorship in the politico-industrial field. (*SPWI*, p.89)

By 1919, however, although Gramsci felt, as noted above, that 'the socialist State already exists potentially in the institutions of social life characteristic of the exploited working class', and although he believed that the influence of the trade unions and the Socialist Party 'grows daily, spreading to previously unexplored popular strata', he nevertheless argued that: 'The traditional institutions of the movement have become incapable of containing such a flowering of revolutionary activity. Their very structure is inadequate to the task of disciplining the forces which have become part of the conscious historical process' (*SPWI*, p.77).

During 1919 and 1920 much of Gramsci's writing is concerned with these structural deficiencies and with how they can be overcome by the factory councils. In the first place, Gramsci argued that although the trade unions had always maintained the overall aim of 'eliminating the capitalist', they had been drawn into the 'competitive' ethos of capitalism at a particular stage in its development and had lost sight of their original aim. They had, in other words, 'directed all their energies to the immediate [aim] of improving the proletariat's living conditions, demanding higher wages, shorter hours of work and a body of social legislation'. However, once the trade unions had in effect limited their practical aims in this way, and once capitalism had moved into its monopoly stage, they had ceased to be a revolutionary force:

> Thus trade union action, within its own sphere and using its own methods, stands revealed as being utterly incapable of overthrowing capitalist society; it stands revealed as being incapable of leading the proletariat to its emancipation, of leading it to accomplish the lofty and universal goal it had itself initially proposed. (*SPWI*, p.105)

This situation was made worse as the urban and industrial workforces began to expand and as a new class consciousness developed. As noted in Chapter 3, Gramsci argued that these new groups lost confidence in the traditional unions who tended to represent the interests of the skilled workers or 'labour aristocracy' rather than the much larger groups of unskilled workers:

> The workers feel that 'their' organization has become such an enormously complex apparatus, that it has ended up obeying only laws of its own, inherent in its structure and complicated functioning, but alien to the masses who have acquired a consciousness of their historical mission as a revolutionary class. (*SPWI*, p.98)

In the second place, Gramsci argued that because the trade unions were originally formed on the basis of particular skills, they tended to perpetuate a number of divisions within and between different sections of the workforce. Consequently, workers were encouraged to see themselves as purveyors of a particular 'labour commodity' rather than as 'producers' in a much more general and universal sense:

The industrial or craft union, by combining the worker with his comrades in the same craft or industry, with men who use the same tools or transform the same material as himself, helps to foster this mentality, so that the worker is even less likely to see himself as a producer. He is led instead to consider himself as a 'commodity' whose price, whose value, is set by the free play of competition in a national and international market. (*SPWI*, p.110)

The main advantage of the factory councils was precisely that by organising the workers on a factory-wide basis they encouraged people to see themselves in universal terms as self-determining producers: 'In the factory council, the worker participates as a producer, i.e. as a consequence of his universal character and of his position and role in society' (*SPWI*, p.295).

Finally, Gramsci argued that because the trade unions had become so heavily integrated and thus dependent upon the present organisation of work, they were highly undemocratic and therefore structurally and intellectually unable to respond to new situations. Consequently, the initiative remained with the capitalist while, through its own organisations and 'false' consciousness, the leadership and administrative hierarchy of the trade unions tended to perpetuate a fatalistic and somewhat submissive acceptance of the status quo:

> The selection of trade-union leaders has never been made on the basis of industrial competence, but rather simply on the basis of juridical, bureaucratic and demagogic competence. . . . Thus a veritable caste of trade-union officials and journalists came into existence, with a group psychology of their own absolutely at odds with that of the workers. (*SPWI*, p.105)[3]

In sum, it is clear that Gramsci felt that, through participation in the factory councils, individuals could overcome the instrumentality and self-centredness of economic-corporate 'trade-union consciousness' and move towards the sympathetic perspective of intellectual-political consciousness discussed above. First, since the councils were not bourgeois institutions they did not suffer from the inherent structural and intellectual limitations of the trade unions. Second, because their structures and organisation were essentially organic rather than static, the factory councils would be able to respond much more quickly to the changing needs of those they represented. Third, in nurturing a strong sense of continuity between the roles of worker and social subject, the councils constituted a way of transcending both the synthetic separation of economic and political institutions, and the conceptual separation of thought and action. Finally, the factory councils would provide an ideal environment within which the working class could develop new organic intellectuals who had first-hand experience of economic production and of political leadership and organisation.

Having looked at Gramsci's suggestions as to how the factory councils can make up for the deficiencies of the trade unions, it is now necessary to consider his views on the second principal representative organisation of the working-class, the political party.

The political party

In the same way that Gramsci's views on workplace representation developed in response to changes in the composition and circumstances of the Italian working class, his views on the political party also passed through a number of stages. Broadly speaking, it is possible to distinguish four main stages: (i) Gramsci and the PSI in 1919; (ii) the need for renewal in 1920; (iii) the Communist Party after 1921; and (iv) the Party in the *Prison Notebooks*. The following discussion will outline each of these stages in turn.

(i) Gramsci and the PSI in 1919
As noted above, during 1919 Gramsci was primarily concerned with organising the factory councils as an eventual replacement for the trade unions. Since the development and characteristics of the PSI were closely related to these organisations, it was inevitable that Gramsci's critique of the PSI shared many of the features discussed above. So, for example, as Femia points out, he believed that the socialist parties 'were ineradicably tainted by their origins in capitalist society and by their tendency to function in accordance with its logic' (Femia, 1981: 142). In July 1919 Gramsci writes that:

> The socialists have simply accepted, and frequently in a supine fashion, the historical reality produced by capitalist initiative. They have acquired the same mistaken mentality as the liberal economists: they believe in the perpetuity and fundamental perfection of the institutions of the democratic State. (*SPWI*, p.76)

At the same time, however, and although the factory councils are given priority, Gramsci at least implies that the PSI can still play an important role in co-ordinating and consolidating the growing spontaneity of the working classes. He writes, for example, that 'These disorderly and chaotic energies must be given a permanent form and discipline. They must be absorbed, organized and strengthened' (*SPWI*, p.66). And again four months later, in November 1919, that: 'The immediate, concrete problem confronting the Socialist Party is the problem of power; the problem of how to organize the whole mass of Italian workers into a hierarchy that reaches its apex in the Party' (*SPWI*, p.133). He even goes so far as to make favourable comparisons between the reformism of the trade unions and the revolutionary potential of the PSI: 'The character of the Socialist Parties is becoming increasingly revolutionary and internationalist; the trade unions, on the other hand are increasingly embodying the theory(!) and tactics of reformist opportunism and becoming merely national bodies' (*SPWI*, p.104).

By the end of 1919 and into 1920, however, Gramsci's attitude towards the PSI and especially towards the relationship between the PSI and the factory councils becomes more ambiguous. He suggests that although 'the vanguard workers and peasants . . . have pointed to the Socialist Party, which represents the ideas and programmes to be accomplished, as their natural political leader', they have also pointed out that 'the road to power' should be based 'not on a Parliament elected by universal suffrage encompassing both exploited and exploiters, but on a system of workers' and peasants' Councils embodying the rule of industrial as well as of political power' (*SPWI*, p.133). Somewhat paradoxically, however, this acceptance of a necessary relationship between the councils, the trade unions and the PSI is referred to even more explicitly the following month. In discussing what he calls 'the network of institutions in which the revolutionary process is unfolding', he describes the Party and the unions in unusually positive terms:

> The trade unions and the Party, voluntary associations, driving forces of the revolutionary process, the 'agents' and 'administrators' of the revolution: the trade unions coordinating and impressing a communistic form on the industrial apparatus; the Socialist Party, the living and dynamic model of a social system that unites discipline with freedom and endows the human

spirit with all the energy and enthusiasm of which it is capable. (*SPWI*, p.146)

To some extent, this apparent ambiguity can be attributed to the fact that Gramsci was still developing his thoughts on the character and function of the political party. As Showstack Sassoon puts it, he was aware of the deficiencies of the PSI 'without being able at this stage of his development to have a clear idea of an alternative' (Showstack Sassoon, 1987: p.45). Although he soon decided that the alternative was to form a separate communist party, we can agree with Showstack Sassoon that, at this stage, Gramsci had made a distinction between the negative and positive functions of the political party.[4] In terms of its negative function, the PSI was at least partially successful to the extent that 'it has succeeded in stirring the masses down to their deepest levels; it has succeeded in focusing the attention of the working people on its programme for revolution and a workers' State'. In terms of its positive function, however, Gramsci clearly feels that the PSI has failed. In January he writes that:

> The Socialist Party has had no success so far as the essential aspect of its historical task is concerned. It has not succeeded in giving a permanent and solid form to the apparatus it had succeeded in building up by its agitation amongst the masses. (*SPWI*, p.154)

By early in 1920, therefore, Gramsci is arguing that the trade unions and the PSI had at least partially fulfilled the tasks for which they had originally been created, but that subsequent phases of the capitalist crisis had now brought about a situation which demanded new solutions. If they were to continue to meet their obligations to the working class, the trade unions and the PSI would have to change. If they failed to do this then they would have to be replaced by new and genuinely revolutionary organisations.

(ii) The need for renewal

As noted in Chapter 3, ever since Serrati had refused to expel Turati and the other reformists at the Bologna Conference in 1919, Gramsci and Bordiga had become increasingly impatient with the PSI. Initially, Gramsci argued that the PSI could be renewed by the 'communist workers' within its own ranks. These elements 'must renew the Party' giving it 'a precise form and a clear direction'. As the situation in Italy became more and more militant and as the need for co-ordination and leadership grew correspondingly more urgent, Gramsci's criticism of the PSI became directly hostile. By the end of January, in the first of two important articles on the subject of 'renewal' written in January and May 1920, he writes that:

> The necessary and sufficient conditions for the proletarian revolution are present on both the national and international levels. But at this crucial moment, the Socialist Party is not up to its task. A party of agitators, negotiators and intransigents in questions of general tactics, a party of apostles of elementary theories, it is incapable of organizing and mobilizing the broad masses into movement. (*SPWI*, p.156)

Throughout the spring of 1920, Gramsci's analysis of the role of the political party, and of the shortcomings of the PSI in particular, had become much more specific. In addition to the Party's role as an organiser of the proletarian masses he suggests, first, that the PSI must align itself much more fully with the Third International of the Comintern: 'The Socialist Party must be a section of the IIIrd International in earnest, and must start by carrying out the latter's programme within itself' (*SPWI*, p.157). Second, the PSI must stop acting as an 'openly reformist and opportunist' parliamentary group, and become instead a genuinely revolutionary party: 'The Party must acquire its own precise and distinct character. From a petty-bourgeois parliamentary party it must become the party of the revolutionary proletariat' (*SPWI*, p.194). Third, Gramsci begins to place greater emphasis upon the leadership role of the political party in general and of its vanguard in particular. Writing after the failure of the April strike in Turin, he suggests that the Party 'needs to be in a position to give real leadership to the movement as a whole and to impress upon the masses the conviction that there is an order within the terrible disorder of the present' (*SPWI*, p.192).

After the failure of the September strike and the rapid collapse of the council movement which followed, Gramsci completely abandons the idea that the PSI could be reformed from within. He argues that during the strike the PSI had effectively forfeited its capacity for leadership, and was therefore ineffectual at the decisive moment when guidance, discipline and organisation were most crucial:

> [The PSI] is exposed . . . to all the pressures of the masses. It shifts and alters its colours as the masses shift and alter their colours. In fact this

Socialist Party, which proclaims itself to be the guide and master of the masses, is nothing but a wretched clerk noting down the operations that the masses spontaneously carry out. This poor Socialist Party, which proclaims itself to be the head of the working class, is nothing but the baggage train of the proletarian army. (*SPWI*, pp.337–8)

From this point on Gramsci joins Bordiga in calling for the formation of an entirely separate Communist Party. Indeed, he begins to define the political party specifically in terms of the communist party: 'The Communist Party, representing the proletarians and the socialized and internationalized economy, is the model party of proletarian society' (*SPWI*, p.167). And again in 1921 that: 'The Communist Party is the historically determined political party of the revolutionary working class' (*SPWII*, p.32). Indeed, he goes so far as to suggest that the revolution in Italy can be brought about *only* with the help of a communist party:

> The existence of a cohesive and highly disciplined communist party with factory, trade-union and co-operative cells, that can co-ordinate and centralize in its executive committee the whole of the proletariat's revolutionary action, is the fundamental and indispensable condition for attempting any experiment with Soviets. (*SPWI*, p.195)

(iii) The Communist Party after 1921

Following the formation of the PCI in January 1921, Gramsci still had to resolve the question of the relationship between the factory councils, the trade unions and the Communist Party. As noted in Chapter 3, Gramsci argued that because the urban proletariat was the vanguard of the working class, the factory-based organisations should take precedence over the Party. Bordiga argued, on the other hand, that although the factory councils represented the *economic* interests of the working class, it was the task of the Party to represent its *political* interests. Having said this, though, Bordiga does make a distinction between the different phases of the revolution, and suggests that, once the political battle has been won, the economic institutions of the working class will play the leading role:

> The system of proletarian representation that has been introduced for the first time ever in Russia has a twofold character: political and economic. Its political role is to struggle against the bourgeoisie until the latter has been totally eradicated. Its economic role is to create the whole novel mechanism

of communist production. As the revolution unfolds and the parasitic classes are gradually eliminated, the political function become less and less important in comparison with their economic counterparts: but in the first instance, *and above all when it is a question of struggling against bourgeois power*, political activity must come first. . . . The authentic instrument of the proletariat's struggle for liberation, and above all of its conquest of political power, is the *communist class party*. (Bordiga, *Il Soviet*, 1 January 1920; *SPWI*, p. 214; original emphasis)

It could be suggested, therefore, that although Gramsci and Bordiga held different views of the role of the factory councils, and although Bordiga may not have appreciated that the factory councils were quite different from the trade unions, they did at least agree that factory-based organisations would be a key feature of the revolution. Indeed, by February 1921 Gramsci seems to see the factory councils and the Party as having a *combined* or *equal* rather than *separate* role. He writes that while the organisation of the 'revolutionary mass' can 'only be the Factory Councils and the nationally organized system of Factory Councils', this organisation is also 'an activity of the historic party of the working class, the Communist Party' (*SPWII*, p.11). Later the same month, Gramsci suggests that the factory councils 'must enable the [communist] party to graft itself directly onto a centralized organization of the working-class masses' (*SPWII*, p.13). He suggests, in other words, that the factory councils and the trade unions 'are one among the many forms of political organization characteristic of modern society', with whose 'consent and support' the Communist Party will be able to bring about 'the dictatorship of the proletariat and the foundation of the workers' State'. Most significantly, by April Gramsci suggests that: 'The party is *the higher organizational form*; the trade union and the factory council are *intermediary organizational forms*, in which the most conscious proletarians enrol for the daily struggle against capital' (*SPWII*, p.33; emphasis added). Broadly speaking, therefore, by 1921 Gramsci still sees the factory councils as an important aspect of working-class organisation especially in terms of gaining control of the economic institutions of society. At the same time, and in light of the fact that the political phase of the struggle has not yet been won, he becomes increasingly convinced of the need for a strong Communist Party.

In the 'Rome Theses' presented to the PCI at its Second Congress in March 1922, the form and function of the PCI is discussed in some detail. Although the Theses were largely drafted by Bordiga and Terracini, and although Gramsci subsequently criticised some aspects of the Party's programme because it tended to contradict the Comintern's new policy of forming a 'united front' with socialist parties and other groups, it is reasonable to assume that Gramsci held a similar view of the Party to that put forward in the Theses. First then, although strictly speaking the Communist Party is the party of 'the most advanced part of the proletarian class',[5] it none the less represents the interests of 'the entire working class' by incorporating them into 'an organism with a unitary action' and 'unitary approach'. This 'unitary collective organism' provides a forum within which individuals can express both their 'critical consciousness' and their 'will' to join forces with others in a 'disciplined and centralized organization'. Second, the aims or programme of the Party are derived from 'a thorough examination and study of the history of human society and its structure in the present capitalist epoch'. Similarly, 'the men to whom the various levels of the party organization are entrusted' are 'a product of the real process which accumulates elements of experience and carries out the preparation and selection of leaders'. The Party's aims and leadership, in other words, are derived from the organic development of critical consciousness and the formation of working-class intellectuals. Like the tactics of the Party, they are not 'dictated by theoretical preconceptions or by ethical and aesthetic preoccupations', imposed as it were 'from above'. If, however, the Party's programme deviates from this organic development, then 'a part of the party', its 'leading hierarchy' must take on the task of reconstituting the Party and of imposing a new 'consciousness and discipline'. Third, with regard to relations with other political parties and groups, although these cannot be 'assimilated *en bloc*', and although the Party must ensure that particular and 'partial' economic-corporate aims are never allowed to displace the overall aims of the revolution, the Party has a duty to create unity between all members of the working class by participating 'in the organizational life of all forms of the proletariat's economic organization open to workers of all political faiths (unions, factory councils, co-operatives, etc.)'. It does this by bringing the leaders of these groups 'into the ranks of the political [Communist] party'.

Many of these features of the role and structure of the PCI were later included in the fourth section of the 'Lyons Theses' drafted by Gramsci and Togliatti, which was accepted by a large majority at the

Third Congress of the PCI in January 1926. Regarding relations with other working-class groups, however, the 'Lyons Theses' stress the need for the proletariat to exercise practical leadership over both the rural proletariat and the southern peasantry:

> One may in general assert . . . that one will pass from the period of revolutionary preparation to an 'immediately' revolutionary period when the industrial and rural proletariat of the North has succeeded in regaining . . . a high level of organization and combativity. As for the peasantry, that of the South and the Islands must be included in the front line among the forces upon which the insurrection against the industrial/landowning dictatorship must rely, although one should not attribute to them decisive importance unless they are allied to the proletariat.[6]

Gramsci and Togliatti go on to emphasise that the Party is not so much 'an organ' or instrument of the working-class as an integral part of it. The Party should not therefore concentrate on producing 'cadres who can lead the masses' and make them accept 'fixed and programmatic positions', but rather it should strive 'to remain in contact with [the masses] through all changes in the objective situation . . . and provide a constant contact with the broadest layers of the working population'. In addition to the Central Committee, there must therefore be a democratically elected 'second element' of 'subordinate leading bodies' who ensure that the Party 'is not ruled from on high with autocratic methods', but that it corresponds 'to a real process of formation of a homogeneous proletarian vanguard linked to the masses'.

In terms of organisation, the 'Lyons Theses' reflect many of the principles of the council movement discussed in above: 'By locating the organizational basis in the place of production, the party performs an act of choice of the class on which it bases itself. It proclaims that it is a class party and the party of a single class, the working class.' In this way, the Party can overcome many of the structural and conceptual divisions associated with the 'traditional' institutions of the working class by establishing close contact 'between the upper and lower strata of the working masses (skilled workers, unskilled workers and labourers), and to create bonds of solidarity which eliminate the basis for any phenomenon of "labour aristocracy" '.

In sum, therefore, at the time of his arrest in 1926, Gramsci sees the PCI as the 'natural' political party and main representative of the working class. Because of the particular features of its development, different groups of the working class can be seen as lying along a continuum of political and organisational development. The most advanced and thus leading or 'vanguard' group is the urban proletariat, followed by the rural proletariat and the peasantry. By virtue of its greater experience and more advanced political-intellectual consciousness, the leading group is responsible for organising the other groups in such a way as to nurture solidarity and stimulate the further development of 'universal' critical consciousness. Because the Party has to be able to respond to changing circumstances, and because the business of analysing these circumstances requires a certain amount of theoretical and tactical judgement – including, for example, an assessment 'of the degree to which that society is ripe for a transformation from capitalism to socialism' (*SPWII*, p.388) – some individuals from within the urban proletariat will have to take on the role of leadership. This leadership will form the apex of a leadership hierarchy wherein other individuals will be responsible for transmitting the instructions of the Central Committee to the lower strata. Other individuals will take on a specifically educative and organisational role within the factory councils and other working-class institutions. Since members of the leading group have themselves originated from within the proletariat, and since they have been democratically elected, both the programme and administration of the Party are an organic reflection of the aims of the working class as a whole.

(iv) The party in the Prison Notebooks
It should be remembered that Gramsci's view of the political party discussed thus far developed in response not only to ongoing changes in the Italian situation, but also to changes in the relationship between the PCI and the Comintern. In contrast, and having been removed from day to day involvement in the revolutionary struggle, his comments on the political party in the *Prison Notebooks* are expressed in a more reflective and philosophical manner, and often emerge as part and parcel of his broader analysis of historical development. So, for example, Gramsci's concern with the wider dimensions and implications of political activity is clearly reflected in his view that the Communist Party, 'The Modern Prince',[7] is 'the first cell in which there come together germs of a collective will tending to become universal and total' (*SPN*, p.129). The Party, in other words, is seen as a catalyst or 'Jacobin' force which will awaken and unite the 'collective will' of the

population to form a new type of society.[8] Most significantly, the Party should not only be concerned with gaining power in the limited sense of taking control of the means of production, it must also devote itself 'to the question of intellectual and moral reform':

> The Modern Prince must be and cannot but be the proclaimer and organiser of an intellectual and moral reform, which also means creating the terrain for a subsequent development of the national-popular collective will towards the realisation of a superior, total form of modern civilisation. (*SPN*, pp. 132–3)

Having said this, the earlier themes of political organisation, leadership and discipline continue to play an important part in the *Notebooks*, and it will be useful to consider what turned out to be Gramsci's final comments on this subject.

In the first place, Gramsci continues to see the political party in terms of the 'convergence' of 'three fundamental elements':

> 1. A mass element, composed of ordinary, average men, whose participation takes the form of discipline and loyalty, rather than any creative spirit or organisational ability. . . . 2. The principal cohesive element, which centralises nationally and renders effective and powerful a complex of forces which left to themselves would count for little or nothing. This element is endowed with great cohesive, centralising and disciplinary powers [and] . . . with the power of innovation. . . . 3. An intermediate element, which articulates the first element with the second and maintains contact between them, not only physically but also morally and intellectually. (*SPN*, pp.152–3)[9]

The relative size of each stratum and the relations between them are not predetermined but, depending upon particular historical circumstances, vary 'according to the level of its culture, independence of mind, spirit of initiative and sense of responsibility, and according to the degree of discipline of its most backward and peripheral members' (*SPN*, p.191).[10]

In the second place, one of the principal activities of the party is to provide leadership; they have the task 'of forming capable leaders': 'They are the mass function which selects, develops, and multiplies the leaders which are necessary if a particular social group . . . is to become articulated, and be transformed from turbulent chaos into an organically prepared political army' (*SPN*, p.191). Indeed, Gramsci goes on to suggest that leaders can *only emerge* from within political parties:

> There cannot be any formation of leaders without the theoretical, doctrinal activity of parties, without a systematic attempt to discover and study the causes which govern the nature of the class represented and the way in which it has developed. (*SPN*, pp.227–8)

Because of the nature of its tasks, this leadership must be made up of a high proportion of intellectuals. As discussed in the previous chapter, Gramsci's notion of an intellectual derives from the need to perform particular functions. In the context of the political party, he sees the functions of organisation, leadership and therefore of theoretical analysis specifically in terms of intellectual activity:

> A human mass does not 'distinguish' itself, does not become independent in its own right without, in the widest sense, organising itself; and there is no organisation without intellectuals, that is without organisers and leaders, in other words without the theoretical aspect of the theory-practice nexus being distinguished concretely by the existence of a group of people 'specialised' in conceptual and philosophical elaboration of ideas. (*SPN*, p.334)

The party leadership, its 'intellectual General Staff' or 'intellectual *élite*' should not however become 'separated from the masses', but should always be conscious 'of being linked organically to a national-popular mass' (*SPN*, p.204). For Gramsci, it is the ability of the working class to generate *a particular kind* of technical and intellectual leadership which distinguishes it from all previous types of political organisation. The leaders of the working class are not leaders in the sense of being 'charismatic' or fanatical individuals supported by an unquestioning and obedient mass, but rather the *party itself* becomes a leader. This new type of 'leadership' is made possible precisely because the 'consent' or 'will' of the population is based upon the critical consciousness it has already developed or is in the process of developing for itself:

> Knowledge and judgement of the importance of this feeling on the part of leaders . . . is acquired by the collective organism through 'active conscious co-participation', through 'compassionality', through experience of immediate particulars, through a system which one could call 'living philology'. In this

way a close link is formed between great mass, party and leading group; and the whole complex, thus articulated, can move forward together as 'collective-man'. (*SPN*, p.429)

Finally, and continuing his emphasis upon the democratic nature of the party and its ability to respond to new circumstances, Gramsci makes a distinction between 'progressive' and 'regressive' political parties:

> When the party is progressive it functions 'democratically' (democratic centralism); when the party is regressive it functions 'bureaucratically' (bureaucratic centralism). The party in this second case is a simple, unthinking executor. It is then technically a policing organism, and its name of 'political party' is simply a metaphor of a mythological character. (*SPN*, p.155)[11]

This is an important distinction as Gramsci clearly wishes to emphasise that, as the representative of the most progressive forces in society, the Communist Party must always remain sensitive to its grass roots:

> 'Organicity' can only be found in democratic centralism, which is so to speak a 'centralism' in movement – i.e. a continual adaption of the organisation to the real movement, a matching of thrusts from below with orders from above, a continuous insertion of elements thrown up from the depths of the rank and file into the solid framework of the leadership apparatus which ensures continuity and the regular accumulation of experience. (*SPN*, pp.188–9)

Although many themes recur througout Gramsci's writings on the political party, and although these themes are intimately related to other topics, such as the development of political consciousness, the nature of hegemony and the appropriateness of different strategies, it is also clear that Gramsci's view of the Communist Party leaves a number of important points unresolved. In particular, and as noted at the start of this chapter, Gramsci can be read as recommending a somewhat disciplinarian and hierarchical form of political organisation. In conclusion, it will be useful to draw attention to a number of these ambiguities.

First, although Gramsci emphasises the democratic nature of the organisational hierarchy of the factory councils and the Communist

Party, he very often associates the need for organisation, co-ordination and leadership specifically with the need for discipline. At various times he writes, for example, that: 'the internal commissions . . . perform functions of arbitration and discipline' (*SPWI*, p.66); 'the working masses must take adequate measures to acquire complete self-government, and the first step along this road consists in disciplining themselves' (*SPWI*, p.95), and that the proletariat must achieve 'a homogeneous, cohesive party, with a doctrine and tactics of its own, and a rigid and implacable discipline' (*SPWI*, p.194). It is not entirely clear, however, either what the limits of this discipline are, and who is responsible for making sure that it is maintained, or how this discipline can be reconciled with the democratic functioning of the Party.

Second, and following on from this, although the Party's programme is seen as being derived in response to the historically-determined aspirations of the working class, these aspirations and the theoretical and tactical means of realising them are always interpreted within a particular ideological framework. In the 'Lyons Theses', for example, Gramsci writes that: 'The Communist Party needs *complete ideological unity* in order to be able at all moments to fulfil its function as leader of the working class. . . . *The basis of ideological unity is the doctrine of Marxism and Leninism*' (*SPWII*, p.358; emphasis added). To this extent, it would seem that the development of intellectual-political consciousness is more a matter of acquiring a *particular* way of looking at the world than of 'free development'. Similarly, the principle of discipline is sometimes used to limit the scope of discussion within the Party. In considering the relationship between the 'intellectually qualified' and the 'intellectually subordinate strata', for example, Gramsci recognises the problem of how to limit or define the acquisition of knowledge:

> It is a question, in other words, *of fixing the limits of freedom of discussion and propaganda*, a freedom which should not be conceived of in the administrative and police sense, but in the sense of self-limitation which the leaders impose on their own activities, or, more strictly, in the sense of fixing the direction of cultural policy. (*SPN*, p.341; emphasis added)

Further still, once this general direction has been fixed, the ideas and suggestions put forward still have to be scrutinised:

Nor is it inconceivable that individual initiatives should be disciplined and subject to an ordered procedure, so that they have to pass through the sieve of academics or cultural institutes of various kinds and only become public after undergoing a process of selection. (*SPN* p.341)

However sympathetically one looks at these problems, there is, in Femia's words: 'an underlying margin of ambiguity in his position on the boundaries of individual freedom, both within the present movement and in the post-revolutionary society' (Femia, 1981: 180).

A third important issue is the question of 'leadership'. As shown above, Gramsci feels that contact between the 'top stratum' of the leadership hierarchy and the intermediary and mass elements below is ensured by the fact that all agents of the Party are organically created from within the proletariat itself. Because these individuals are untainted by bourgeois ideology, their motives and actions are taken to be above reproach. Clearly, however, not all agents of the Party have personal and 'hands-on' experience of production, and even if they have, this does not guarantee their good will. Gramsci's polemic against the pre-Leninist organisations of the working class is a clear acknowledgement of this difficulty. With regard to the élitist overtones associated with leadership, Gramsci is quite specific that 'there really do exist rulers and ruled, leaders and led. The entire science and art of politics are based on this primordial, and . . . irreducible fact' (*SPN*, p.144). Although Gramsci implies that this fact applies to capitalist or *class* societies, and that since communism is a class-*less* society the distinction between rulers and ruled will no longer apply (he goes on to ask whether 'it is the intention that there should always be rulers and ruled, or is the objective to create the conditions in which this division is no longer necessary?'),[12] it seems clear enough that this division between the rulers and the ruled is likely to be maintained for some time to come.

Taking these points together, it would seem that although all members of the working class are *potentially* able to take on a leading role, only a minority of them will *actually* reach this point. Because experience of the political and organisational aspects of the struggle is one, if not the most important, qualification for leadership, then it is likely that a large proportion of this stratum will be made up of individuals (like Gramsci and Togliatti, for example) who perform specifically 'intellectual' rather than 'technical' functions. Indeed, in his essay on the 'southern question' Gramsci goes so far as to suggest that: 'The proletariat, as a class, is poor in organizing elements. It does not have its own stratum of intellectuals, and can only create one very slowly, very painfully, *after the winning of State power*' (*SPWII*, p.462; emphasis added). Although, in other words, Gramsci repeatedly expresses great confidence in the creative abilities of individuals, he is sometimes less than convinced that this really is the case:

> But innovation cannot come from the mass, at least at the beginning, except through the mediation of an *élite* for whom the conception implicit in human activity has already become to a certain degree a coherent and systematic ever-present awareness and a precise and decisive will. (*SPN*, p.335)

We can again agree with Femia that:

> Gramsci never really solved the problem of who would define the new world-view; nor did he manage to delineate clearly the appropriate region of human liberty. All his formulations are unsatisfactory to those who do not share his boundless faith in a dialectical interplay between a central authority and the aspirations of a mass movement. (Femia, 1981: 188–9)

Summary

This chapter has given a brief outline of the organisations through which the working class can develop the kind of hegemonic solidarity and leadership necessary for the transformation of society. It has been shown that in building upon the educational principles of the common school Gramsci argued that adult participation in the factory councils, and subsequently in the political party, would provide individuals not only with an opportunity to develop critical consciousness, but also with a model of post-revolutionary society. The discussion has also shown that, in common with other aspects of his analysis, Gramsci's views on this subject passed through a number of stages. In response to changes in the conditions and composition of the Italian working class, and particularly the emergence of an urban proletariat in Turin and elsewhere, Gramsci believed that the factory councils constituted a new and progressive forum for revolutionary practice. Although he continued to include important elements of the council movement in his proposals after its formal collapse in 1920, Gramsci turned his attention towards the problems of leading and co-ordinating the working class as a whole, rather than of concentrating upon the organisation of its most advanced elements. In trying to solve these problems, he first looked towards the PSI. As noted in Chapter 3, Gramsci had been somewhat critical of the reformist tendencies of the PSI both during and after the First World War. During the period of the council movement, and although many of his criticisms of the trade unions were equally applicable to the PSI, he continued to imply that the PSI still had an important role to play if only in terms of representing the working class within the bourgeois political system. After 1920, however, Gramsci became much more critical of the PSI, particularly in terms of its inability to provide leadership, and began to argue that the PSI could remain truly representative only if it 'renewed itself'. Initially, he felt that this renewal could be brought about with the help of the factory councils. Subsequently, and as the PSI continued to resist demands from both within its own ranks and from the Comintern to expel its reformist wing, Gramsci completely rejected the PSI as a revolutionary force and joined Bordiga in demanding that a separate communist party should be formed. Following the formation of the PCI in January 1921, he adopted a much more overtly Leninist or Bolshevik concept of the Party within which the factory councils played a supporting rather than leading role. Following his imprisonment in 1926, and as part of his more general study of Italian history and political processes, Gramsci continued to discuss the Party in these terms but warned against the dangers of the kind of bureaucratic ossification which had taken place under Stalin.

Notes

1. See, for example, Femia (1981): 130–89; Davidson (1974): 138–9; Davidson (1972); and Adamson (1978): 432. The early interpretation of Gramsci's writings in Italy has been discussed in Chapter 1 above.
2. In July 1919 Gramsci writes that 'the traditional institutions of the movement . . . are not dead' but that they 'must continue to exist until the last remnant of competition has been wiped out, until classes and parties have been completely suppressed and national proletarian dictatorships have been fused in the Communist International' (*SPWI*, p.77).
3. This is a clear example of how the 'traditional intellectuals' of the working class can themselves become a reactionary force. See Chapter 7 above.

4. For a detailed analysis of this distinction see Showstack Sassoon (1987): 44ff.
5. The following references are taken from 'Theses on the Tactics of the PCI' ('Rome Theses') by Bordiga and Terracini (*SPWII*, pp.93–117).
6. This and the following references are taken from 'The Italian Situation and the Tasks of the PCI' ('Lyons Theses'), by Gramsci and Togliatti (*SPWII*, 340–75).
7. Gramsci uses the term 'The Modern Prince' in order to draw a number of comparisons with Machiavelli's political theory as set out in his principal work *The Prince*, published in 1532. For a detailed discussion of this topic see Femia (1981): ch.4; and Showstack Sassoon (1987): ch. 8.
8. As Femia points out, Gramsci uses the term 'Jacobin' in a particular way to denote 'strong leadership tied to democratic mission' (Femia, 1981: 134). In Gramsci's words, Jacobinism should be used in a constructive sense to denote someone who has 'made the demands of the popular masses' the 'national political element' his or her own (*SPN*, p.65–6). He often uses this concept to explain why different political parties such as the Italian Action Party of the *Risorgimento* lacked the kind of leadership necessary for attracting popular support. See, for example, *SPN* pp. 74–86.
9. This view is very similar to that expressed in August 1926 when Gramsci suggested that:

> In every party, and especially in the democratic and social-democratic parties in which the organizational apparatus is very loose, there exist three strata. The very tiny top stratum, which is usually made up of parliamentary deputies and intellectuals often closely linked to the ruling class. The bottom stratum, made up of workers, peasants and urban petty-bourgeois, which provides the mass of party members or the mass of those influenced by the party. An intermediate stratum, which . . . maintains the link between the leading group at the top, and the mass of members and those influenced by the party. It is on the solidarity of this middle stratum that the leading groups are counting, for a future renewal of these various parties and their reconstruction on a broad basis. (*SPWII*, p.401)

10. This flexibility or variability had been recognised in the 'Rome Theses' of 1922:

> One cannot insist that by a given time, or on the eve of undertaking general actions, the party must have realized the condition of incorporating under its leadership – or actually in its own ranks – the majority of the proletariat. Such a postulate cannot be put forward aprioristically, abstracting from the real dialectical course of the party's process of development. (*SWPII*, p.98)

11. As both Femia and Showstack Sassoon point out, Gramsci's comments on bureaucratic centralism and particularly his comment that a bureaucratic and regressive party 'tends to hold back the vital forces of history and to maintain a legality which has been superseded, which is anti-historical, which has become extrinsic' (*SPN*, p.155), may be a taken as a critique of the degeneration of the CPSU and the Comintern under Stalin. See, for example, Femia (1981): 158; Showstack Sassoon (1987): 162ff.
12. Elsewhere Gramsci suggests that:

> In reality, only the social group that poses the end of the State and its own end as the target to be achieved can create an ethical State – i.e. one which tends to put an end to the internal divisions of the ruled, etc., and to create a technically and morally unitary social organism. (*SPN*, p.259)

Conclusion

In Chapter 1 it was shown that from the 1960s onwards a Gramscian perspective has been very evident in Marxist accounts of social change. In Britain, for example, the characterisation of Thatcherism as a form of hegemony established an orbit within which the discourses and strategies of the Left were circulated and analysed. If the New Right maintained its authority and control by responding to the apparent cultural and ideological predispositions of the population at large, then the solution or antidote was to challenge this world-view by developing an alternative hegemony. Similarly, in the context of an increasingly plural and fragmented socio-political atmosphere, this hegemony would not only have to encompass a wide range of apparently non-economic issues, but would have to acknowledge the weakening of the association between particular classes and particular forms of political organisation and motivation. The new hegemony would, in other words, have to be based on a system of alliances between groups whose perspectives were not necessarily derived from their positions in the relations of production. Although at least some aspects of these developments can be traced back to Gramsci, it is evident that they have now developed well beyond what Gramsci may have intended. It is unlikely, for example, that he would have sanctioned a relegation of the influence of material and structural phenomena to quite the extent that some contemporary accounts may suggest. Nor would he have been particularly happy with the idea that the organisations and perspectives of the working class would come to play a reduced if not subordinate role in the formation of an alternative hegemony. To this extent, and as Forgacs has pointed out, the assimilation of Gramsci by the British New Left in particular has involved considerable 'elaborations' and 'recastings of Gramscian concepts' (Forgacs, 1989: 86).

At the same time, it is important to recognise that while this remodelling has tried to make significant revisions and additions to the Marxist tool kit, it has also inherited a number of the problems which Gramsci failed to resolve. Emphasising the consensual and ideological aspects of hegemony, for example, may provide a useful framework within which to describe and characterise prevailing forms of social control and manipulation, but it may be less useful as a means of predicting or specifying what the new society of the future may be like. Having emphasised that the dictatorship of the proletariat will usher in a new intellectual and moral order, it is less clear precisely what form it will take. In the same way that Marx was less than forthcoming in his predictions for socialist society, Gramsci seems equally reluctant to discuss the nature of the moral and cultural milieu of the future.

One of the implications of this recent reliance on a sometimes ill-defined and vaguely expressed notion of alternative hegemony is that it may distract attention from those aspects of social change *which can be predicted* with reasonable accuracy. In contemporary society, for example, the development and adoption of microelectronic technologies may offer an unprecedented degree of choice as to how goods and services are produced. Although control over the actual implementation of these technologies currently remains with the employer, it is none the less the case that the nature of the technology itself requires a much greater degree of negotiation and flexibility which could in turn result in a profound transformation not only of the labour process itself, but also of the mechanisms through which it is organised and controlled. Similarly, persistently high levels of unemployment and recurrent economic crises could lead to a radical reassessment of the whole idea of formal paid employment as the most appropriate mechanism through which individuals gain access to the means of survival. Although these developments cannot be taken for granted, and although their precise path will involve political intervention, understanding and analysing the form and nature of these changes could provide a concrete and practical basis upon which to develop a proscriptive plan for the radical transformation of capitalist society.

In terms of its broad features, there are clear reflections of the Gramscian perspective in many aspects of modern society. The Green movement, for example, is characterised by a strong sense of 'the universal' both in terms of the geographical implications of local events, and in terms of the long-term effects of present actions. Similarly, the movement away from single party and single programme politics towards negotiation and compromise indicates a transition towards more participatory forms of political organisation. The recent overthrow of authoritarian regimes in eastern Europe provides clear examples of how the popular and political dimensions of revolutionary change can take a leading role. At the same time, however, the profound economic crises now facing the new democracies of eastern Europe forcefully confirm the fact that lasting social transformation cannot be achieved unless the economic structure *is itself transformed*. Demands for political and ideological 'superstructural' reform, in other words, may play a leading role in developing important aspects of the trajectory of social change, but these changes are likely to remain incomplete if the economic base is insufficiently strong to support them.

Despite the fact that the Gramscian perspective sometimes creates as many problems as it solves, and although the relationship between Gramsci and his successors has not been entirely straightforward, it is certainly true that his work has had a profound effect on contemporary accounts of social control. To the extent that Gramsci's ideas provide Marxism with a new degree of flexibility and adaptability, it is likely that his influence will be felt for some time to come. Gramsci, it seems, has not been 'relegated to the attic'.

Further reading

The following section lists a number of books and articles which, in addition to those already referred to in the chapter notes above, will give an indication of where to look for more detailed treatments of the topics introduced in this volume. The short references refer to books which are also included in the main Bibliography.

Chapter one: Central themes and debates

For an introduction to the debate on ideological consensus see:
Abercrombie, N. (1980), *Class, Structure and Knowledge: Problems in the sociology of knowledge*, Oxford: Basil Blackwell.
Abercrombie, N., S. Hill and B. S. Turner (1980), *The Dominant Ideology Thesis*, London: Allen & Unwin.
Lodziak, C. (1987), *The Power of Television: A critical appraisal*, London: Frances Pinter.
Mann, M. (1973), *Consciousness and Action Among the Western Working Class*, London: Macmillan.

For introductions to linguistics and semiotics see:
Fiske, J. (1982), *Introduction to Communication Studies*, London: Methuen.
Lyons, J. (1981), *Language and Linguistics: An introduction*, Cambridge University Press.

For discussions of Thatcherism see:

Gamble, A. (1988), *The Free Economy and the Strong State: The politics of Thatcherism*, London: Macmillan.
Hall, S. (1988), *The Hard Road to Renewal: Thatcherism and the crisis of the left*, London: Verso.
Hall, S. and M. Jacques (eds.), (1983) *The Politics of Thatcherism*, London: Lawrence & Wishart. (Published in association with *Marxism Today*.)
Jessop, B., K. Bonnett, S. Bromley and T. Ling (1988), *Thatcherism: A tale of two nations*, Cambridge: Polity Press.

For a critique of Hall's thesis see:
Hall, S. (1985), 'Authoritarian populism: a reply to Jessop *et al*.', *New Left Review*, no.151: 115–124.
Jessop, B., K. Bonnett, S. Bromley, and T. Ling (1984), 'Authoritarian populism, two nations and Thatcherism', *New Left Review*, no.147: 32–60.
Jessop, B., K. Bonnett, S. Bromley and T. Ling (1985), 'Thatcherism and the politics of hegemony: a reply to Stuart Hall', *New Left Review*, no.153: 87–101.

On new social movements see:
Frankel, B. (1987), *The Post-Industrial Utopians*, Cambridge: Polity Press.
Giddens, A. (1990), *The Consequences of Modernity*, Cambridge: Polity Press.

For examples of the Frankfurt School see:
Adorno, T. and M. Horkheimer (1947), 'The culture industry: entertainment as mass deception', in *Dialectic of Enlightenment* (trans. by J. Cummings), New York: Herder & Herder, 1972.
Benjamin, W. (1978), 'The author as producer', in A. Arato and E. Gebhert (eds), *The Essential Frankfurt School Reader*, Oxford: Basil Blackwell.
Fromm, E. (1956), *The Sane Society*. London: Routledge & Kegan Paul.
Marcuse, H. (1972), *One Dimensional Man*, London: Abacus. (First published by Routledge & Kegan Paul, London, 1964.)

Chapter two: The development of modern Italy, 1861–1914

For a general introduction to the history of this period in Europe and in Italy see:

Bertrand, C. L. (ed.) (1977), *Revolutionary Situations in Europe, 1917–1922: Germany, Italy, Austria-Hungary*, Montreal: International University Centre for European Studies.

Joll, J. (1976), *Europe Since 1870: An international history*, Harmondsworth: Penguin Books.

Mack Smith, D. (1969), *Italy: A modern history*, Ann Arbor MI: University of Michigan Press.

Taylor, A. J. P. (1954), *The Struggle for Mastery in Europe: 1848–1918*, (Oxford History of Modern Europe), Oxford: Oxford University Press.

For an outline of Sardinian history see:
Davidson (1977): 1–12.

For a thorough treatment of Italian history from Mussolini to the present day see:

Ginsborg, P. (1990), *A History of Contemporary Italy: Society and politics 1943–1988*, Harmondsworth: Penguin Books.

On the social history of the period see:

Engels, F. (1973), *The Condition of the Working Class in England*, London: Lawrence & Wishart.

Hobsbawm, E. (1968), *Labouring Men: Studies in the history of labour*, London: Weidenfeld & Nicolson.

Thompson (1963).

On the development of Soviet Russia and the Russian Revolution see:

Carr, E.H. (1979), *The Russian Revolution: From Lenin to Stalin (1917–1929)*, London: Macmillan.

Kochan, L. (1967), *Russia in Revolution: 1890–1918*, London: Weidenfeld & Nicolson. (Subsequently published by Paladin, London, 1970.)

Trotsky, L. (1965), *The History of the Russian Revolution* (trans. by M. Eastman), London: Victor Gollancz. (First published in 3 vols., 1932–33.)

Trotsky, L. (1973), *1905* (trans. by A. Bostock), Harmondsworth: Penguin Books.

For an account of the development of Marxist theory during the Second and Third Internationals see:
Colletti, L. (1972), *From Rousseau to Lenin*, New York: Monthly Review Press, esp. pp.45–108.
Joll, J. (1955), *The Second International: 1889–1914*, New York: Praeger. (Rev. ed. 1975.)
Kolakowski, (1978): vol.2, *The Golden Age*.
Lindemann, A. S. (1974), *The 'Red Years': European socialism versus Bolshevism, 1919–1921*. Berkeley CA: University of California Press.

Chapter three: Gramsci's life and work, 1891–1937

For brief discussions of Croce's influence on Gramsci see:
Adamson (1980): 120–30 and 179–84.
Davidson (1977): 50–7 and 94–8.

For more extensive discussions see:
Femia (1981), ch.3.
Finocchiaro, M. A. (1988), *Gramsci and the History of Dialectical Thought*, Cambridge: Cambridge University Press, chs. 1 and 2.
Jacobitti, E. E. (1981), *Revolutionary Humanism and Historicism in Modern Italy*, London: Yale University Press.

For detailed accounts of the period of the factory councils see:
Cammett (1967).
Clark (1977).
Spriano, P. (1975), *The Occupation of the Factories* (trans. by G. Williams), London: Pluto Press. (Originally published as *L'Occupazione della fabriche*, Turin: Einaudi, 1964.)
Williams (1975).

On the development of the PCI see:
Amyott, G. (1981), *The Italian Communist Party: The crisis of the popular front strategy*, London: Croom Helm.
Cammett (1967): 123–200.
Davidson (1982): vol. 1, chs. 7 and 8.

For an account of the evolution of Marxism–Leninism during the Stalinist period see:
Kolakowski (1978): vol.3, *The Breakdown*, esp. chs. 1–3.
Spriano, P. (1985), *Stalin and the European Communists* (trans by J. Rothschild), London: Verso.
Trotsky, L. (1957), *The Third International After Lenin*, New York: Pioneer Publishers. (1st ed. 1936.)

On Italian fascism see:
Forgacs, D. (ed.) (1986), *Rethinking Italian Fascism: Capitalism, populism and culture*, London: Lawrence & Wishart.
Rossi, A. (1976), *The Rise of Italian Fascism, 1918–1922* (trans. by P. and D. Wait), New York: Gordon Press. (Originally published by Methuen, London, 1938.)
Tannenbaum, E.R. (1972), *Fascism in Italy: Society and culture 1922–1945*, London: Allen Lane.

Chapter four: Ideology and the concept hegemony

For an introduction to the problem of ideology see:
Hall, S. (1978), 'The hinterland of science: ideology and the "sociology of knowledge"', in Centre for Contemporary Cultural Studies (1978), *On Ideology*, London: Hutchinson. (Originally published by Centre for Contemporary Cultural Studies, *Working Papers in Cultural Studies*, no. 10: 9–32, 1977.)
Hall, S., B. Lumley and G. McLennan (1978), 'Politics and ideology: Gramsci', in Centre for Contemporary Cultural Studies (1978), *On Ideology*, London: Hutchinson, pp. 45–76.

On Lukács see:
Lichtheim, G. (1970), *Lukács* (Fontana Modern Masters), London: Fontana.
McDonough R. (1978), 'Ideology as false consciousness: Lukács', in Centre for Contemporary Cultural Studies (1978), *On Ideology*, London: Hutchinson, pp. 33–44.
Steadman Jones, G. 'Marxism of the early Lukács', *New Left Review*, no.70: 27–64.

See also:

Bocock, R. (1986), *Hegemony*. London: Tavistock Publications.
Buci-Glucksmann (1980): esp. ch.2, 'State class and apparatuses of hegemony', pp.47–68.
Mouffe (ed). (1979): esp. ch.5, 'Hegemony and ideology in Gramsci', pp.168–204.

Chapter five: The concept hegemony: a variable definition

On the definition of the concept hegemony see:
Bates, T. R. 'Gramsci and the theory of hegemony', *Journal of the History of Ideas*, vol.36: 351–66.
Williams, G. (1960).
Williams, R. (1977), parts 1 and 2.

On Althusser see:
Callinicos, A. (1976), *Althusser's Marxism*, London: Pluto Press.
McLennan, G., V. Molina and R. Peters (1978), 'Althusser's theory of ideology', in Centre for Contemporary Cultural Studies (1978), *On Ideology*, London: Hutchinson, pp.77–105.
Mouffe (1981).

For more detailed accounts of the issues discussed in this chapter see:
Boggs, C. (1976), *Gramsci's Marxism*, London: Pluto Press, ch.2.
Buci-Glucksmann (1980): esp. chs. 2 and 3, 7, 13 and 14.
Buci-Glucksmann, C. (1982), 'Hegemony and consent: a political strategy', in Showstack Sassoon, A. (1982), *Appoaches to Gramsci*, London: Writers & Readers Publishing Cooperative Society, pp.116–26.
Hoffman (1984).
Merrington, J. (1974), 'Theory and practice in Gramsci's marxism', in Miliband and Saville (eds) (1968): 145–176.
Showstack Sassoon, A. (1982), 'Hegemony, war of position and political intervention', in Showstack Sassoon, A. (1982), *Approaches to Gramsci*. London: Writers and Readers Publishing Cooperative Society, pp.94–115.

For an interesting discussion of the application of the concept of 'cultural hegemony' in contemporary America see:
Jackson Lears, T. J. (1985), 'The Concept of cultural hegemony: problems and possibilities', *American Historical Review*, vol.90: 567–93.

Chapter six: Structure and Superstructure

The most comprehensive account of Gramsci's theory of the superstructure is given in:
Femia (1981): ch.3.

See also:
Buci-Glucksmann (1980).
Laclau and Mouffe (1985).
Mouffe (1981).

For a discussion of Laclau and Mouffe's interpretation of Gramsci and the structure–superstructure debate see:
Geras, N. (1987), 'Post-Marxism?', *New Left Review*, no.163: 40–82.
Geras, N. (1988), 'Ex-Marxism without substance: being a real reply to Laclau and Mouffe', *New Left Review*, no.169: 34–61.
Laclau and Mouffe's (1987) reply appeared as: 'Post-Marxism without apologies', *New Left Review*, no.166: 79–106.
Morera (1990): esp. Ch. 3.
Mouzelis, N. (1988), 'Marxism or Post-Marxism?', *New Left Review*, no.167: 107–23.

Chapter seven: Political Consciousness: education and the intellectuals

For an outline discusion of the problem of 'mass consciousness' see:
Boggs (1976), *Gramsci's Marxism*, London: Pluto, ch.3.

On the intellectuals see:
Buci-Glucksmann (1980): ch.1.
Cammett (1967): ch.10.

Vacca, G. 'Intellectuals and Marxist theory of the State', in Showstack Sassoon, A. (1982), *Approaches to Gramsci*, London: Writers & Readers Publishing Cooperative Society, pp.37–69.

For an interesting although now dated account of the 'role of the intellectuals' in Britain see:
Jacques, M. (1971), 'Intellectuals and their role today', *Marxism Today*, October: 307–6.

Chapter eight: Political participation: the council movements and the political party

On the problem of the political party see:
Boggs, C. (1976), *Gramsci's Marxism*, London: Pluto, ch.5.
Giovani, B. de (1979), 'Lenin and Gramsci: State, politics and party', in Mouffe (1979): 259–88.
Molyneux, J. (1978), *Marxism and the Party*, London: Pluto Press.
Spriano, P. (1979), *Antonio Gramsci and the Party: The prison years*, London: Lawrence & Wishart.

For an introductory discussion of the development of bureaucracy see:
Migliaro, L. R. and P. Misurca, 'The theory of modern bureaucracy', in Showstack Sasson, A. (1982), *Approaches to Gramsci*, London: Writers & Readers Cooperative Society, pp.70–91.

Bibliography

Adamson, W.L. (1978), 'Beyond "reform and revolution": notes on political education in Gramsci, Habermas and Arendt', *Theory and Society*, no. 3: 429-60.

Adamson W.L. (1980), *Hegemony and Revolution: Antonio Gramsci's political and cultural theory*, London: University of California Press.

Althusser, L. (1971), 'Ideology and ideological state apparatuses', in *Lenin and Philosophy and Other Essays* (trans. by B. Brewster), London: New Left Books, pp. 121-73.

Anderson, P. (1964), 'Origins of the present crisis', *New Left Review*, no. 23: 26-53.

Anderson, P. (1966) 'Socialism and pseudo-empiricism', *New Left Review*, no. 35:pp. 2-42.

Anderson, P. (1976), 'The antinomies of Antonio Gramsci', New Left Review, no. 100: 5-79.

Anderson, P. (1980), *Arguments Within English Marxism*, London: Verso.

Bennett, T., G. Martin, C. Mercer and J. Woollacott (eds) (1981), *Culture, Ideology and Social Process: A Reader*, London: Batsford.

Bloomfield, J. (ed.) (1977), *Class, Hegemony and Party* (the Communist University of London), London: Lawerence & Wishart.

Bobbio, N. (1979), 'Gramsci and the conception of civil society', in Mouffe (ed.) (1979): 21-47.

Bridges, G. and R. Brunt (eds.) (1981), *Silver Linings: Some strategies for the eighties* (Contributions to the Communist University of London), London: Lawrence & Wishart.

Buci-Glucksmann, C. (1979), 'State, transition and passive revolution', in Mouffe (ed.) (1979): 207-36.

Buci-Glucksmann, C. (1980), *Gramsci and the State* (trans. by D. Fernbach), London: Lawrence & Wishart. (Originally published as *Gramsci et L'Etat*, Paris: Arthème Fayard, 1975.)

Cammett, J.M. (1967), *Antonio Gramsci and the Origins of Italian Communism*, Stanford, CA: Stanford University Press.
Carrillo, S. (1977), *'Eurocommunism' and the State*, London: Lawerance & Wishart. (Originally published as *'Eurocomunismo' y Estado*, Barcelona: Editorial Critica, 1977.)
Clark, M. (1977), *Antonio Gramsci and the Revolution that Failed*, London: Yale University Press.
Claudin, F. (1978), *Eurocommunism and Socialism* (trans. by J.Wakeham), London: New Left Books. (Originally published as *Eurocomunismo y Socialismo*, Madrid: Siglo Veintiuno Editores, 1977.)
Colletti, L.(1971), 'Antonio Gramsci and the Italian Revolution', *New Left Review*, no.65: 87–94.
Communist Party of Great Britian (1978), *The British Road to Socialism*, London: CPGB. (Earlier edns pud. 1951, 1952, 1958, 1968.)
Communist Party of Great Britain (1989), *Manifesto for New Times: A Communist Party strategy for the 1990s*, London: CPGB.
Davidson, A. (1972), 'The varying seasons of Gramscian studies', *Political Studies*, vol. 20, no. 4: 448–61.
Davidson, A. (1974), 'Gramsci and Lenin 1917–1922', in Miliband and Saville (eds) (1974): 125–50.
Davidson, A. (1977), *Antonio Gramsci: Towards an intellectual biography*, London: Merlin Press.
Davidson, A. (1982), *The Theory and Practice of Italian Communism*,vol.1, London: Mercury Press.
Eley, G. (1984), 'Reading Gramsci in English: observations on the reception of Antonio Gramsci in the English-speaking world 1957–82', *European History Quarterly*, vol. 14, no.4: 441–77.
Femia, J. V. (1981), *Gramsci's Political Thought: Hegemony, consciousness and the revolutionary process*, Oxford: Clarendon Press.
Fiori, G. (1990), *Antonio Gramsci: Life of a revolutionary* (trans. by T. Nairn), London: Verso. (First published as *Vita di Antonio Gramsci*, Bari: Laterza, 1965.)
Forgacs, D. (1989), 'Gramsci and Marxism in Britian', *New Left Review*, no. 176: 70–88.
Freire, P. (1972a), *Pedagogy of the Oppressed*, (trans. by Myra Bergman Ramos), Harmondsworth: Penguin Books.
Freire, P. (1972a), *Cultural Action for Freedom*, Harmondsworth: Penguin Books.
Freire, P. (1974), *Education for Critical Consciousness*, London: Sheed & Ward.
Gorz, A. (1989), *Critique of Economic Reason* (trans. by G.Handyside and C. Turner), London: Verso. (Originally published as *Métamorphoses du travail*, Galilée: Quête du sens, 1988.)
Gramsci, A. (1947), *Lettere dal Carcere*, vol.1 of *Opere di Antonio Gramsci* (1947–72), Turin: Einaudi. (Rev. ed. 1965, ed. by S. Caprioglio and E. Fubini, Turin: Nuovo Universale Einaudi.)

Gramsci, A. (1949), *Il materialismo storico e la filosofia di Benedetto Croce*, vol. 2 of *Opere di Antonio Gramsci*, (1947–72), Turin: Einaudi.
Gramsci A. (1951), *Passato e Presente*, vol. 7 of *Opere di Antonio Gramsci* (1947–72),Turin: Einaudi.
Gramsci A. (1954), *L'Ordine Nuovo, 1919–1920* vol.9 of *Opere di Antonio Gramsci* (1947–72), Turin: Einaudi.
Gramsci, A. (1957) *The Modern Prince and Other Writings* (trans. and introduced by L. Marks), New York: International Publishers.
Gramsci, A. (1971), *Selections from the Prison Notebooks*, (ed. and trans. by Q. Hoare and G. Nowell Smith), London: Lawrence & Wishart.
Gramsci, A. (1973), *Letters from Prison* (selected, trans. and introduced by L. Lawner), New York: Harper & Row. (Subsequently published by Jonathan Cape, London, 1975.)
Gramsci, A. (1977), *Selections from Political Writings: 1910–1920* (selected and ed. by Quintin Hoare, trans. by John Mathews), London: Lawrence & Wishart.
Gramsci A. (1978), *Selections from Political Writings: 1921–1926* (trans. and ed. by Quintin Hoare), London: Lawrence & Wishart.
Hall, S. (1977), 'Re-thinking the base and superstructure metaphor', in Bloomfield (1977): 43–71.
Hall, S. (1981), 'Cultural Studies: Two paradigms', in Bennett *et al.* (1981): 19–37. (A longer version was published in *Media, Culture and Society*, no. 2, 1980: 57–72.)
Henderson, H. (trans.) (1974), *Prison Letters, etc.*, in three special editions on Gramsci in the *New Edinburgh Review*, pp. 3–47 and 1–44.
Hobsbawm, E. (1968), *Industry and Empire: An economic history of Britain since 1750*, London: Weidenfeld & Nicolson. (Subsequently published by Penguin Books, Harmondsworth, 1969).
Hoffman, J. (1984), *The Gramscian Challenge: Coercion and consent in Marxist political theory*, Oxford: Basil Blackwell.
Hoggart, R. (1958), *The Uses of Literacy*, Harmondsworth: Penguin Books.
Hyman, R. (1984), *Strikes*, London Fontana. (3rd ed.)
Jakubowski, F. (1976), *Ideology and Superstructure in Historical Materialism*, London: Allison & Busby.
Jaszi, O. (1969), *Revolution and Counter-Revolution in Hungary*, New York: Howard Fertig.
Karabel, J. (1976), 'Revolutionary contradications: Antonio Gramsci and the problem of the intellectuals', *Politics and Society*, no. 6, pp. 125–72.
Kaye, H. J. (1981), 'Antonio Gramsci: An annotated bibliography of studies in English', *Politics and Society*, vol. 10, no. 3: 335–53.
Kolakowski, L. (1978), *Main Currents of Marxism: Its origins, growth and dissolutiom*, 3 vols.: *The Founders, The Golden Age, The Breakdown* (trans. by P. S. Fella), Oxford: Oxford University Press.

Laclau, E. and C. Mouffe (1985), *Hegemony and Socialist Strategy: Towards a radical democratic politics* (trans. by W. Moor), London: Verso.
Larrain, J, (1979), *The Concept of Ideology*, London: Hutchinson.
Larrian, J. (1983), *Marxism and Ideology*, London: Macmillian.
Lenin, V. I. (1947), *What is to be Done?*, Moscow: Progress Publishers.
Lenin, V. I. (1963), *Collected Works*, vol. 17, London: Lawrence & Wishart.
Lenin, V. I. (1965), *Collected Works*, vol. 32, London: Lawrence & Wishart.
Lukács, G. (1968), *History and Class Consciousness: Studies in Marxist dialectics*, (trans. by R. Livingstone), London: Merlin Press.
Lukács, G. (1970), *Lenin: A study in the unity of his thought*, London: New Left Books.
Mackie, R. (ed.) (1980), Literacy and Revolution: The pedagogy of Paulo Freire, London: Pluto Press.
McLellan, D. (ed.), (1977), *Karl Marx: Selected Writings*, Oxford: Oxford University Press.
Magri, L. (1970), 'Problems of the Marxist theory of the revolutionary party', *New Left Review*, no. 60: 97–128.
Marx, K. (1954), *Capital I*, London: Lawrence & Wishart.
Marx, K. (1959), *Capital III*, London: Lawrence & Wishart.
Marx, K. (1975), *Early Writings* (Introduction by Lucio Colletti, trans. by R. Livingstone and G. Benton), Harmondsworth: Penguin Books.
Marx, K. (1977), 'Preface to *A Critique of Political Economy*' in McLellan (ed.) (1977): 388–91. (First published 1859.)
Marx, K. and F. Engels (1935), 'The German Ideology', *Selected Works*, vol. 1. Moscow.
Marx, K. and F. Engels. (1977a), *Selected Letters*, Peking: Foreign Language Press.
Marx, K. and F. Engels (1977b), 'The German Ideology', in McLellan (ed.) (1977): 159–91. (First published 1932.)
Miliband, R. (1982), *Capitalist Democracy in Britian*, Oxford University Press.
Miliband, R. and J. Saville, (eds) (1965), *The Socialist Register*. London: Merlin Press.
Miliband, R. and J. Saville (eds) (1968), *The Socialist Register*, London: Merlin Press.
Miliband, R. and J. Saville (eds) (1974), *The Socialist Register*, London: Merlin Press.
Morera, E. (1990), *Gramsci's Historicism: A reaslist interpretation*, London: Routledge.
Mouffe, C. (ed.) (1979), *Gramsci and Marxist Theory*, London: Routledge & Kegan Paul.
Mouffe, C. (1981), 'Hegemony and the integral State in Gramsci: towards a new concept of politics', in Bridges and Brunt (eds) (1981): 167–87.
Mouffe, C. and A. Showstack Sassoon (1977), 'Gramsci in France and Italy: A review of the literature', *Economy and Society*, vol. 6 no. 1: 31–68.

Nairn, T. (1964a), 'The English working class', *New Left Review*, no. 24: 43–57.
Nairn, T. (1964b), 'The anatomy of the Labour Party', *New Left Review*, no. 27: 38–65, and no. 28: 33–62.
Rustin, M. (1985), *For a Pluralist Socialism*, London: Verso.
Ryder, A. J. (1967), *The German Revolution of 1918: A study of German socialism in war and revolt*, London: Cambridge University Press.
Sarte, J.–P. (1974), *Between Existentialism and Marxism*, London: Verso.
Schwarz, B. and C. Mercer (1981), 'Popular politics and Marxist theory in Britain: the History Men', in Bridges and Brunt (eds) (1981): 143–66.
Seton-Watson, C. (1967), *Italy from Liberalism to Fascism: 1870–1925*, London: Methuen.
Showstack Sassoon, A. (1987), *Gramsci's Politics*, London: Hutchinson. (1st ed., London: Croom Helm, 1980).
Smart, B. (1976), *Sociology, Phenomenology and Marxian Analysis: A critical discussion of the theory and practice of a science of society*, London: Routledge & Kegan Paul.
Texier, J. (1979), 'Gramsci, theoretician of the superstructure', in Mouffe, (ed.) (1979): 48–79.
Thompson, E. P. (1961), 'Reviews of Raymond Williams' *The Long Revolution*', *New Left Review*, nos. 9 and 10: 24–33; 34–9.
Thompson, E. P. (1963), *The Making of the English Working Class*, London: Victor Gollancz. (Subsequently published by Penguin Books, Harmondsworth, 1968.)
Thompson, E. P. (1965), 'The peculiarities of the English', in Miliband and Saville (eds) (1965). (Subsequently included in Thompson 1978:35–91.)
Thompson, E. P. (1978), *The Poverty of Theory and Other Essays*, London: Merlin Press.
Thompson, P. (1983), *The Nature of Work: An introduction to debates on the labour process*, London:Macmillan.
Togliatti, P. (1979), *On Gramsci and Other Writings*, (ed. and introduced by D. Sassoon), London: Lawrence & Wishart.
Trotsky, L. (1945), 'The main lessons of the Third Congress', in *The First Five Years of the Communist International*, vol. 1, New York.
Trotsky, L. (1969), *Military Writings*, New York.
Williams, G. (1960), 'The concept of egemonia in the thought of Antonio Gramsci', *Journal of the History of Ideas*, vol. 21: 586–99.
Williams, G. (1975), *Proletarian Order: Antonio Gramsci, facrory councils and the origins of Italian communism 1911–1921*, London: Pluto Press.
Williams, R. (1958), *Culture and Society: 1780–1950*, London: Chatto & Windus. (Subsequently published by Penguin Books, Harmondsworth, 1961.)
Williams, R. (1961), *The Long Revolution*, London: Chatto & Windus. (Subsequently published by Penguin Books, Harmondsworth, 1965.)

Williams, R. (1973),"Base and superstructure in Marxist cultural theory', *New Left Review*, no. 82: 3–16.
Williams, R. (1977), *Marxism and Literature*, Oxford: Oxford University Press.
Williams, R. (1979), *Politics and Letters: Interviews with New Left Review*, London:Verso.
Williams, R. (1981), 'The analysis of culture', in Bennett *et al.* (1981): 43–52.
Zucaro, D. (ed.) (1961), *Il processone: Gramsci e i dirigenti comunisti dinanzi al tribunale speciale*, Rome: Riuniti.

Index

abstentionists, 81, 84
Abyssinia, 41
Action Party, 31, 33, 168, 225 n.8
Adowa, battle of, 41, 46
Adriatic, 34, 48, 64, 87
Aegean, 47
Africa
 colonial rivalry in, 30, 46
 Italian interests in, 34, 41, 42, 87
Ales, Gramsci born at, 56
Algeria, 34
alienation, 116
 see also Marxism; consciousness, revolutionary
Althusser, L., 15, 143
Ancona, 48
Anderson, P., 6, 7, 14, 133, 139ff
Anti-Nazi League, 17
Arditi, 75, 88, 89
Association for Social Policy (in Germany), 37
Austria, 30, 31, 32, 34, 46, 48, 77
 and First World War, 64, 65, 66, 69, 75, 76
Avanti!, 44, 48, 65, 71, 73, 74
Aventine Secession, 100, 101, 102, 104

Bakunin, M., 38, 52 n.5
Balkan States, Balkans, 34, 47
Bartoli, M., 63

Bebel, A., 38
Belgium, 48, 65, 92
Berlin
 Congress of, 34
 Communist uprisings in, 77
Bissolati, L., 43, 44, 47, 64
Blanqui, L.-A., 38
Bobbio, N., 7, 157, 166–9
Bolsheviks, 10, 38, 68, 69, 73, 74, 76, 77, 129, 139, 145, 201, 203
 see also Russian Revolution.
Bonomi, I., 90
Bordiga, A., 78, 81, 84, 100, 147, 149
 arrested by fascists, 96
 calls for formation of separate communist party, 86
 criticised by Lenin for abstentionist attitude, 84
 criticises reformism of the PSI, 82
 expelled from Comintern, 107
 Gramsci and, 75, 83, 92, 93, 95, 97, 100, 203, 211, 213, 214, 215
Boselli, P., 66, 75
Bosnia, 48
bourgeoisie, bourgeois society, *see* capitalism
Brest-Litovsk, Treaty of, 70
Britain, *see* Great Britain
British Labour Party, 14, 16, 38
British New Left, 6, 13ff, 227
 see also Marxism, British

Bugerru, miner's strike at, 43, 59
  see also strikes
Bukharin, N., 99, 107
Bulgaria, 31, 53 n.10, 65, 76

Cagliari, 57, 59, 60, 61, 64
Camera del Lavoro (Chambers of Labour), 45, 78
Campaign for Nuclear Disarmament (CND), 16
capitalism, capitalist society, 20ff, 39, 50, 92, 100, 104, 114ff, 171, 188, 193, 205
Caporetto, battle of, 75
Catholics, Catholic Church, 42, 43, 47, 87
Catholic Action Party, 43, 53 n.11
  see also Italian Popular Party
Cavour, Count Camillo Bensi di, 31
CGL (General Confederation of Labour), 44, 45, 48, 65, 66, 78ff, 89, 91, 97, 155 n.18, 203
civil society, 7, 114, 138ff, 157ff, 166ff
  see also political society; State
Club di Vita Morale, 72, 202
Cobden, R., 37
coercion, 135, 137ff, 146, 156, 161, 192
  see also consent; war of manoeuvre
Comintern, *see* Communist International
Commissioni interne, *see* internal committees
Como, 99
common school, Gramsci's theory of, 7, 179–186, 201
  see also education, political
Communist International (Comintern), 55, 81, 82, 86, 93, 94, 96, 97, 98, 99, 100, 102, 134, 147, 212, 217, 226 n.11
  Lenin proposes formation of, 68
  First Congress, 77
  Second Congress, 77, 84
  Third Congress, 92
  Fourth Congress, 94
  Fifth Congress, 100
  Sixth Congress, 107
  Seventh Congress, 10

  see also Second International; Third International
Communist Party of Great Britain, 12, 16, 17, 25
Communist Party of the Soviet Union, 9, 15, 99, 100, 106, 226 n.11
Confédération Générale du Travail (CGT), 38
Confederazione Generale del Lavoro, *see* CGL
Confederazione Italiana del Lavoro (CIL), 43, 78
Confindustria (General Confederation of Industry), 81
consciousness
  political, 7, 71, 109, 113–29, 157, 201, 216, 219
  development of, 179ff, 162ff
  development of among European working class, 36ff, 42
  moments and levels of, 163
  revolutionary, 24, 39, 113–29, 201, 216
    see also revolution;
  trade union, 122, 124, 126, 133, 184;
    see also reformism
  universal, 5, 18, 27, 124, 134, 136, 167, 204;
    see also economic-corporate
    see also education, political
consent, 4, 6, 22, 24, 26, 135, 137ff, 146, 156, 161, 192
  see also coercion; war of position
consigli di fabbrica, *see* factory councils
consumer society, 25, 36
Cosmo, U., 63
council movement, *see* factory councils
Crispi, F., 40, 41, 42
Croce, B., 11, 61, 63
Czechoslovakia, 15, 67, 75, 111 n.5, 111, n.6

Dalmatia, 6
D'Annunzio, G., 87, 89, 91
De Leon, D., 79
Depretis, A., 33, 34, 40
De Sanctis, F., 63
Dettori, Gramsci attends *liceo* at, 60

East/West

Gramsci draws distinction between, 139ff, 144
Ebert, F., 76
economic-corporate, 134, 136, 149, 162, 164, 167, 190, 201, 204, 205, 208, 215
  see also reformism;
  consciousness, political, development of
economic determinism, *see* Marxism
economism, *see* reformism
education, political, 7, 72, 179–186, 202
  see also consciousness, political; common school
Emilia-Romagna, 31, 43, 48
Engels, F., 143, 157, 160, 175
Eritrea, Italian colony of, 41
Eurocommunism, 6, 15, 17, 155

Fabian Society, 37
Facta, L., 91
factory councils (*consigli di fabbrica*), 8, 11, 85, 91, 92, 97, 103, 109, 129, 149, 201ff
  Gramsci establishes, 80
  and relationship with Party, 83, 202, 209ff
Farinelli, A., 63
Fasci, Fasci Italiani di Combattimento, 65, 88
fascism, fascists, 87, 89, 90, 91, 97, 98, 100, 105, 107, 109, 149
  Gramsci analyses, 95, 101, 103, 169
Federazione Impiegati Operai Metallurgici (Italian metalworkers' union), *see* FIOM
Federterra (National Federation of Landworkers), 45
Ferrara, 44
Ferri, Enrico, 44
Feuerbach, L., 115
FIAT (*Fabbrica Italiana Automobili Torino*), 79, 81
FIOM, 78, 80, 81, 85
First International, 39, 52 n.4
  see also Marxism, international dimension of
First World War, 6, 45, 49, 64–76, 205
Fiume, 87

Florence, 74
Formia, Gramsci attends clinic at, 108
France, 15, 30, 31, 32, 34, 35, 36, 38, 41, 58, 76, 77
  and First World War, 65, 67, 75
Franco–Prussian War, 30
Frankfurt School, 15, 25
Franz Ferdinand, Austrian Archduke, 48
Franz Joseph, Austro-Hungarian Emperor, 31
Freire, P., 183, 185ff

Gaeta, 55
Garibaldi, G., 31, 32
Garzia, R., 60
General Confederation of Labour, *see* CGL
General Elections (Italian)
  1892, 1895, 1900, 52 n.6
  1909, 44
  1913, 48
  1919, 78, 85
  1921, 90
  1924, 98
Genoa, 32, 33, 79
Gentile, G., 11
Germany, 30, 31, 34, 35, 36, 45, 46, 48, 77, 145
  and communist uprisings, 76, 92
  and First World War, 65, 67, 69, 75, 76
Ghilarza, 56, 57, 59
Giolitti, G., 41, 42, 44, 46, 48, 65, 85, 86, 90, 91, 169
Gramsci, Antonio
  analyses fascism, 95, 101, 103, 169
  arrest and trial, 104–5
  attitude towards Russian Revolution, 72–3
  attitude towards War, 65
  becomes Secretary-General of PCI, 100
  becomes Secretary of Turin branch of PSI, 74
  begins life as political activist, 71
  calls for renewal of PSI, 82
  criticisms of PSI endorsed by Lenin, 84
  elected to Italian Parliament, 98
  establishes factory councils and internal committees, 80, 81

failing health and death, 108
founds *L'Ordine Nouvo*, 78
imprisonment, 105–7
influence on British Marxism, 12ff, 227
influence on PCI after 1945, 9ff, 201
Lyons Theses adopted at PCI Congress, 104
after Mussolini's rise to power, 93
meets and marries Julia Schucht, 94
proposes new strategy for PCI, 97
foundation of PCI, 86
joins PSI, 64
publication of work in English, 11, 15
returns to Italy for secret meeting of PCI at Como, 99
returns to Rome to speak in parliament, 103
role in factory occupations in Turin, 85
Sardism and early socialism, 60, 63
studies in Turin, 11, 61, 62
travels to Moscow as PCI representative, 94
unhappy childhood and schooling, 56–60
moves to Vienna, 98
writes on Southern Question, 104, 103, 63
Gramsci, Carlo, 56
Gramsci, Delio, 99, 102, 103
Gramsci, Emma, 56
Gramsci, Francesco, 55, 56, 58
Gramsci, Gennaro, 56, 57, 59, 60, 61, 106
Gramsci, Giuliano, 106
Gramsci, Giuseppina, *née* Marcias, 56
Gramsci, Grazia, 56, 71
Gramsci, Julia, *née* Schucht, 94, 98, 101, 102, 103, 104, 105, 107
Gramsci, Mario, 56
Gramsci, Terresina, 56
Great Britain, 30, 34, 35, 36, 46, 49, 76, 92
and First World War, 65, 67, 75
Greece, 53 n.10, 65
Il Grido del Popolo, 65, 71, 72

Hall, S., 14, 157, 158, 170

Hegel, G. W. F., 40, 114, 139, 166
hegemony, 3, 7, 10, 103, 104, 132–138, 142, 146, 147, 156, 162, 172, 186, 194, 196, 201, 205
and ideology, 25, 26 113ff, 128–30
historical bloc, 7, 27, 133–8, 147, 148, 162, 164, 168, 169, 171, 172, 173, 179, 186, 197, 201, 205
Hobsbawm, E., 12
Hungary, 12, 77, 92, 111 n.5, 145

ideology, 4, 6, 19, 23ff, 113–29, 140ff, 168ff, 184
Independent Social Democratic Party of Germany (USPD), 67, 76, 77
intellectuals, 7, 104, 129, 179, 183, 186–98, 215, 219
organic, 188ff
traditional, 189ff
intellectual and moral unity, Gramsci's theory of, 134, 135, 218
intellectual vanguard, 82, 93, 122, 124, 127, 129, 184, 213, 215, 216, 219
see also revolution, Leninist theory of; leadership
internal committees (*commissioni interne*), 80, 83, 97, 103
Istria, 66
Italian Communist Party (PCI), 9, 15, 55, 72, 83, 84, 85, 86, 88, 90, 93, 94, 100, 103, 107, 109, 147, 149, 213ff
and Aventine Secession, 100, 101
contests 1924 General Election, 98
formation of, 86
Second Congress, 93
secret conference at Como, 103
suppression by fascists, 96
Third Congress, 103
Italian Confederation of Labour, *see Confederazione Italiana del Lavoro* (CIL)
Italian Popular Party (*Partito Poplare Italiano*), 43, 87, 90, 91, 101
Italian Socialist Party (PSI), 39, 41, 42, 43, 44, 45, 47, 48, 61, 64, 71, 77, 78, 80, 81, 83, 84, 87, 90, 96, 147, 149, 205, 206, 209ff
and April strike in Turin, 81, 82

and attitude towards First World War, 64ff
and attitude towards invasion of Tripoli, 47
and the Aventine Secession, 100, 101
contests 1924 General Election, 98
expels reformists, 94
expulsion from Comintern, 93
and factory occupations and General Strike in September, 85
loses popular support, 89
Party split by communist minority at Livorno Congress, 86
reformist tendencies criticised by Lenin, 84
tries to form anti-fascist coalition, 91
Italian Somaliland, 41
Italy, 6, 40, 76, 86, 91
  economic development of, 32, 35, 44, 45, 205
  economic problems, 32, 35, 45, 77
  and First World War, 64ff, 75, 76
  and foreign affairs, 34, 41, 46
  reform process, 33, 41, 43, 44
  and social unrest, 35, 40, 42, 45, 48, 74, 81, 85; *see also* strikes
  unification of, 31ff; *see also* *Risorgimento*
Italian Syndicalist Union, *see* USI
IWW (International Workers of the World), 79

Jacobins, Jacobinism, 217
Jakubowski, F., 160, 171

Kamenev, L., 107
Kautsky, K., 38, 154, n.13, 184
Kerensky, A., 70, 74
Kommunistische Partei Deutschlands (Communist Party of Germany, KPD), 77, 130 n.6, 145
Kun, B., 111 n.6

Labour Party, *see* British Labour Party
Labriola, A., 40, 63
Labriola, A., 44
Larrain, J., 114ff

Lassalle, F., 38
Lazzari, C., 93
leadership
  as practical and theoretical problem, 8, 42, 81, 85, 129, 133, 137, 146, 166, 186, 195, 197, 212ff
  see also historical bloc; intellectuals
Leghorn, *see* Livorno
Lenin, V I., 6, 7, 38, 73, 74, 93, 99, 135, 140, 145, 146, 147, 184
  approves Gramsci's critique of PSI, 84
  and concept of ideology, 113, 121–9
  proposes formation of Third International, 68, 77
  proposes policy of united front, 92
  puts forward April Theses, 69
  puts forward twenty-one conditions, 84
  see also party, Leninist theory of
Libya, Italian conquest of, 47, 64, 87
Liebknecht, K., 77
Liebknecht, W., 38
Livorno, 86, 93
Lombardy, 31, 32
London, Treaty of, 66, 77
Lukács, G., 7, 15, 113, 119, 121, 123–9, 138, 145
Luxemburg, R., 77, 154 n.13, 184
Lyons, PCI Congress at, 103, 104

Machiavelli, N., 63, 136, 161, 225 n.7
Marcias, Giuseppina, *see* Gramsci, Giuseppina *née* Marcias
Marinetti, F., 88
Marx, Karl, 7, 26, 38, 39, 40, 63, 159ff, 168, 170, 171, 173, 183, 184
  and concept of ideology, 113ff, 168, 173
Marxism, 1, 8, 9, 10, 18, 26, 55, 79, 139
  and economic determinism, 13, 19ff, 39, 113, 120, 156ff
  British, 6, 9, 11ff, *see also* British New Left
  deficiencies of, 26, 113, 120
  Gramsci studies, 63
  impact in Italy, 40ff, 64, 68
  international dimension of, 39, 65, 68, 50 *see also* First International
  see also revolution; ideology

Il Marzocco, 61
Matteotti, G., 100, 101, 149
maximalists, 75, 81, 93
Mazzini, G., 31, 148
Menelik, Abyssinian king, 41
Mensheviks, 38, 69, 70, 133
Metalworkers, Italian Federation of, *see* FIOM
Milan, 32, 33, 79, 81, 88, 91, 93, 105
   strikes at, 44, 66, 85
Moderate Party, 31, 33, 168
Montenegro, 31, 53 n.10, 65
Morocco, 46
Moscow, 77, 94, 96, 97, 99, 100, 102, 109
Mussolini, B., 39, 47, 64, 74, 88, 90, 94, 98, 103, 108, 199 n.2
   achieves total control, 102
   changes attitude towards War, 65, 66
   elected to PSI executive, 48
   expelled from PSI, 65
   forms Partito Nazionale Fascista, 91
   March on Rome, 91
   and Matteotti crisis, 100

Nairn, T., 6, 11, 14
Naples, 31, 32, 46, 108
National Federation of Landworkers, *see* Federterra
nationalism
   development of in Europe, 34, 48, 75, 76
   in Italy, 42, 46, 47, 87, 89
   see also PNF; fascism
New Left, *see* British New Left
Nicefero, A., 63
Nitti, F., 63, 78, 85, 87
North/South
   uneven development of in Italy, *see* southern problem

October Revolution, *see* Russian Revolution
Opera dei Congressi, 43
   see also Catholics
L'Ordine Nuovo, 55, 78, 82, 92, 97, 98, 101, 202
Ordine group, 72, 79, 81, 83, 86, 98, 101, 109

Orlando, V., 75, 78

Papal States, 31, 32
Paris Commune, 38
Parma City, 44
Partito Communista Italiano (PCI), *see* Italian Communist Party
Partito Nazionale Fascista (National Fascist Party), *see* PNF
Partito Popolare Italiano, *see* Italian Popular Party
Partito Socialista Italiano (PSI), *see* Italian Socialist Party
party, 8, 201ff
   Gramsci's theory of, 83, 97, 101, 104, 201, 209ff
   Marxist theory of, 38, 73
   Leninist theory of, 73, 74, 103, 121ff, 184, 201
   and relationship with factory councils, 202ff
   see also historical bloc.
Pastore, A., 63
peasantry, 79, 97, 101, 102, 103, 104, 124, 147, 216
PCI, *see* Italian Communist Party
Piedmont, 31, 32, 81
Plekhanov, G., 38, 184
PNF (National Fascist Party), 39, 91, 100, 110
   see also fascism; nationalism
Poland, 12, 15, 69., 111 n.5, 92
political consciousness, *see* consciousness, political
political education, *see* education, political
political society, 7, 114, 122, 136, 138ff, 157ff, 166ff;
   see also civil society; State
Il Popolo d'Italia, 65, 88
Popular Front, policy of, 10
Popular Party, *see* Italian Popular Party
Prison Notebooks (*Quaderni del Carcere*), 7, 55, 71, 106, 109, 144, 147, 173, 209, 217
   problems of interpretation, 3, 132, 152 n.5, 139
Proudhon, P.-J., 38
Prussia, 32

PSI, *see* Italian Socialist Party

Quisisana clinic, Gramsci transferred to, 108

Reformism, 39, 43, 79, 93, 133, 147, 149, 169, 203, 205, 207
  criticisms of, 82, 124, 126
  development of reformist organisations, 38
  reformists expelled from PSI, 94
  and factory occupations, 81
  as political strategy, 39
  and the PSI, 43
Reggio E., 66
revolution, 21, 23, 107
  Gramsci's theory of, *see* war of position; war of manoeuvre
  Leninist theory of, 26, 73, 121, 122, 144ff *see also* intellectual vanguard
  Marxist theory of, 20, 39, 68, 73, 113, 115, 116, 117, 119
revolutionary consciousness, *see* consciousness
Risorgimento, 10, 31, 33, 42, 87, 148, 169, 225 n.8
  see also Italy
Rome, 32, 55, 66, 93, 94, 103, 104, 108
  march on, 91, 108
Romania, 31, 53 n.10, 65, 67, 75, 111 n.5, 111 n.6
Rudin, A. di, 41
Russia, 30, 41, 46, 48, 54, 65, 75, 79, 214
  Soviet, 92
  Tsarist, 27, 50, 51 n.1, 69, 146
Russian Revolution, 39, 139, 144
  Gramsci writes on, 73–5, 139, 145
  October Revolution 1917, 39, 68–70
  St. Petersburg 1905, 50, 69
  see also Soviet Union

Salandra, A., 48, 65, 66
Salvemini, G., 46, 61
San Vittore, Gramsci held at prison at, 105, 106
Santu Lissurgiu, Gramsci attends school at, 58
Sard (language), Gramsci's knowledge of, 57, 63

Sardinia, 35, 43, 55, 56, 58, 60, 62, 181
Sardinia-Piedmont, 31
Sardism, Sard nationalism, 61, 63, 71
Sartre, J.-P., 15
Schucht, E., 102, 103, 104, 107
Schucht, Julia, *see* Gramsci, Julia *née* Schucht
Schucht, T., 103, 104, 105, 106, 107, 109
Second International, 65, 68, 73, 77, 184
  see also Marxism, international dimension of
Serbia, 31, 48, 53 n.10, 65, 111 n.5
Serrati, G., 74, 75, 78, 81, 84, 86, 93, 94, 211
shop steward movement (English), 79
Sicily, 31, 34, 41, 87, 104
Silvery Wood, Gramsci attends sanatorium at, 94, 103
Sozialdemokratische Partei Deutschlands (Social Democratic Party of Germany), *see* SPD
Social Democratic Workers' Party (Russian), 38, 67
Social-Revolutionaries, 69, 70
socialism, 38, 107
  development of in Europe, 38, 50, 76
  in Italy, 39ff, 59
  see also Marxism
Socialist Workers Party (Great Britain), 16
southern problem, 32, 35, 45, 46, 53 n.8, 58, 59, 61, 63
  Gramsci writes on, 63, 103, 104
SPD, 38, 76
Il Soviet, 82
Soviet Union, 12, 100, 103, 108
  see also Russia
soviets, 69, 79, 203
  and internal committees, 83, 129, 213
  see also factory councils
Spain, 15
Spartakus League, 77
Squadre, squadristi, 89, 90, 91
  see also fascism
St. Petersburg, 50
  see also Russian Revolution
Stalin, J., 10, 15, 99, 106, 109, 150, 226 n.11

State, 37, 133ff, 157ff, 166ff, 181, 194, 114
  see also civil society and political society
strikes
  at Bugerru 1904, 43, 59
  in Northern Italy 1906 and 1908, 44
  'red week' June 1914, 48
  against First World War, 66
  throughout Italy 1919, 81
  at FIAT works March 1920, 81
  factory occupations and General Strike September 1920, 85, 212
structure (economic 'base'), 4, 7, 19, 114, 120, 136, 138ff, 156–78, 201
Sulcis-Iglesiente, 58, 59
superstructure, 4, 7, 19, 114, 120, 136, 138ff, 156–78, 201
syndicalism, 44, 65

Tasca, A., 64, 78, 83, 84, 96, 99, 107, 147
Terracini, U., 64, 78, 83, 84, 86, 93, 95, 96, 215
Terzini, Terzinternationalisti (Third Internationalist fraction of PSI), 94, 95, 96, 98
Texier, J., 7, 157, 170–4
Thatcherism, 25, 227
Third International, 68, 77, 81, 212
  see also Communist International
Thompson, E. P., 6, 12, 13, 14, 16
Togliatti, P., 9, 11, 64, 78, 83, 84, 96, 98, 99, 107, 109, 144, 215
Toscanini, A., 88
trade unions, Italian, 43, 44, 59, 80, 83, 91
  British, 38, 79
  Gramsci criticises, 206ff
  see also consciousness
Trafoi, Gramsci's family moves to, 104
Trasformismo, 33, 34, 35, 39, 40, 41
Trentino, 66
Tripple Alliance, 34, 46, 64, 65
Tripoli, 34, 47
Trotsky, L., 16, 38, 70, 99, 103, 107, 145, 146, 147, 149
Tunis, 34, 47
Turati, F., 40, 43, 44, 47, 61, 68, 75, 78, 81, 93, 211
Turi, Gramsci imprisoned at, 55, 105, 106

Turin, 11, 33, 44, 55, 60, 74, 79, 84, 91, 95, 98
  strikes at, 66, 81, 85, 212
Turkey, 47, 49, 55, 76, 78
Tuscany, 31
Twenty-One Conditions, 84, 86

UIL (*Unione Italiana di Lavoro*), 65, 78, 88, 89, 91
L'Unione sarda, 60
Unione Sindicale Italiana, see USI
L'Unita, 97, 98, 101
Unitary Socialist Party, 94, 98
united front, policy of, 92, 93, 107, 147
United States of America, 67
universal consciousness, see consciousness, universal
USI (*Unione Sindicale Italiana*), 65, 78, 91
USPD see Independent Social Democratic Party of Germany
Usticia, Gramsci imprisoned on, 55, 104

vanguard, see intellectual vanguard
Vatican, 32, 43, 104, 108
Venetia, 31, 32
Veneto, Gramsci elected at, 98
Vienna, 98, 102, 144
Vietnam Solidarity Campaign (VSO), 16
La Voce del Popolo, 61

war of manoeuvre, 7, 27, 144–51
  see also coercion
war of position, 7, 27, 144–51, 161
  see also consent
Weber, M., 143
Williams, R., 6, 12, 13, 14, 16, 158, 159, 170
Wilson, W. (US President), 67, 76
working class, 6, 36ff, 50
  British, 12, 14
  Italian, 42, 43, 44, 78, 79, 93, 109
  organisations of, 8, 21, 38, 39, 76, 202ff
  see also trade unions; consciousness; socialism
  role in revolutionary change, 21, 39, 117, 119–29, 141, 162ff, 202

Yugoslavia, 67, 75, 111 n.5, 111 n.6

Zimmerwald, 68
Zinoviev, G. 107

262541

QL666
L5Q2
48/48076